THE 100 BEST
NONFICTION BOOKS
OF ALL TIME

As featured in **The Observer**

THE 100 BEST NONFICTION BOOKS OF ALL TIME

Robert McCrum

G

Galileo Publishers
Cambridge, UK

Galileo Publishers
16 Woodlands Road
Great Shelford
Cambridge CB22 5LW
UK

www.galileopublishing.co.uk

ISBN 978-1-903385-83-8

First published in the UK 2018

2 3 4 5 6 7 8 9

Printed and bound in the UK

Cover Illustration by Rockwell Kent

CONTENTS

INTRODUCTION

What part of mankind's stone age brain, we might wonder, is wired to get excited by a list? Is it the delightfully named hippocampus? Neurologists would dispute that. Or the parietal lobe, an interpretative centre for words and language? Possibly. The inner working of the brain remains the dark side of the moon and, in truth, no one knows. Somewhere in the mysterious recesses of our anonymous "grey matter", there are many cortical sub-sections that respond to indexes, catalogues and league tables, to inventories, registers and lists. The human brain likes to make sense of chaos.

I know this from experience. Between 2012 and 2018, for approximately five years, I spent successive weeks compiling first a fiction, and then a nonfiction, Top 100 Books list for the *Observer* & *Guardian*. Say what you like about these two lists – writing on-line, people from all over the world didn't hesitate to vent a mix of contempt, joy, rage, frustration, approval, and dismay at my selection – there has been no shortage of interest. In fact, the reverse. My virtual readership, worldwide, has been numbered in the low millions.

★★★

On reflection, the literary lists that are wired into our consciousness often find a more than neurological expression. "How do I love thee?" muses Elizabeth Barrett Browning. "Let me count the ways." Indeed, you quickly find that lists are a literary form closely woven into fiction, opera and popular verse.

In *The Great Gatsby*, for instance, F. Scott Fitzgerald creates a classic list with Nick Carraway's impressionable naming of "those who came to Gatsby's house":

> From West Egg came the Poles and the Mulreadys and Cecil Roebuck and Cecil Shoen and Gulick the State senator and Newton Orchid, who controlled Films Par Excellence, and Eckhaust and Clyde Cohen and Don S. Schwartz (the son) and Arthur McCarty, all connected with the movies in one way or another....

Again, there's another famous list in *Don Giovanni:* Leporello's breathless catalogue of his master's sexual conquests, ("100 in France, in Turkey 91"), is a high point of Mozart's opera. Elsewhere, among other, more sentimental lyrics, there's Paul Simon's "Fifty Ways to Leave Your Lover", and also from *The Sound of Music*, Maria's saccharine recitation of her "Favourite Things". More astringent, in *The Mikado*, W.S. Gilbert gives Ko-Ko his immortal "I've Got A Little List" – a famous *tour-de-force* sung by a Lord High Executioner always on the look-out for fresh meat:

> As some day it may happen that a victim must be found,
> I've got a little list – I've got a little list....

Another lyric, from the Arctic Monkeys, possibly supplies a more contemporary clue to the relationship between art and lists:

> *There's only music*
> *So that there's new ringtones.*

***

So much for the history and theory of lists. The practice is equally persuasive. There was a moment in mid-2017 when a counter-cultural icon – Bob Dylan no less – belatedly publishing his Nobel lecture, admitted to "an informed view of the world" based on another list, a text that was itself borrowed from elesewhere.

"I had had that for a while," he writes, "learned it all in grammar school. *Ivanhoe, Robinson Crusoe, Gulliver's Travels, Tale of Two Cities*, all the rest – typical grammar school reading that gave you a way of looking at life, an understanding of human nature, and a standard to measure things by." Dylan continued:

> "I took all that with me when I started composing lyrics. And the themes from those books worked their way into many of my songs, either knowingly or unintentionally. I wanted to write songs unlike anything anybody ever heard, and these themes were fundamental."

The great novelist and critic, Umberto Eco, renowned for *The Name of the Rose*, has also addressed this theme. Less familiar as the author of *The Infinity of Lists,* Eco writes that "The list is the origin of the culture." He adds that culture wants "to make infinity comprehensible" and "to create order – not always, but often." He points out that Homer and Shakespeare have this in common: neither is afraid of a catalogue, either in *The Iliad,* or in *The History plays.* In *Macbeth,* we find the playwright in a playful mood when two murderers declare "we are men, my liege." To which Macbeth makes this sardonic reply:

> Ay, in the catalogue ye go for men,
> As hounds and greyhounds, mongrels, spaniels, curs,
> Shoughs, water-rugs, and demi-wolves are clept
> All by the name of dogs.

"We like lists," says Eco, rather mysteriously, "because we don't want to die". This is possibly an allusion to W.H. Auden's suggestive remark that the pleasure we derive from literature is to wrapped up in "communing with the dead".

***

Some weeks into the compilation of the *100 Best Nonfiction Books of all Time,* one mischievous *Observer* colleague with a penchant for the arcane posed this wild-card challenge: "What are you going to do about Betty McDonald?"

"Who she?"

"Haven't you read *The Egg & I?*"

Well, no, I hadn't, but in 1945 Betty McDonald's whimsical autobiography was as popular as baked beans. Now it's almost completely forgotten, but – tellingly – still in print. Alas, after an hour or two with *The Egg & I,* it was excruciatingly obvious that Betty McDonald is not a classic. If only the other ninety-nine choices had been as painless.

Literary classics cluster on the north face of Parnassus. For this vertiginous terrain there are different sherpas. Italo Calvino says that a classic is "a book that has never finished what it wants to say". Ezra Pound identifies "a certain eternal and irresponsible freshness"; TS Eliot, more astringent, observed in *The Sacred Wood* that "No modern language can hope to produce a classic, in the sense I have called Virgil a classic." Alan Bennett wryly notes: "Definition of a classic: a book everyone is assumed to have read and often thinks they have read themselves."

***

Among nonfiction classics, the most treacherous category is the creature beloved of publishers – "the contemporary classic", a second cousin to that notorious impostor, the "instant classic". Such books will have been judged by slippery criteria: popular and literary critical fashion; a changing marketplace and new technology; bestseller lists, and hype. In the 20th century, a familiar palette of blurbish adjectives gives shape and colour to a moving target: provocative, outrageous, prophetic, ground-breaking, funny, disturbing, revolutionary, moving, inspiring, life-changing, subversive... A literary classic will always have a mix of these qualities.

Such a list raises another troubling question. Is nonfiction "the new fiction"? There are some good writers who will argue that this is so, but I believe that nonfiction (which can sometimes successfully bring together many genres) is not, strictly speaking, a genre of its own. Creatively – yes – using narrative techniques borrowed from fiction, it's possible to give certain kinds of nonfiction the aura of a distinct new genre. Yet, at the end of the day, "nonfiction" fractures into time-hallowed categories such as philosophy, history, reportage, etc. This is particularly true of "nonfiction classics" from the 18th and 19th centuries, titles such as *A Treatise of Human Nature* by David Hume or *On Liberty* by J.S. Mill. By that yardstick, a recent classic will be quite distinct, chiefly because its literary and cultural milieu is so different.

***

Literature will always mirror social and political upheaval. In a rare, and possibly thrilling, moment of historical disruption, our own cultural matrix is so much in flux that we'd be wise to rule nothing out. While multi-cultural diversity slowly transforms the canon, new readers are likely to frame "nonfiction" in a new way. As Kazuo Ishiguro observed in Stockholm, during his Nobel prize lecture in December 2017:

> "We must take great care not to set too narrowly or conser-vatively our definitions of what constitutes good literature. The next generation will come with all sorts of new, sometimes bewildering ways to tell important and wonderful stories. We must keep our minds open to them, especially regarding genre

and form, so that we can nurture and celebrate the best of them. Good writing and good reading will break down barriers. We may even find a new idea, a great humane vision, around which to rally."

Definitions of "good literature" start with critics and publishers. In the UK, the book industry is just beginning to reject patterns of exclusion that permeate the literary establishment. A recent "Spread the Word" report has already drawn attention to the dominance of white, middle-class males not merely in festivals and prizes but also in the upper echelons of book publishing. Not coincidentally, Penguin, Faber and Bloomsbury (to name three) are now addressing the issue of diversity in their commissioning cadres. Diversify the editors and you will diversify the books.

Disruption plus innovation equals confusion: we have been here before. In the spring of 1886, the young and iconoclastic Oscar Wilde, writing in the *Pall Mall Gazette*, declared: "Books today may be conveniently divided into three classes." There were, he went on, "books to read" and "books to re-read". Finally, there were "books not to read at all... argumentative books, and books that try to prove anything." This, Wilde decided, was "an age that reads so much that it has no time to admire, and writes so much that it has no time to think." His solution was typically Wildean. "Whosoever will select out of the chaos of our modern curricula 'The Worst 100 Books', and publish a list of them, will confer on the rising generation a real and lasting benefit."

The Observer's two series (fiction and nonfiction) have had more serious intentions. In the first, my choice of classic novels, a taxonomic spree could become an elevated discussion, based on comparative criticism. Later, with my choice of the *The 100 Best Nonfiction Books of all Time*, the debate became broader. Where fiction is a discrete and well-defined genre with established criteria, as manageable and satisfying as a spacious country-house garden, "nonfiction" remains the Wild West. To put it another way: choosing it became an infuriating case of "As I Please", driven by whim and caprice as much as taste. One thing is certain: the classic in all genres, must, uniquely, express something about its subject in a way that was previously unexpressed. It must, in Pound's famous injunction, "Make it new." Read it for the first time now, and still be thrilled by its vigour, originality and wisdom.

***

Whatever the influence of some basic literary criteria, there's no escaping the *zeitgeist*. To put that another way, I cannot disguise the inescapable fact that this 100 best nonfiction book list first appeared in the pages of a British national newspaper during the years 2015-18. It has, for instance, been interesting to discover how some of these classics, unforced, speak quite directly to the twin challenges of Trump and Brexit.

Your list-maker, then, is a creature of his or her times. They will have the appetites of a butterfly-collector, the instincts of a gambler, and the mind of a missionary or saboteur – perhaps with more than a hint of the cultural dictator. They are also part anthologist and part antiquarian.

There's an additional difficulty: almost any selection of "classic nonfiction" from library shelves that includes History; Film; Biography; Cookery; Politics; Fashion; Sociology; Art History; Reportage; Feminism; Drama; Biology; Philosophy; Economics and Poetry (which I included because poetry is catalogued as "nonfiction" by most libraries) is going to be either perverse and disappointing, or stupid and enraging, or downright baffling. As everyone knows, there is (thank God) no accounting for taste.

With so much choice, and so many available options, the free range of taste in Nonfiction was always going to be more debatable than with Fiction. Looking back at both lists as a whole, I recognise that (in nonfiction) I have displayed an adventitious bias towards memoir and biography. I must also concede certain deficiencies.

Granted: I am not fully equipped to cover the potentialities of theology, philosophy or economics. Not being a woman, or a person of colour, and – perhaps worse – being a citizen of the UK, I am condemned to the role of an Anglo-centric middle-aged white male raised on Beatrix Potter, Lewis Carroll, George Orwell, and Winston Churchill. This has doubtless conditioned my choice of – for example – Edward Lear, C.S. Lewis and Oscar Wilde.

On top of socio-cultural bias, there's this iron law of lost times: history is unforgiving. History remains – at least in part – the record of genocide, slavery, torture and sinister, unspeakable barbarities. Why should the literature that springs from such a record be immune to the influence of crimes against humanity? The great books from the western tradition will, inevitably, mirror this inconvenient truth.

On the positive side, history also provides the common reader with a brilliant tapestry of fascinating complexity. One of the unintended pleasures of my reading for this series was to uncover the debts of influence and association shared among many of my chosen writers. The Anglo-American literary canon is replete with such connections. Thus the American spelling maven Noah Webster is in hock to Dr Johnson, the great lexicographer; Jefferson acquires added consequence from Locke; Boswell takes inspiration from Hume; Orwell owes a debt to Swift and Jack London; and almost everyone looks over their shoulder at Shakespeare. In addition, nonfiction also nourishes fiction. Mark Twain wrote *Life on the Mississippi* (1883) before completing *The Adventures of Huckleberry Finn* (1886). Mrs Gaskell worked on her life of Charlotte Bronte (1857) while also publishing *North and South* (1855). And so on. You will make your own private pairings: that's part of the pleasure such a sequence can offer.

★★★

Among many serendipitous discoveries, there are some periodic clusters of greatness. 1962 is notable for the emergence of Rachel Carson and Thomas Kuhn; the post-war year 1919 stands out for the polemical genius of John Reed, J.M. Keynes and H.L. Mencken; 1859 is an *annus mirabilis* marking the publication of *The Tale of Two Cities*, *Self-Help*, *The Origin of Species* and *On Liberty*. Almost a century before, 1776 looms large for many reasons, including the appearance of Tom Paine's *Common Sense*, Adam Smith's *The Wealth of Nations*, and the first volume of Gibbon's *Decline and Fall*. It has been aptly said that great literature is always characterised by an unmistakeable air of inevitability.

It was my claim, in 100 Great Novels, that the classics of English and American fiction were often written in extremis. The same holds good for nonfiction: from *Birthday Letters* (1998), *Dispatches* (1977), and *Silent Spring* (1962), to *The Road to Wigan Pier* (1937), *A Room of One's Own* (1929), and *De Profundis* (1905). Unique in this list, the latter was actually written from prison. Further back, we find Mary Wollstonecraft, Edmund Burke, Jonathan Swift, Samuel Pepys, Thomas Hobbes, and especially John Milton all writing to the present moment. One 21st century lesson for the would-be writer to take home and reflect on: make sure you have something to say.

***

A list can be satisfying, but it should never be a source of complacency (i.e. the Last Word). One thing a good list can – indeed must – do is challenge its own existence. In the choice of a time-hallowed genre, such as fiction, this can become an elevated discussion, based on comparative criticism. With nonfiction, the debate is more wide-ranging.

In this much looser category, the world is your oyster. If your list-maker is a creature of his or her times, any compilation of nonfiction "classics" will be idiosyncratic and personal. Reviewing the complete list, with the benefit of hindsight, I discover that I selected books from as many as thirty distinct genres, from philosophy (Hobbes and Hume) to food (MFK Fisher).

When a nonfiction classic is whatever takes your fancy, according to your own self-imposed criteria, then the subtitle to such a project might be "Anything Goes". It could be a book that reported a great revolution – John Reed's *Ten Days That Shook the World* – or a masterpiece of magazine journalism that exposed the truth about a humanitarian catastrophe such as John Hersey's *Hiroshima*. Some of the classics catalogued here have caused shock and outrage: Carson's *Silent Spring*, for example, or Said's *Orientalism*. Others, notably Berlin's *The Hedgehog and the Fox*, and de Quincy's *Confessions*, I've listed as a diversion, to vary the pace. Still others – Greer's *The Female Eunuch* and Carson's *Silent Spring* – have broken down barriers and turned worlds upside down. Some titles (*A Grief Observed*; *A Room of One's Own*) have expressed a new idea sotto voce; others at maximum decibels: *A Vindication of the Rights of Women; The Feminine Mystique; The Double Helix; The Making of the English Working Class;* and *Common Sense*. Some classics live on, imperishably, as works of sheer entertainment: *How to Cook a Wolf* or *Eminent Victorians, Domestic Manners of the Americans*, and *Goodbye to All That*. Some classics were written in extremis, and carry their scars all too visibly (*Dispatches; Birthday Letters, De Profundis*), others are more reflective (*The Uses of Literacy; Awakenings*). Each is original, and speaks for itself.

***

Towards the end of compiling this series, I chanced upon *The Oxford Book of English Prose* (1998), and edited by the late and great John Gross. Working on my own list of nonfiction books, I had strenuously avoided making comparisons with similar exercises. Now – with all my entries read and written – I could not resist a sneak peek at some tantalising alternatives. Should we have neglected William Morris, John Ruskin, and Fraser's *Golden Bough*? How could we have omitted Neville Cardus, Rebecca West, and Nirad Chaudhuri?

The Oxford Book of English Prose has more than five hundred entries. We had just 100 slots to play with. Furthermore, my list was constructed for a newspaper audience, with the added gimmick that it unspools in a remorseless chronological sequence: it was always intended to entertain, tantalise and provoke. And there is, of course, the vagary of taste, the intangible thing we inherit that's shaped by character, education, class, gender and race.

Such influences marked the crossroads of a fierce internal debate. Would it be possible, I often asked myself, to re-shape the contours of the canon by assertively promoting forgotten kinds of writer? If there was a choice, say, between a neglected woman writer and a dead white male, should I automatically favour the former? And what about writers of colour? What about African-American slaves such as Olaudah Equiano (no. 22)?

If we are true to the historical record, the inconvenient truth is that such affirmative action on behalf of the forgotten and the ignored becomes mission impossible. Lists such as this one (and its fiction predecessor) cannot escape the past. From a 21st century perspective, those times to do not make a pretty sight. The history of our literature is shaped by patriarchal traditions and Anglo-Saxon attitudes or – to put it another way – xenophobia, misogyny, racism, religious intolerance, and sexism.

Before the 19th century, there are very few published women, and virtually no English language writers from India, Africa or the Far East. That's not a complacent assertion, but a simple statement of fact. The alternative titles one would need to construct an alternative canon simply do not exist. Where they do, as in the case of African-Americans such as Equiano, they are in a minority. Even to list the outstanding half a dozen African-American writers of consequence is still hardly to redress the injustices of the past.

***

In the evolution of English and American prose, there are at least three turning-points in our literature. First, there's the shift from the courtly, Latinate eloquence of Bacon, Donne, and Milton towards the crisper, vernacular clarity of Pepys, Defoe and the notable writers of a self-confident Great Britain. Between the years 1660-1688, from the Restoration to the Glorious Revolution, English prose becomes plainer, more demotic, and robust – to suit the times.

A hundred years later, there's the dramatic expansion of English as a future world language after the American Revolution. Finally, during the last century, as English culture, disseminated by colonialism, began to flourish worldwide and find local Indian and African expression, the Anglo-American hegemony starts to morph into a more global expression of English, infused by the literary traditions of India, Australia and the Far East, Canada, and sub-Saharan Africa. In our own century, this process is still ongoing…

***

If you break this list into its constituent parts, you will find that genres such as Philosophy (nos. 7, 11, 14, 32, 40, 66 and 48) and History (nos. 2, 18, 69, 95 and 92) have a disproportionate representation, followed by Travel (12, 27, 31, 44 and 61) and Autobiography (26, 29, 37, 45, 46, 49, 57, 58, 59, 96 and 99). Controversially, I also included occasional titles of poetry (43, 55, 84, 90 and 97). Cookery got just one entry: no. 71, MFK Fisher's *How To Cook a Wolf*. I had intended to include Mrs Beeton's *Book of Household Management*, but finally omitted her in favour of Matthew Arnold's *Culture and Anarchy* (no. 42).

Other notable omissions include: Robert Hooke: *Micrographia*; JH Newman: *Apologia Pro Vita Sua;* Marie Stopes: *Married Love;* Ronald Blythe: *Akenfield;* Hannah Arendt: *Eichmann in Jerusalem*; Hunter S. Thompson: *Fear and Loathing in Las Vegas*; Vance Packard: *The Hidden Persuaders*; DW Winnicott: *The Child and the Family*; Alex Comfort: *The Joy of Sex*; Paul Fussell: *The Great War and Modern Memory*; George Steiner: *Language and Silence*; Nancy Mitford: *Noblesse Oblige*; Hannah Arendt: *The Origins of Totalitarianism*; Richard Mabey: *Flora Britannica*; and William Goldman: *Adventures in the Screen Trade*.

I wish there had been more entries for "Biology", "Science", and "Literary Criticism" (why no Hazlitt or Leavis?). Some tough decisions were very tough: Cyril Connolly had to be on my list, but to prefer *Enemies of Promise* over *The Unquiet Grave* was painful. J.M. Keynes' *The General Theory of Employment, Interest and Money*, published in 1936 in the depths of the Great Depression, is beyond question a landmark volume of the 20th century. But every nominated author is only allowed one title, so I chose the less well-known but more readable Keynes essay, *The Economic Consequences of the Peace*.

Then there's what I think of as the "Thorstein Veblen Question". The neurotic author of *The Theory of the Leisure Class,* (as well as the far-seeing *The Engineers and the Price System*, 1921), Veblen is remembered as a cantankerous theorist with a penchant for the wives of his colleagues on the Stanford campus. Among many phrases, he coined "conspicuous consumption", and is a guru of American technology, but his books now seem weirdly dated. Veblen – in or out? In golfing parlance, he did not survive the cut-off.

Some other titles I could not find space for include: Alexander Pope: *Essay on Man*; William Wordsworth: *The Prelude;* Booker T. Washington: *Up From Slavery;* William Blake: *Songs of Innocence;* Beatrice Webb: *Women and the Factory Acts.* CLR James: *The Black Jacobins;* Edmund Wilson: *To the Finland Station*; Noam Chomsky: *Syntactic Structures*; Nancy Mitford: *Madame de Pompadour;* Julia Child: *Mastering the Art of French Cooking;* Ayn Rand: *The Virtue of Selfishness*; Bertrand Russell: *Autobiography, volume 1;* John Carey: *The Intellectuals & The Masses*; Janet Malcolm: *The Journalist and the Murderer*; Malcolm Gladwell: *The Tipping Point*; Richard Feynman: *What Do You Care What Other People Think?*; Francis Fukuyama: *The End of History*; and Adam Phillips: *On Kissing, Tickling and Being Bored.* This remains a moving target. Ask me again tomorrow and you'll find me wondering why we did not include Jung Chang: *Wild Swans* or E.M.Forster: *Aspects of the Novel.*

Another regret, bricked into the structure of both these series: no translations. With fiction, the language problem was simply unsurmountable. With inadequate language skills and limited resources, how could one possibly compare a Russian, with a Spanish, or with a Chinese novelist? What useful insights could be gained from an inevitably imperfect knowledge of world literature? With nonfiction, the same rule holds good, but it still seems odd, even perverse, not to include Karl Marx: *Capital*, or Sigmund Freud: *The Interpretation of Dreams.* No question, these (and some others such as Descartes' *Meditations* and Kant's *Critique*) are every bit as influential, and important, as the work of Hobbes, Darwin and Keynes. My justification of this limitation was always that each selection for both series (fiction and nonfiction) must express an English literary sensibility illustrating who we are and how we got here.

★★★

Working from title to title, through the centuries, the list evolved from week to week. Some choices reflect the *zeitgeist*. The passage of time will undoubtedly winnow a lot of titles inspired by the Great War once that apocalypse takes its long-term place in history.

The year 1900 marked a turning-point. A "modern classic" may easily turn out not be literature, and get forgotten; a 19th or 18th century classic will be part of the canon almost by definition. As survivors from another age, such books have a special consequence. Among 20th century classics, it's more difficult to achieve both influence and true greatness, though *The Waste Land* is a title with a strong claim on posterity.

What, finally, do I take away from nearly five years on the north face of Parnassus? The vitality, richness, depth and variety of the Anglo-American literary tradition continues to astonish. And because it has shaped who we are, and why we are here, it also educates and instructs. At times a chore, occasionally a headache, and always a looming deadline, I would not have missed it.

Sometimes, I wonder what such an exercise will look like in 2117. For now, this list will survive here and on-line, a snapshot of taste at the beginning of the 21st century. It will, no doubt, continue to provoke and infuriate. That's partly its *raison d'etre*. More seriously, it will also continue to mine a treasury of prose that has been seasoned by adversity, guarded by devoted readers of all kinds, and cherished for expressing the shock of the new, in the greatest language the world has ever known.

Now, having completed this long journey into the fathomless interior of our literature, I make no apology for the Anglo-centricity of these lists, though some die-hards will no doubt continue to dispute it. For better or worse, my choices have the texture and colouring of their origins. Furthermore, they must have a focus. From a broader perspective, I will continue to insist that these 100 titles, added to our 100 Great Novels, will have had a decisive influence on the shaping of the "English imagination". Braided together, these lists add up to the beginnings of an explanation of our culture.

As far as that canon goes, we are possibly at a moment of transition. Now it's up to another, and more diverse generation of readers to frame the literary canon in another way. To every literary expression of an idea (and this series has seen many) there is always a range of possible optimistic and pessimistic responses, a ceaseless and invaluable dialectic. It will always be a lively ride – and a great read.

★★★

At the conclusion of *100 Best Novels,* to provoke my readers with yet another set of literary verdicts, I chose an "All Time Top Ten" list of novels. With the caveat, already stated, about the profound difference between Fiction and Nonfiction, here is my chronological top ten of All Time Nonfiction Greats:

1. *The King James Bible* (1611)
2. Thomas Hobbes: *Leviathan* (1651)
3. Samuel Pepys: *Diary* (1660)
4. Adam Smith: *The Wealth of Nations* (1776)
5. Edward Gibbon: *The History of the Decline and Fall of the Roman Empire* (1776-88)
6. Mary Wollstonecraft: *A Vindication of the Rights of Women* (1792)
7. Charles Darwin: *On the Origin of Species* (1859)
8. Oscar Wilde: *De Profundis* (1905)
9. Virginia Woolf: *A Room of One's Own* (1929)
10. Joan Didion: *The Year of Magical Thinking* (2005)

Robert McCrum, London
October 2018

1. King James Bible:
The Authorised Version (1611)

In the beginning God created the heaven and the earth. And the earth was

without form, and void; and darkness was upon the face of the deep.

In the making of the world's English, only the King James Bible has been as universal and influential as Shakespeare and *The Book of Common Prayer*. It is, indeed, almost impossible to imagine the English-speaking world we celebrate in this series without the glittering majesty of this bible's most sonorous passages, the austere beauty of its

prose, and the endlessly quoted phrases that have become braided into the texture of contemporary reference:

To every thing there is a season, and a time to every purpose under the heaven: A time to be born, and a time to die; a time to plant, and a time to pluck up that which is planted ...

Again:

But as it is written, the eye hath not seen, nor ear heard, neither have entered into the heart of man, the things which God hath prepared for them that love him.

And again:

But lay up for yourselves treasures in heaven, where neither moth nor rust doth corrupt, and where thieves do not break through nor steal.

Some passages in the Authorised Version hover on the edge of poetry:

Consider the lilies how they grow: they toil not, they spin not; and yet I say unto you, that Solomon in all his glory was not arrayed like one of these.

Other lines have become seamlessly absorbed into the collective unconscious surrounding the language:

Finally, brethren, whatsoever things are true, whatsoever things are honest, whatsoever things are just, whatsoever things are pure, whatsoever things are lovely, whatsoever things are of good report; if there be any virtue, and if there be any praise, think on these things.

Thus our series begins here, in 1611, coincidentally, the year Shakespeare probably completed *The Winter's Tale* and staged *The Tempest*. The language has emerged from its centuries-long gestation since the subjugation of Anglo-Saxon after the Norman conquest, and is now recognisably modern in a way that Chaucer's English is not.

Remarkably, in a startling testament to the vigour of the vernacular at the beginning of the 17th century, the Authorised Version was written by a committee. In 1604, the Hampton Court conference, chaired by Elizabeth's successor, King James I, decided that the bitter doctrinal friction between Anglicans and Puritans should be soothed by "one uniforme translation".

In an act of entrepreneurial collaboration, typical of the age, six trans-lating teams were instructed to base their "authorised" versions upon previous English editions, translating afresh, but also comparing their work with previous vernacular bibles, from Tyndale to Parker.

In the final stages of its work, this committee would go through the drafts of their translation, reworking it so that it would not only read better, but sound better – the quality for which it is world famous. The transla-tors relished this instruction. In their preface to the reader, they remarked: "Why should we be in bondage to them [words and syllables], if we may be free, use one precisely when we may use another no less fit, as commo-diously?"

Such was the versatility of English society and its language at this moment that the power of the *Authorised Version* could spring from the quills not of a single writer – a Marlowe, a Jonson or a Shakespeare – but a team. In some famous passages, these anonymous translators were touched with genius:

In the beginning was the Word, and the Word was with God, and the Word was God. The same was in the beginning with God. All things were made by him; and without him was not anything made that was made. In him was life; and the life was the light of men. And the light shineth in darkness; and the darkness compre-hended it not.

The *King James Bible* became, as Adam Nicolson has written, "England's equivalent of the great baroque cathedral it never built, an enormous and magnificent verbal artifice, its huge structures embracing all 4 million Englishmen, its orderliness and richness a kind of national shrine built only of words."

Three to compare:
Jeremy Taylor: *Holy Living and Holy Dying* (1651)
Thomas Cranmer: *The Book of Common Prayer* (1662)
The New English Bible (1970)

2. The History of the World
by Walter Raleigh (1614)

"When Sir Walter Raleigh was imprisoned in the Tower of London," writes George Orwell in his As I Please column for 4 February 1944, "he occupied himself with writing a history of the world. He had finished the first volume, and was at work on the second, when there was a scuffle between some workmen beneath the window of his cell, and one of the men was killed. In spite of diligent inquiries, and in spite of the fact that he had actually seen the thing happen, Sir Walter was never able to discover what the quarrel was about: whereupon, so it is said – and if the story is not true it certainly ought to be – he burned what he had written, and abandoned the project."

Raleigh is one of those larger-than-life characters – an inveterate buccaneer and a gifted poet, parodied by Shakespeare in *Love's Labours Lost* – who has long been an object of awestruck anecdote. See, for instance, John Aubrey's sexual gossip about Raleigh in *Brief Lives* (*No. 47*). Nevertheless, in the composition of Raleigh's *History of the World*, Orwell's apocryphal tale does not quite square with the facts.

Sir Walter, who came from the West Country, had sprung to prominence under Elizabeth I, for whom he acted as an explorer and coloniser, notably in Virginia. His devotion to his queen ("My fidelity towards Her," he writes in his preface to the *History*, "whom I must still honour in the dust") always made him suspect in the eyes of her successor. On the death of the queen in 1603, he was tried for high treason on trumped-up charges and imprisoned in the Tower of London.

This was hardly an ideal research centre, but with characteristic energy Raleigh devoted years of work to his *History of the World*. Created with the aid of several assistants and a library of more than 500 books that Raleigh was allowed to keep in his quarters, this remarkable work of English vernacular would become a bestseller, with nearly 20 editions, and abridgments, in the years that followed its author's execution.

Written during the first seven years of his long (1603-1616) incarceration, *The History of the World* is Raleigh's most important prose work. It was originally intended as a multi-volume project, covering the creation of the world through Greek, Egyptian and biblical history to 146 BC. Initially, the book seems to have been intended as an educational tool for Henry, Prince of Wales (1594-1612), with many references to warfare, kingship and strategy: "Whosoever commands the sea commands the trade; whosoever commands the trade of the world commands the riches of the world, and consequently the world itself."

Thanks to its association with the prince, the book was entered on the list of officially approved books held at Stationers' Hall in 1611 and all seemed set fair. But when Henry died in 1612, Raleigh was forced to bring the project to a sudden and premature conclusion. His narrative ends abruptly with the second Macedonian war instead of continuing through two more volumes as originally intended.

Whatever the full explanation for this curtailment, it seems that Raleigh had already provoked some serious regal displeasure. In addition to his advice to the Prince of Wales, like many writers at this time, Raleigh used ancient history as a sly commentary on contemporary issues. The work, close to a million words in total, was eventually published in 1614. His work exemplifies the culture of history writing and historical thinking in the late Renaissance.

Like many early modern Europeans, Raleigh placed a special value on the study of the past. He was a scholar and a politico who saw historical expertise as not just a foundation for political practice and theory, but as a means of advancing his power in the court.

It's for these reasons, principally, that Raleigh's work was construed by King James as critical of the new Stuart dynasty. Several months after publication in 1614, James ordered further sales of the book suppressed and all unsold copies to be confiscated "for divers exceptions, but especially for being too saucy in censuring Princes". Once the king had suppressed it, it would later be subsequently reissued with no title page and no authorial identification. This did not prevent it from becoming a hot seller.

In 1616, through another twist, Raleigh was released from the Tower to lead one final expedition to South America. The expedition was a disaster; his men attacked a Spanish outpost and in the battle his eldest son was killed. A commission of inquiry set up under Spanish pressure, revived the 1603 charge of treason. Raleigh was executed upon his return to England in 1618. This event has also entered folklore.

On feeling the edge of the axe before his execution, he is said to have remarked "'Tis a sharp remedy, but a sure one for all ills." Reportedly, his last words were: "I have a long journey to take, and must bid the company farewell."

After his death, Raleigh's *History of the World* had a bibliographical history almost as exotic as its author, replete with success, controversy and more royal disapprobation. Despite James I's ambivalence about the book, it survived through sheer popularity and the posthumous reputation of its swashbuckling author.

Three to compare:
Edward Gibbon: *The History of the Decline and Fall of the Roman Empire* (1776)
TB Macaulay: *The History of England From the Accession of James the Second* (1848)
EH Gombrich: *A Little History of the World* (1935)

3. THE ANATOMY OF MELANCHOLY
BY ROBERT BURTON (1621)

From the eccentric compulsion of its full title onwards (*The Anatomy of Melancholy, What it is: With all the Kinds, Causes, Symptomes, Prognostickes, and Several Cures of it. In Three Partitions with their severall Sections, Members, and Subsections. Philosophically, Medicinally, Historically, Opened and Cut Up*), Burton's masterpiece is garrulous, repetitive and often exasperating, but strangely addictive. I imagine that some readers of Karl Ove Knausgaard will understand the fascination of this book.

Ostensibly a medical study of melancholia, a subject first captured in a celebrated engraving by Dürer in 1514, it becomes a sublime literary doorstop (some 1,400 pages in my paperback edition) that exploits every facet of its subject, to explore humanity in all its paradoxical complexity, drawing from the science of the age and mixing it with astrology, meteorology, psychology, theology and rich, old-fashioned kidology. Teasingly, Burton describes himself as "a loose, plain, rude writer … I call a spade a spade". He may say "all poets are mad", but he is neither plain nor rude. Parts of *The Anatomy* are outstandingly comic: no surprise that Laurence Sterne should send up Burton in *Tristram Shandy*. Indeed, Burton's voice is never less than inimitable:

"I might indeed (had I wisely done) observed that precept of the poet [blank] – nonumque prematur in annum – and have taken more care: or, as Alexander the physician would have done by lapis lazuli, fifty times washed before it be used, I should have revised, corrected and amended this tract, but I had not (as I said) that happy leisure, no amanuenses or assistants."

According to Boswell, Dr Johnson said that *The Anatomy* was "the only book that ever took him out of bed two hours sooner than he wished to rise". Keats derived the story of his poem *Lamia* wholesale from Burton and claimed this to be his favourite book.

Literature and melancholy are intimately related, as Graham Greene suggests when he writes (in *Ways of Escape*): "Writing is a form of therapy; sometimes I wonder how all those who do not write, compose or paint can manage to escape the madness, the melancholia, the panic and fear which is inherent in the human situation."

Also from the 20th century, Samuel Beckett was another devotee. Burton's *Anatomy* lurks behind the writing of his first novel, *Murphy*. Other 20th century admirers include (it is said): Jorge Luis Borges, Philip Pullman, the poet Jay Parini, William Gass, and the American artist Cy Twombly.

Burton's *Anatomy* is among the strangest books on this list, but in its day it was cult reading: wildly popular among the Jacobean reading class. Subsequently, it has influenced figures as diverse as Charles Lamb and General Custer. It continues to exert a spell over the susceptible imagination as an offbeat, encyclopedic, stream-of-consciousness meditation on the mysteries of existence.

As advertised in its subtitle, the book falls into a long introduction and three parts (on the symptoms of melancholy; on its cure; and thirdly, on "love-melancholy" and religious melancholy). Rather in the manner of Montaigne, Burton, who was a highly educated man, stuffs his exposition with quotations from a remarkable range of writers. He also adopts a playful pseudonym ("Democritus Junior", a pointed allusion to the classical writer known as "the laughing philosopher").

To the contemporary reader, *The Anatomy of Melancholy* is less a work of humour, more a bizarre masterpiece of late Renaissance English prose, replete with wonderful nuggets of observation, sardonic utterances on the human condition: "I may not here omit those two main plagues, and common dotage of human kind, wine and women, which have infatuated and besotted myriads of people. They commonly go together."

Aside from many asides about the battle of the sexes, Burton is ironic about his chosen profession: "From this it is clear how much the pen is worse than the sword." He closes with some good advice to all his readers: "Be not solitary, be not idle."

Three to compare:

Laurence Sterne: *The Life & Opinions of Tristram Shandy, Gentleman* (1759)

Holbrook Jackson: *Anatomy of Bibliomania* (1930)

WG Sebald: *The Rings of Saturn* (1995)

4. THE FIRST FOLIO
BY WILLIAM SHAKESPEARE (1623)

The coming of age of English at the beginning of the 17th century,

after a golden generation of extraordinary growth and innovation, is symbolised by the publication of a landmark edition that the playwright himself had never bothered with in his own lifetime. Indeed, it was not until seven years after his death, thanks to the *First Folio*, that his work began slowly to acquire the canonical status it enjoys today.

Towards the end of November 1623, the bookseller Edward Blount, who traded at the sign of the Black Bear near St Paul's, finally held in his hands the text of a great volume for which he had long been waiting: *Mr William Shakespeares Comedies, Histories & Tragedies. Published according to the True Originall Copies.* In the words of one critic: "It is hard to overstate the importance of this literary, cultural and commercial moment."

The book now known as the *First Folio* (the first authoritative edition of Shakespeare's plays) established "Shakespeare" for all time and it did this in two principal ways. First, it collects some 36 plays, including 18 scripts (notably *Macbeth, Julius Caesar, As You Like It* and *The Tempest*) which would be otherwise unknown. The trove of work thus assembled gave posterity not just a cast of immortal characters (Bottom, Falstaff, Lear, Portia, Jaques, Prospero et al), but also a heap of new words (including, for example, catastrophe, exaggerate, assassinate, indifference, monopoly and paradox).

Second, it definitively connects his contemporary Ben Jonson (who declared his rival to be "the soul of the age") and some of the actors who had first performed these plays with the historical person, the playwright himself, a figure helpfully illustrated by a famous frontispiece, the engraved portrait of the artist that has become an icon of "Shakespeare studies".

Other facts about the *First Folio*, a canon of incomparable power and authority, and the text that would help launch Shakespeare's global literary afterlife are indisputable: both its value (somewhere north of $5m in rare books' sales) and its comparative rarity (approximately 240 copies survive worldwide in public and private collections). This *First Folio* also does not include collaborations such as *Pericles* or *The Two Noble Kinsmen*. On the other hand, it does establish three categories for Shakespeare's work – comedies, histories and tragedies – that survive to the present. Furthermore, it promotes a seductive myth of the artist's genius, as "a happy imitator of nature". According to John Heminges and Henry Condell, the two actors from the acting company the King's Men responsible for putting this volume together: "His mind and hand went together and what he thought he uttered with that easiness that we have scarce received from him a blot in his papers."

This is a particularly tantalising reference. All the contemporary, working manuscript materials of Shakespeare's plays are lost. We have his signature on several legal documents but – apart from one scene, his contribution to *Sir Thomas More* – nothing in his hand: no prompt copy, no printer's proofs, nothing. As so often with Shakespeare, when you look closely at his work, you find layer upon layer of mystery, entwined with fathomless ambiguity.

The *First Folio* does, however, have one significant and unequivocal characteristic. Unlike Shakespeare's producers, Heminges and Condell were determined to promote the poet's authorship. The name of Shakespeare had not been much of a selling point among Elizabethan playgoers, as the sometimes anonymous Quarto editions of his work indicate. For this Jacobean edition, however, his publishers wanted to create a literary artefact, a legacy volume. This, triumphantly, is what the *First Folio* achieves. After 1623, Shakespeare and his works are on the march across the English-speaking world.

Which brings us to that frontispiece by the Dutch engraver Martin Droeshout. As the Shakespeare scholar Emma Smith has noted, this portrait "exists in three separate states", indicating the trouble taken with the likeness. Droeshout's engraving projects what Smith calls "an abiding sense that the man and his plays must be deeply interconnected ... The book [the *First Folio*] presents us with a person, a personality, through his work." In thus branding their volume, his publishers were leaning on a secure and careful image of Shakespeare himself to encourage its market and champion its contents.

This in turn, brings us back to Ben Jonson, whose salute to Shakespeare faces the Droeshout portrait. Jonson's role is crucial because his testament to Shakespeare and his work dominates the opening page of the *First Folio*. "Who is Ben Jonson?" we might ask. In brief, he is Shakespeare's great rival, a playwright who had already gone to great lengths to oversee a collected edition of his own dramatic works, a man convinced of his own importance, mildly obsessed with posterity. Garrulous, argumentative, jealous, proud and deeply committed to exposing hypocrisy and corruption, Jonson is never a man to kowtow to nobility or privilege.

How does Jonson make his contribution to this collected works? He writes in strikingly generous (almost awestruck) terms about a man he had mercilessly satirised in his lifetime. Opposite the portrait of his friend, he identifies the image of a writer whose work, he declares, far surpasses the quotidian limits of his ordinary life. It's Jonson who coins the "sweet Swan of Avon" and it's Jonson who declares that he is "the applause, the delight, the wonder of our stage", and then – a few lines later – that he is "not of an age, but for all time" and claims him, with proprietorial certainty, as "my gentle Shakespeare". Here, beyond question, is one great literary figure paying posthumous tribute to another. This must confound those conspiracy theorists for whom "Shakespeare" is simply an alias, an elaborate code for other hands.

You have to ask yourself, confronted with this documentary evidence, why on earth would Jonson, who had competed with Shakespeare throughout his professional life, take part in a cover-up. There are countless examples of how impossible it is to imagine Sir Francis Bacon or Edward de Vere (the 17th Earl of Oxford) or anyone else writing these plays. Tiny details betray the work of a man steeped in everyday life: for instance, the brilliant detail from the history plays of the problem of fleas breeding in the corners of taverns where men have been pissing.

This brings us back to Shakespeare's provincial origins. As many have noted, it's been hard for some to accept that a man from the lower orders, not formally educated at Oxford or Cambridge, could be a genius, the greatest playwright who ever lived. Combined with a natural human appetite for mystery, this has flourished into the "Anonymous" fantasy maintained by the Shakespeare-deniers. The *First Folio* is the obvious refutation of this nonsense. In the real world of serious literary criticism, it remains, in the words of the RSC's *Complete Works*, "unquestionably the most important single book in the history of world drama".

Three to compare:
Stephen Greenblatt: *Will in the World* (2004)
James Shapiro: *Contested Will* (2010)
Emma Smith: *The Making of Shakespeare's First Folio* (2015)

5. DEVOTIONS UPON EMERGENT OCCASIONS BY JOHN DONNE (1624)

On the eve of his daughter's wedding, in late November 1623, the

poet John Donne was struck down by a mysterious "relapsing fever" (so-called because the patient often died during convalescence) and reduced to many weeks of frailty, in which he was "barred of my ordinary diet, which is reading".

What exactly it was that Donne suffered from, and survived, is not known. Some say typhus. The patient himself believed that he was on his deathbed, that the illness reflected his own sinfulness and amounted to a divine rebuke. His response was at once pious and literary: he asked for pen and paper in order to record, for himself, the experience of this "emergent occasion". (He also wrote Hymne to God my God, in my Sicknesse.)

As well as hymns, in this enfeebled condition, the poet also turned to a new and sombre kind of prose, his urgent response to the threat of imminent extinction. Incredibly, he planned, wrote, and finally published, *Devotions Upon Emergent Occasions*, his intense meditation on the meaning of life and death, in a matter of days, while still convalescing. Written with astonishing speed and intensity, the work was registered with the Stationers' Company on 9 January 1624 and published without delay: rarely has such a dramatic affliction had such an immediate literary outcome.

Many of the books in this series are an answer to a crisis of one kind or another. Donne's *Devotions*, a neglected classic, actually braids the author's personal "emergency" into the title. Writing to a friend, he described the process whereby the thoughts sponsored by his "relapsing fever" brought this book into the world:

> "Though I have left my bed, I have not left my bedside; I sit there still, and as a prisoner discharged sits at the prison door to beg fees, so I sit here to gather crumbs. I have used this leisure, to put the meditations I had in my sickness into some such order as may minister some holy delight. They arise to so many sheets (perchance 20) as that without staying for that furniture of an epistle, that my friends importun'd me to print them, I importune my friends to receive them printed."

Like all Donne's greatest writing, these *Devotions*, as the poet and critic Andrew Motion has written, "are a performance, and because they are a performance, we feel held at arm's length. To put it another way: Donne's sickbed is a stage and we admire the patient as if we were looking at him across footlights."

The shape of the *Devotions* helps condition this response. The 23 sections correspond to the 23 days of the poet's fever. Entitled "The Stations of the Sickness", each of these is divided into three parts: "Meditations upon our Humane Condition", "Expostulations, and Debatements with God" and "Prayers, upon several occasions, to him".

Within these sections, the reader encounters a succession of dazzling observations:

> "We study health, and we deliberate upon our meats, and drink, and air, and exercises; and we hew, and we polish every stone, that goes to that building; and so our health is a long and regular work. But in a minute a cannon batters all, overthrows all, demolishes all; a sickness unprevented for all our diligence, unsuspected for all our curiosity; nay, undeserved if we consider only disorder, summons us, seizes us, possesses us, destroys us in an instant."

As well as reflecting on the shocking propinquity of life and death, Donne is tormented by his isolation, as a patient:

"As sickness is the greatest misery, so the greatest misery of sickness is solitude … Solitude is a torment which is not threatened in hell itself."

From his sickbed, he hears the bell in the neighbouring square and translates the moment into one of his most famous lines: "Never send to know for whom the bell tolls, it tolls for thee."

Donne needs God. "Enable me by thy grace to look forward to mine end," he writes, confronting his mortality. If that seems alien and remote, in an age dominated by agnosticism and aetheism, other some other passages are both touching and strikingly modern:

"Death is in an old man's door, he appears and tells him so, and death is at a young man's back, and says nothing; age is a sickness, and youth is an ambush; and we need so many physicians as may make up a watch, and spy every inconvenience. There is scarce any thing that hath not killed somebody; a hair, a feather hath done it; nay, that which is our best antidote against it hath done it, the best cordial hath been deadly poison."

Three to compare:
Jeremy Taylor: *The Rule and Exercises of Holy Living* (1650)
Sir Thomas Browne: *Urn Burial* (1658)
Thomas Cranmer: *The Book of Common Prayer* (1662)

6. Areopagitica
by John Milton (1644)

Throughout England and Europe, the 17th century was notable

for its violence, instability and profound social upheavals. On the continent, a whole generation became traumatised by the thirty years' war. In England, the civil war divided the country and executed a king. There are some moments when, as is happening again now, the forces of history seem to be on the march. In England, several writers (notably Browne, Burton, Hobbes and Marvell) who lived through these dangerous times produced work that is clearly influenced by the experience of chaos, conflict and revolution.

John Milton is perhaps most notable of these. Born the son of a scrivener in Cheapside, London, in 1608, and educated at Cambridge, he devoted many years in mid-life to the politics of the Commonwealth, was arrested during the Restoration, but was released, had blindness in old age, and died in 1674.

Milton today is remembered as the author of *Lycidas, Paradise Lost,* and *Paradise Regained* – a supremely great English poet. To his contemporaries, however, he was pre-eminently a rhetorical writer – a fiery pamphleteer in an age of religious and political argument, whose tireless defence of divorce, progressive education, regicide and the Commonwealth marked him out as a natural, and brilliant, English radical.

For Milton himself, his gifts were complementary. He said he could write with his left hand (prose) or his right hand (poetry). To understand him better, and to locate him in the England of the civil war and subsequent Restoration, his readers need to reconcile these two parts of his genius, the polemical master as much as the subtle lyricist. Milton's *Areopagitica* is the mature text that displays both parts of his creative imagination at full pitch, and adds another dimension to our appreciation of his poetry – in the words of one critic "a monument to the ideal of free speech". As Milton himself writes: "A good book is the precious life-blood of a master spirit, embalmed and treasured up on purpose to a life beyond life."

Subtitled "A speech of Mr John Milton for the liberty of the unlicensed printing, to the Parliament of England", the title of *Areopagitica* pays deliberate homage to the Areopagiticus of the famous Greek orator Isocrates. Like all his contemporaries, notably Sir Thomas Browne, Milton believed that referencing the classics was one way of guaranteeing the permanence of his prose.

Milton was writing in response to parliament's licensing order of 14 June 1643, a repressive measure that had shockingly re-established the press restrictions of the hated Stuart dynasty. His attack on censorship and call for a free press asserted the ideals of liberty and free speech in a tour de force of English prose that's at once fierce and poetic: "As good almost kill a man as kill a good book: who kills a man kills a reasonable creature, God's image; but he who destroys a good book, kills reason itself, kills the image of God, as it were in the eye."

For Milton, as for all great libertarians, true freedom is indivisible, a point that he argues with polemical brilliance.

Areopagitica opens with a survey of press licensing, satirically linking the practice to the Spanish Inquisition. Why, he asks, should the common reader not be free to judge for themselves between a good and bad book? Is it not the condition of virtue to recognise evil and resist it? In a celebrated passage, he writes that he has no time for "a fugitive and cloistered virtue". The exercise of freedom for Milton was a moral and dynamic right: free citizens must always strive to earn their freedom. Any regulation of reading, he continues, broadening the argument against the licensing of the press, should logically include all recreations.

> "If we think to regulate printing, thereby to rectify manners, we must regulate all recreations and pastimes, all that is delightful to man … And who shall silence all the airs and madrigals, that whisper softness in chambers?"

This passage is an apt reminder that the cultural changes wrought by the Puritan revolution did not eliminate a lingering attachment to a courtly style that would survive (just) into the 18th century. Milton's work is expressive of a society in transition.

Areopagitica builds over some 40 pages (in my Penguin edition) to a rousing appeal to "the Lords and Commons" to consider "what Nation it is we are". Milton's answer is both patriotic and inspiring: "A nation not slow and dull, but of a quick, ingenious and piercing spirit … methinks I see in my mind a noble and puissant nation rousing herself after sleep, and shaking her invincible locks."

His optimism, however, is freighted with anxiety at the prospect of a breakdown between rival political and religious interests. He concludes that there can be no limits to tolerance. Freedom must be unlimited, and without restriction – inalienable and indivisible:"Give me the liberty to know, to utter, and to argue freely, according to conscience, above all liberties."

Three to compare:
John Locke: *Letters on Toleration* (1689-92)
John Stuart Mill: *On Liberty* (1859)
George Orwell: *Politics and the English Language* (1946

7. LEVIATHON
BY THOMAS HOBBES (1651)

According to the 17th century historian and gossip John Aubrey,

Thomas Hobbes "was wont to say that if he had read as much as other men, he should have known no more than other men." As a great thinker, Hobbes epitomises English common sense and the amateur spirit, and is all the more appealing for deriving his philosophy from his experience as a scholar and man of letters, a contemporary and occasional associate of Galileo, Descartes and the young Charles Stuart, prince of Wales, before the Restoration.

Hobbes himself was born an Elizabethan, and liked to say that his premature birth in 1588 was caused by his mother's anxiety at the threat of the Spanish Armada:

… it was my mother dear
Did bring forth twins at once, both me, and fear.

Throughout his long life, Hobbes was never far either from the jeopardy of the times (notably the thirty years' war and the English civil war) or the jeopardy sponsored by the brooding realism and pragmatic clarity of his philosophy. What, asked Hobbes, was the form of politics that would provide the security that he and his contemporaries longed for, but were always denied?

Subtitled *The Matter, Forme and Power of a Commonwealth Ecclesiasticall and Civil, Leviathan* first appeared in 1651, during the Cromwell years, with perhaps the most famous title page in the English canon, an engraving of an omnipotent giant, composed of myriad tiny human figures, looming above a pastoral landscape with sword and crosier erect.

Thus "the Leviathan" (sovereign power) entered the English lexicon, and Hobbes's vision of man as not naturally a social being, animated by a respect for community, but a purely selfish creature, motivated by personal advantage, became condensed into his celebrated summary of mankind's existence as "solitary, poore, nasty, brutish, and short".

It was Hobbes's argument that, to ameliorate these conditions, man should adopt certain "Laws of Nature" by which human society would be forbidden to do "that which is destructive" of life, whereby virtue would be the means of "peaceful, sociable and comfortable living."

The first law of nature is: "every man ought to endeavour peace". This, he argues, will be a hard goal: the general inclination of all mankind is "a perpetual and restless desire of power after power, that ceaseth only in death". The second law of nature is: "a man [must] be willing when others are so too ... to lay down his right to all things; and be contented with so much liberty against other men, as he would allow other men against himself." The third law of nature is: "men performe their Covenants made."

This, in essence, adds up to Hobbes's social contract, enforced by an external power. Accordingly, members of civil society should enter into a contract to confer their power and strength "upon one Man, or upon an Assembly of men ... This done, the Multitude so united in one Person, is called a Common-wealth." For Hobbes, the contracting of such power is the only guarantee of peace and prosperity: "During the time men live without a common power to keep them all in awe, they are in that condition which is called war; and such a war as is every man against every man."

Having witnessed the English revolution at first hand, it is war above all that Hobbes most fears. Social warfare empowers mankind's darkest side: "Force, and fraud, are in war the two cardinal virtues."

Hobbes is never less than ironical in his attitude to humanity's appetite for "government". He had seen too much debate, before and after the execution of Charles I, about the relationship between, citizen, church and state to be anything but pragmatic: "they that are discontented under monarchy, call it tyranny; and they that are displeased with aristocracy, call it oligarchy; so also, they which find themselves grieved under a democracy, call it anarchy, which signifies the want of government; and yet I think no man believes, that want of government, is any new kind of government."

For Hobbes, the "political community" is paramount, and individuals must surrender themselves for their own further and better protection.

As numerous commentators have observed, *Leviathan* is the founding document of the "social contract theory" that would eventually flourish in the western intellectual tradition. It is also a majestic monument of 17th century English prose, at once sinewy and vivid:

Riches, knowledge and honour are but several sorts of power.

Hobbes also illuminates his argument with many delicious asides:

The Papacy is not other than the Ghost of the deceased Roman Empire, sittig crowned upon the grave thereof.

This comparison of the papacy with the kingdom of fairies ("that is, to the old wives' fables in England concerning ghosts and spirits") is a reminder of the philosopher's pre-eminent wit and imagination. Combined with the economy, candour and irony of *Leviathan* as a whole, it marks Hobbes out as one of the truly great writers in the English literary canon. But he is also a giant of western philosophy whose influence can be found in the work of Rousseau and Kant.

Three to compare:
John Locke: *Two Treatises of Government* (1690)
David Hume: *A Treatise of Human Nature* (1739)
Paul Auster: *Leviathan* (1992)

8. HYDRIOTAPHIA, URN BURIAL, OR A BRIEF
DISCOURSE OF THE SEPULCHRAL
URNS LATELY FOUND IN NORFOLK
BY SIR THOMAS BROWNE (1658)

Sir Thomas Browne is one of those major-minor figures in the story

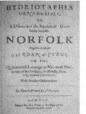

of these great books, a writer whose afterlife vindicates the power of an enchanted, idiosyncratic, and – the gift that holds one key to the success of the writing life – deeply humane imagination. Browne's reputation among admirers as various as Johnson, Coleridge, De Quincey, Lytton Strachey and, most recently, WG Sebald, confirms him as an early example of "the writer's writer".

Browne himself, whose life spanned the 17th century, was a learned, proto-Romantic, nomadic figure with a scholarly, metropolitan pedigree. He told John Aubrey that he had been born in Cheapside, educated at Oxford, then "spent some years in foreign parts" before joining the college of physicians. He also proudly reports that he was "knighted September 1671, when Charles II, the Queen and court" visited Norwich, the city to which he had retired in old age. Another fan, Dr Johnson, who wrote a brief "life" of Browne, supplied a good summary of his subject's inimitable style, which the plain-spoken critic described as "a tissue of many languages; a mixture of heterogeneous words, brought together from distant regions, with terms originally appropriated to one art, and drawn by violence into the service of another."

After an education at Winchester and Oxford, Browne – who appears to have had private means, as the son of a London merchant – travelled in Ireland, studied medicine in France and Italy, and received a doctorate in Germany from the university of Leiden. His first book, *Religio Medici* (The Religion of a Doctor), was an eccentric devotional meditation, directed by its author towards his own attitudes to faith, reason and the classical tradition. In his preface, he protests that it was composed without "the assistance of any good book whereby to promote my invention or relieve my memory", but it's still a genre-defying tour de force that quickly made his name in literary circles. In the words of one critic, it was "the expression of a peculiarly individual personality at a particular stage of his development as a scholar and a writer in a notably idiosyncratic age".

From *Religio Medici*, it's a short step, after a long and unusual life, to Browne's masterpiece, written after his move to Norfolk in old age, and published in 1658, a book devoted to "old mortality, the ruins of forgotten times".

Urn Burial, dedicated to two friends, members of the East Anglian gentry, is a strange and witty excursion by a scholarly mind into the burial customs of the past, a peculiar meditation on death and dying that becomes an essay on the nature of identity and humanity's vain quest for immortality. Browne – like Shakespeare's Jaques – is at once ironical and melancholy, a winning combination: "Were the happiness of the next world as closely apprehended as the felicities of this, it were a martyrdom to live." For many subsequent writers, especially WG Sebald, it was Browne's superb melancholy that has been most influential.

The Victorian writer, Edmund Gosse, describes Browne as "the laureate of the forgotten dead". If literary culture, as Auden says, is about "communing with the dead", then Browne is indeed the enchanted high priest of a secular faith, with all the mystery of a sublime hierophant. In the words of another critic, "the subject of *Urn Burial* is death, its dimension is time, and its articulation is music". At fewer than 50 pages in most editions, this is a meditation for the ages: "The iniquity of oblivion blindly scattereth her poppy, and deals with the memory of men without distinction to merit perpetuity."

Is melancholy, following Freud, merely an unproductive form of mourning? Or can it be an uplifting form of sadness that infuses consciousness with new possibilities? These are the kinds of questions sponsored by *Urn Burial.* Furthermore, Browne's prose is never less than beautiful, and always arresting. "Man is a noble animal," he writes, "splendid in ashes and pompous in the grave, solemnising nativities and deaths with equal lustre, nor omitting ceremonies of bravery in the infamy of his nature."

Browne is obsessed by the passage of history: "The night of time far surpasseth the day, and who knows when was the equinox?" In the closing pages of *Urn Burial,* after numerous brilliant passages, he concludes in a kind of sombre ecstasy: "Life is a pure flame; and we live by an invisible sun within us. A small fire sufficeth for life: great flames seemed too little after death, while men vainly affected precious pyres, and to burn like Sardanapulus."

Despite the sobriety of his mood, and its style, Browne never fails to find sympathy with humanity's deepest predicament, that we are ill equipped for old age: "The long habit of living indisposeth us for dying." Rarely have the addictions of melancholy seemed more appealing.

Three to compare:
Robert Burton: *The Anatomy of Melancholy* (1621)
Francis Bacon: *Essays* (1625)
WG Sebald: *The Rings of Saturn* (1995)

9. THE DIARY OF SAMUEL PEPYS (1660)

One day in December 1659, a young civil servant and Cambridge graduate named Samuel Pepys went to the shop in Cornhill in the City of London, where the stationer John Cade sold paper and pens, and bought himself a paper-covered notebook too fat for his pockets and took it home to his lodgings in Westminster. There, having ruled in red ink a left-hand margin down some 282 pages, he was ready. Thus it was that on 1 January 1660 the 27-year-old Pepys made his first diary entry:

"Blessed be God, at the end of the last year, I was in very good health, without any sense of my old pain [in 1658, he'd endured an operation for the removal of a stone], but upon taking of cold. I lived in Axe Yard, having my wife and servant Jane, and no more in family than us three."

Soon, however, this sober narrative became transformed by the diarist's exuberant character and his enthusiastic discovery of his "unequalled self". Pepys's determination to place himself – in all his contradictory and intoxicating vigour – at the centre of his own life, with its splendour, shame, variety and vanity, had taken over. For the next nine and a half years, Pepys's diary, the greatest in English literature, became the seething receptacle for its author's loves and hates, anxieties, frustrations and expectations, triumphs and disasters, as well as a faithful record of everyday life:

"This morning Mr Sheply and I did eat our breakfast at Mrs Harper's, (my brother John being with me,) upon a cold turkey-pie and a goose. From thence I went to my office, where we paid money to the soldiers till one o'clock, at which time we made an end, and I went home and took my wife and went to my cosen, Thomas Pepys, and found them just sat down to dinner, which was very good; only the venison pasty was palpable beef, which was not handsome. After dinner I took my leave, leaving my wife with my cozen Stradwick, and went to Westminster to Mr Vines. After that my wife and I bid adieu and came home, it being still a great frost."

As well as giving the language the catchphrase "And so to bed", Pepys also paints an unforgettable portrait of a society putting itself back together after the Puritan experiment:

"I went out to Charing Cross, to see major-general Harrison [a regicide] hanged, drawn and quartered; which was done there, he looking as cheerful as any man could do in that condition."

Pepys was a government servant and a man of business who liked to regulate his life. The diary was Pepys's informal system: tidying up the chaos of personal experience and reducing it to a meticulous shorthand. (You can still see the manuscript in Cambridge, the crown jewels of the Magdalene College library.) Later, when the cipher – Shelton's shorthand – was broken in 1825 and a full transcript completed, something very far from a system emerged: a portrait of an extraordinary Englishman at an extraordinary moment of English history.

Pepys was a man of his time who revelled in its politics, its opportunities and its adventures. He loved music and women, taverns and good wine, metropolitan pleasures and the boisterous company of the new generation coming to prominence around Charles II.

We don't know what it was that prompted Pepys to pick up his pen and keep a daily record of his life and times, but it was, in the words of one scholar, the "by-product of his energetic pursuit of happiness". Keeping the diary intensified his enjoyment of the present moment, giving him first the experience, then his account of it, as well as, eventually, the chance to recollect his experiences in tranquillity.

By chance, Pepys was writing at a pivotal moment in English

history. On 25 April 1660, the new parliament demanded by public opinion had met, then General Monck and the exiled court had reached a secret agreement. On 11 May, the fleet sailed to Holland to bring Charles Stuart back to his throne as Charles II.

Pepys's career prospered. His job as clerk of the acts to the Navy Board put him at the centre of the second Dutch war (1665-1667). Living in Westminster, close to the seat of government, he had first-hand experience of the 1665 plague:

> "I saw a dead corpse in a coffin lie in the close unburied – and a watch is constantly kept there, night and day, to keep the people in – the plague making us cruel dogs to one another … In the height of the plague bold people there were to go in sport to one another's burials. And in spite to well people, would breathe in the faces of well people going by."

Then, in September 1666, Pepys witnessed the Great Fire, a celebrated set-piece in the diary, describing how he had gone to the Tower of London to get a better view of the unfolding disaster:

> "I down to the water-side, and there got a boat, and there saw a lamentable fire. Poor Michell's house, as far as the Old Swan, already burned that way, and the fire running further, that in a very little time it got as far as the Steeleyard, while I was there. Everybody endeavouring to remove their goods, and flinging into the river or bringing them into lighters that lay off; poor people staying in their houses as long as till the very fire touched them, and then running into boats, or clambering from one pair of stairs by the water-side to another. And among other things, the poor pigeons, I perceive, were loth to leave their houses, but hovered about the windows and balconys till they were, some of them burned, their wings, and fell down. Having staid, and in an hour's time seen the fire: rage every way, and nobody, to my sight, endeavouring to quench it, but to remove their goods, and leave all to the fire, and having seen it get as far as the Steele-yard, and the wind mighty high and driving it into the City; and every thing, after so long a drought, proving combustible, even the very stones of churches…"

Pepys's diary, however, is more than just an invaluable record of stirring times. It's a vivid portrait of an ambitious young man becoming a great public official ("one of the most important naval administrators in England's history", according to one biographer).

And then again, it's an enthralling account of one man's life, from the inside out. Vanity must be one motivation for the diarist. Pepys translated his vanity first into intimate reportage and then into art. Yes, he places himself at the centre of events, but not in a self-important way. He gives himself no airs or special dignity. He is as frank about his frailties as he is about every other aspect of the world around him. Famously, he reports his sexual adventures with impressive candour, using a mix of the English vernacular and Latin to report his sexual exploits. His seduction of Deborah Willet, a young woman engaged by his wife for company, is probably the most dramatic. On 25 October 1668, Pepys was surprised at home as he embraced Miss Willet. He describes his wife coming upon them "suddenly" while in *flagrante delicto:*

> "She did find me embracing the girl con [with] my hand sub [under] su [her]coats; and indeed I was with my main [hand] in her cunny. I was at a wonderful loss upon it and the girl also..."

Deborah Willet was sacked; Pepys fell into deep remorse; he did not, however, entirely give up his dalliances. Elizabeth, his long-suffering wife, died in 1669. Fearful for his failing eyesight, or so he claimed, he closed his diary on 31 May 1669, but it's clear that something had changed. His life had reached a turning point – he no longer had the same appetites. He would live to see in the new century, dying in 1703, having happily resisted the temptation to destroy his youthful masterpiece. As a unique literary figure, he always remained, in the fullest and deepest sense, an artist open to the rare mysteries of everyday life. His diary is the work of a special kind of English genius: mundane, humble, brilliantly improvised and profound.

Three to compare:
John Evelyn: *Diary* (1818)
Virginia Woolf: *A Writer's Diary* (1953)
Claire Tomalin: *Samuel Pepys: The Unequalled Self* (2002)

10. THE BOOK OF COMMON PRAYER (1662)

The Book of Common Prayer is, arguably, the most influential and widely read book in English culture.

It emerged from medieval religious practice as a vernacular aid to devotion. The first prayer books with the Litany in English (probably the work of Thomas Cranmer) appeared in 1544, with decisive new editions in 1549 and 1552, both largely owed to Cranmer. In the words of one commentator, this book "has one of the most complicated textual histories of any printed book anywhere in the world ... There were more than 350 different imprints before the date often referred to as the 'first' edition of 1662."

This, the definitive version of Common Prayer, which established uniformity of worship and also renewed the old liturgical tradition, occurred with the restoration of Charles II and was widely seen as an integral part of the Stuart settlement, an assertion of the vernacular traditions of the common man. From this moment on, the magnificent cadences of this simple volume became indistinguishable from the expression of the English language, wherever in the world it took root.

By some estimates, such passages have enjoyed a wider, and larger, audience even than the works of Shakespeare. Perhaps *The Book of Common Prayer*'s only rival is the King James Version of the Bible (1611). Like the Bible, this prayer book was scattered far and wide by empire, trade and Anglicanism through a process that we would now describe as "soft power". Its most famous lines have reverberated round log cabin, quarterdeck and field of battle.

The Book of Common Prayer has indeed been translated into many languages, including Gaelic, Urdu, Hausa, Latin – and three varieties of Inuit. In its English version, it has never been out of print in 500 years, and its age-old rhythms have punctuated the experiences of the Anglo-American community:

> "Wilt thou have this Woman to thy wedded wife, to live together after God's ordinance in the holy estate of Matrimony? Wilt thou love her, comfort her, honour, and keep her in sickness and in health; and, forsaking all other, keep thee only unto her, so long as ye both shall live?"

What might we take from these pages today? Most notably, for a modern audience, *The Book of Common Prayer* is, in some ways, quite secular or, at least, humanistic in spirit. Its language expresses an everyday reconciliation to loss and sorrow, pain and despair, as well as love, joy, childbirth and marriage.

Although this is a text that continues to enjoy an afterlife within the Anglican communion, it bears the marks of its beginnings. The 1662 version was a self-conscious act of nostalgia for a golden age under Elizabeth I and James I. And its backward-looking instinct was reinforced by the antique appearance of "black-letter" or gothic script, reminiscent of a bygone age. It was also a force for modernisation, marrying strands of Catholic and Protestant faith into the work in progress that was Anglicanism, and executing a national ecclesiastical compromise. Its language, now rare, even special, to a modern audience, was the ordinary vernacular of its day, the speech of the people. Wherever you look in the best moments of the English tradition, you tend to find the language of the common man and woman predominant and irrepressible. On this account, the Normans did English culture and society a huge favour.

Three to compare:
Devotions Upon Emergent Occasions by John Donne (1624)
The New English Bible (1970)
The Alternative Service Book (1980)

11. AN ESSAY CONCERNING HUMAN UNDERSTANDING BY JOHN LOCKE (1689)

This celebrated essay, available to its first readers in December 1689,

though formally dated 1690, could hardly be more topical today. It is an examination of the nature of the human mind, and its powers of understanding expressed in brilliant, lapidary prose: "General propositions are seldom mentioned in the huts of Indians: much less are they to be found in the thoughts of children."

In the first two books, the argument moves through the source of ideas, the substance of experience (the origin of ideas), leading to a discussion of "the freedom of the will": "No man's knowledge here can go beyond his experience". In book three, Locke proceeds to discuss language, and in book four he defines knowledge as our perception of the agreement or disagreement between ideas.

Eventually, after several arguments of great intricacy and subtlety, Locke establishes good arguments for empirical knowledge, and moves to explore the existence of God, discussing the relations between faith and reason: "Reason is natural revelation, whereby the eternal Father of light, and fountain of all knowledge, communicates to mankind that portion of truth which he has laid within the reach of their natural faculties."

The *Essay* is a challenging read, made greatly more appealing by the elegance and comparative simplicity of Locke's prose. The discourse eventually became a popular classic, and also a set text among university students. In 1700, when the young student George Berkeley, who would eventually reject so much of Locke's thinking, entered Trinity College Dublin, it was among the prescribed texts. In 1700, the *Essay* was translated into French; a year later it was rendered in Latin, the supreme Age of Reason accolade.

Together, Locke and Newton would become English figureheads of the Enlightenment. With Newton, Locke did so much to sponsor the 18th century picture of the world as a kind of celestial clock, a vast and mechanical assembly of matter in motion, with man taking his place as an element, like a cog, in a regular and predetermined universe.

Locke's portrait of man as part of, not separate from, the rest of nature is also owed to the *Essay*. He had, of course, been anticipated in this by his predecessor Thomas Hobbes, but he went further. In the *Essay* he treats man as an appropriate subject for objective investigation. Thus, in his examination of human understanding, he follows a "plain, historical method" of careful observation, a method that would be adopted by later thinkers as various as Jefferson and Darwin.

It is hardly a surprise, therefore, that Locke should have had an important effect not merely on philosophy and psychology, but also on thought and literature. You can trace Locke's influence, through the *Essay*, on the writing of Addison, the prose and poetry of Pope, the fiction of Laurence Sterne, especially *Tristram Shandy*, and perhaps above all in the writing of Dr Johnson's great *Dictionary of the English Language*.

Bertrand Russell once said, possibly speaking for effect, that Locke had made a bigger difference to the intellectual climate of mankind than anyone since Aristotle. He added that "no one ever had Common Sense before John Locke" – and common sense was the watchword of much 18th and 19th century English endeavour. A sentence such as "I have always thought the actions of men the best interpreters of their thoughts" could equally have been written by Johnson.

Nonetheless, there is really no writer in this series who more impressively embodies the English spirit than Locke, in the sense that it is he who teaches us to think for ourselves, to weigh evidence empirically, to keep belief within limits, and to put all things to the test of reason and experience. He is also witty: "All men are liable to error; and most men are, in many points, by passion or interest, under temptation to it."

Three to compare:
Samuel Johnson: *A Dictionary of the English Language* (1755)
Maurice Cranston: *John Locke: A Biography* (1957)
John Yolton: *John Locke and the Way of Ideas* (1956)

12. A Tour Through the Whole Island of Great Britain by Daniel Defoe (1727)

Daniel Defoe, who also features in our previous series, *The 100 Best*

Novels with *Robinson Crusoe*, was first and foremost a great reporter, who marshalled the English language to describe the variety and wonders of a changing world: Defoe's astonishing career spanned the making of the society that came to call itself, with a certain insular pride, Great Britain.

Defoe is great, too. With his near contemporaries Swift, Johnson and Pope, he is one of those English writers who invented our literary tradition, and whose work resonates down the centuries. As a writer in many genres, he embodies the spirit of the English amateur, and some of his nonfiction is suffused with a quasi-lyrical sensibility.

Defoe's *Tour* was first published in three volumes at intervals of just above a year, in 1724-26. The third volume was dated 1727 (which explains the bibliographical detail), but actually first appeared in August 1726. Another complication: the *Tour* was indeed based on Defoe's extensive travels, but the last of these (Defoe was getting on; he would die in 1731) seems to have occurred in 1722. In fact, the *Tour* had a life long after Defoe's death. The novelist and printer Samuel Richardson, with an eye to the market, published new editions with new material in both 1738 and 1742.

Defoe's *Tour* was an outstanding version of an established genre, the literary travel guide to these islands. As Great Britain acquired its first empire and domestic tourism took off there was no shortage of new, informative surveys of the kingdom, from Arthur Young to William Cobbett. It's a long tradition. English topographic writing flourishes to this day in the writing of Iain Sinclair and Robert Macfarlane. Defoe is their mysterious godfather, a rackety, cross-grained, indomitable writer mildly obsessed with the peculiar and intangible character of the indefinable entity known as England (or Albion, or Britain or – now – the United Kingdom).

Defoe was an instinctive stylist, when he needed to be; he was also at pains to arrange his material into a most engaging narrative, pleasing his audience: the Tour is superbly well organised to satisfy his readers. Cast in the form of "a letter", each journey – at least to start with – begins and ends in his native London. Letter 3, which goes as far west as Land's End, opens:

I intended once to have gone due west on this journey; but then I should have been obliged to crowd my observations so close (to bring Hampton Court, Windsor, Blenheim, Oxford, the Bath and Bristol, all into one letter ...) as to have made my letter too long, or my observations too light and superficial, as others have done before me ...

By Letter 8, he is roaming the Midlands, from 11 to 13, he is in Scotland, a country in the process of merging its fortunes with England, after the Act of Union, a treaty signed and sealed in Defoe's lifetime.

Defoe's aim, throughout, was to report on "the present state" of his country. About 300 years on, his portrait is both an elegy for a lost world and a thrilling advertisement for an extraordinary society on the brink of greatness.

Three to compare:
William Cobbett: *Rural Rides* (Two Vols), (1830)
Henry Mayhew: *London Labour and the London Poor* (1851)
George Orwell: *The Road to Wigan Pier* (1937)

13. A MODEST PROPOSAL
BY JONATHAN SWIFT (1729)

Jonathan Swift, "the gloomy dean", was a great satirist, a Tory essayist and poet, renowned for *Gulliver's Travels*, whose work has not only remained almost continuously in print, but also influenced writers as varied as Thackeray and Orwell. He is also one of a select handful of writers who also appeared in the *Observer's* 100 top novels.

When he died in 1745, Swift was buried in his native Dublin with the celebrated epitaph *"ubi saeva indignatio ulterius cor lacerare nequit"* (where fierce indignation cannot further tear apart his heart), inscribed on his tomb.

Fierce indignation was undoubtedly the chief inspiration for Swift's blistering Juvenalian satire *A Modest Proposal for Preventing the Children of Poor People in Ireland, from Being a Burthen to Their Parents or Country; and for Making Them Beneficial to the Publick,* one of the most savage and powerful tracts in the English language, a masterpiece of sustained, even relentless, irony. Swift published it anonymously, but his authorship soon got out. Besides, it bore the unmistakable marks of his style:

> "It is a melancholly Object to those who walk through this great Town [Dublin], or travel in the Country; when they see the Streets, the Roads, and Cabbin-doors crowded with Beggars of the Female Sex, followed by three, four, or six Children, all in Rags, and importuning every Passenger for an Alms."

Juvenal aside, scholarly debate about the inspiration for the *Modest Proposal* fingers several classical sources, particularly the Roman essayist Tertullian's *Apology,* a satirical attack against Roman persecution of the early Christians. Some critics suggest that Swift saw major similarities between the plight of the Irish poor and the helpless Christians, and note that he felt an obvious affinity for Tertullian. But, finally, this approximately 4,000-word essay exhibits Swift at his merciless best, satirising his society's heartless indifference to the plight of the poor as well as the long-term cruelty of the British government's policies towards its Irish neighbour.

Swift's opening is a brilliant rhetorical feint, apparently inviting the reader into a well-researched examination of Ireland's social conditions, especially among its beggars. After Swift's painstaking calculations about the numbers of destitute children, their cost to the state, and the likely poor return on their potential sale into slavery, his conclusion is a both a stunning *coup de théâtre* and a brilliantly shocking reversal, which he offers very "humbly" in the hope that it will "not be liable to the least Objection". He goes on:

> "I have been assured by a very knowing American of my Acquaintance in London; that a young healthy child well nursed, is, at a year old, a most delicious nourishing and wholesome food, whether Stewed, Roasted, Baked, or Boiled; and I make no doubt that it will equally serve in a Fricasee or a Ragout."

From here – with his readers gasping – he develops his argument with logical precision and macabre brilliance. Swift proceeds to suggest that the indigent Irish might improve their economic prospects by selling their children as food for the rich, elaborating the idea with pitiless forensic zest. He cleverly concludes this outrageous case before the reader has wearied of the conceit. His final paragraph makes a wonderfully ironic conclusion:

> "I profess, in the Sincerity of my Heart, that I have not the least personal interest, in endeavouring to promote this necessary Work; having no other Motive than the publick Good of my Country, by advancing our Trade, providing for Infants, relieving the Poor, and giving some pleasure to the Rich. I have no Children, by which I can propose to get a single Penny; the youngest being nine Years old, and my Wife past Child-bearing."

Three to compare:
Jonathan Swift: *A Tale of a Tub* (1704)
Daniel Defoe: *The Generous Projector or, A Friendly Proposal to Prevent Murder and Other Enormous Abuses, By Erecting an Hospital for Foundlings and Bastard Children* (1728)
George Orwell: *Animal Farm* (1945

14. A TREATISE OF HUMAN NATURE
BY DAVID HUME (1739)

The career of the Scottish philosopher David Hume is a parable of

the writing life that speaks with eloquence about the strange and inexplicable progress of ideas in the marketplace of free debate. His career, moreover, is one that runs almost to the day he died, in 1776, just after the outbreak of the American revolution.

Hume was born and educated in Edinburgh, the son of a successful lawyer, and acquired a fierce appetite for philosophy at a precociously young age. After a mental breakdown as a student, and despite limited personal means, he spent three years of private study in France. Thereafter, he worked for four years on *A Treatise of Human Nature*. It was his first major work as a philosopher, and it bore the unwieldy subtitle "Being an Attempt to Introduce the Experimental Method of Reasoning into Moral Subjects". Hume completed *Treatise* in 1738, aged 28, and published it anonymously in two volumes the following year.

His ambitious intention was to construct a pragmatic science of man, a wholesale system of thought by which to appraise the psychological basis of human nature. In opposition to the rationalists of the day, Hume argued that it was passion rather than reason that moderates human behaviour: "Reason is, and ought only to be the slave of the passions, and can never pretend to any other office than to serve and obey them."

From this position, Hume advanced the idea that human knowledge must ultimately be located in mankind's quotidian experience. "It is not contrary to reason to prefer the destruction of the whole world to the scratching of my finger," he wrote.

The publication of Hume's *Treatise* was a disaster. Its wit and clarity ("Poets … though liars by profession, always endeavour to give an air of truth to their fictions") were overlooked; his majestic philosophical rigour misunderstood. He himself later observed that it "fell dead-born from the press". Today, however, *Treatise* is widely considered to be Hume's most important work, one of the keystone books of western philosophy, in the words of one commentator, "the founding document of cognitive science" and possibly the "most important philosophical work" in the English language.

In 1740, however, the critics were savage, describing his work as "abstract and unintelligible". It's not hard to see why. Even today, the Treatise is notably dry, and makes few concessions to the reader.

Organised in three parts (Of the Understanding, Of the Passions and Of Morals), with many sub-sections such as "Of Ideas, Their Origin, Composition, Connexion, Abstraction, Etc."; "Of the Ideas of Space and Time"; "Of Knowledge and Probability" and "Of the Sceptical and Other Systems of Philosophy Etc", it concludes with a recapitulation with Hume's reasoning for his thesis that "sympathy is the chief source of moral distinctions".

With impressive *sang froid*, having determined that the problem with the *Treatise* was one of style not content, Hume reworked his material into two rather more accessible essays entitled *An Enquiry Concerning Human Understanding* (1748) and *An Enquiry Concerning the Principles of Morals* (1751). These, Hume wrote, with typical brio, were "of all my writings, historical, philosophical, or literary, incomparably the best". Next, in 1752, he published his *Political Discourses*, which was translated into French and made Hume famous throughout Europe. Now on a roll, in 1754 he published the brilliant first volume of his *History of Great Britain*, a narrative largely devoted to the early Stuart kings followed by further volumes in 1757, 1759, and 1762.

His optimism, however, is freighted with anxiety at the prospect of a breakdown between rival political and religious interests. He concludes that there can be no limits to tolerance. Freedom must be unlimited, and without restriction – inalienable and indivisible: "Give me the liberty to know, to utter, and to argue freely, according to conscience, above all liberties."

Three to compare:
Thomas Hobbes: *Leviathan* (1651)
John Locke: *An Essay Concerning Human Understanding* (1689)
David Hume: *History of Great Britain* (1754)

15. A DICTIONARY OF THE ENGLISH LANGUAGE
BY SAMUEL JOHNSON (1755)

British national self-confidence boomed throughout the 18th century, with that familiar mix of pride and insecurity. Now, more than ever, the educated English reader needed a dictionary. In the new world of global trade and global warfare, a language that was becoming seeded throughout the first British empire required an authoritative act of definition by a vigorous and practical champion. Enter Dr Johnson.

Samuel Johnson, born in Lichfield in 1709, was a pioneer who raised common sense to heights of genius, and a man of robust popular instincts whose watchwords were clarity, precision and simplicity. The Johnson who challenged Bishop Berkeley's solipsist theory of the nonexistence of matter by kicking a large stone ("I refute it thus") is the same Johnson for whom language must have a daily practical use, and a ready application to the everyday world of the common man.

The would-be lexicographer signed the contract for his *Dictionary* with the bookseller Robert Dodsley at a breakfast held at The Golden Anchor in Holborn on 18 June 1746. He was to be paid £1,575 in installments, and from this he took money to rent 17 Gough Square in which he set up his "dictionary workshop".

James Boswell described the garret where Johnson worked as "fitted up like a counting house" with a long desk at which his clerks could work standing up. Johnson himself was stationed on a rickety chair surrounded by a chaos of borrowed books. He was helped by six assistants (five of them Scots, one an expert in "low cant phrases").

The work was immense. Writing in some 80 large notebooks (and without a library to hand), Johnson wrote the definitions of more than 40,000 words, illustrating their many meanings with about 114,000 quotations drawn from English writing on every subject, on food, philosophy, fashion and frivolity, from Shakespeare and the Elizabethans, via Milton, to his own time. He did not, he admitted, expect to achieve complete originality. Working to a deadline, essentially on his own, he had to draw on the best of all previous dictionaries, making his work a heroic synthesis. In fact, it was very much more. Unlike his predecessors, Johnson treated English very practically, as a

53

living language, with many different shades of meaning. He adopted his definitions on the principle of English common law – according to precedent.

With the *Dictionary*, the author and his subject achieved a remarkable, unfettered unanimity. Both were adaptable, populist and instinctively subversive (or, to put it another way, libertarian). As a result, in the decades after its publication, the *Dictionary* was not seriously rivalled until the coming of *The Oxford English Dictionary* (1884), by which time some of Johnson's definitions had passed into folklore:

> Lexicographer: A writer of dictionaries, a harmless drudge ...
> Oats: A grain, which in England is generally given to horses,
> but in Scotland supports the people.
> Whigs: The name of a faction.

For all its eccentricity, this two-volume work is a masterpiece and a landmark, in Johnson's own words, "setting the orthography, displaying the analogy, regulating the structures, and ascertaining the significations of English words".

It was an achievement that, in Boswell's words, "conferred stability on the language of his country", a stability that would be invaluable in the decades to come. However, though it made Johnson famous and well esteemed, the Dictionary did not allay his incessant money troubles. By 1759 Johnson was so hard up that he was forced to dash off the potboiling fable *Rasselas* to pay, he said, for his mother's funeral.

Three to compare:
James Boswell: *The Life of Samuel Johnson LL D* (1791)
Noah Webster: *An American Dictionary of the English Language* (1828)
James Murray (ed): *The Oxford English Dictionary* (1884)

16. COMMON SENSE
BY TOM PAINE (1776)

The American Revolution was always a rhetorical as well as a political

upheaval. The Founding Fathers transformed a mood of sullen opposition into a convulsion of revolutionary fury as much in print as on the field of battle. Thomas Jefferson's catalyst for the conflict in the Declaration of Independence was a masterpiece of English prose.

If there was to be a storm, there first had to be a lightning strike. The necessary explosion was ignited by a little book, attributed to an anonymous "Englishman", and published by Robert Bell from a print shop on

Third Street, Philadelphia, on 9 January 1776. The book was *Common Sense*, the bestselling American pamphlet of the 18th century. In no time at all, there were more than 120,000 copies in circulation, some 25 editions in 1776 alone, and its ideas were the talk of the eastern seaboard. "Who is the author of *Common Sense?*" asked the Philadelphia Evening Post. "He deserves a statue in gold."

Thomas Paine, unmasked as the author of this sensational broadside, is a key figure in the making of the Anglo-American tradition, a man of fierce libertarian language and mercenary political instincts. He made his name by out-Englishing the English: exaggerating the most distinctive traits and selling it as a basis for revolt. A down-on-his-luck emigrant, landing in Philadelphia with few prospects, he had written *Common Sense* (the title belonged to another colonial revolutionary, Benjamin Rush) in a few hectic weeks.

Rarely has a single volume achieved such an instantaneous effect, possibly because it was published on the same day that George III pledged in parliament to put "a speedy end to these disorders" in the 13 colonies.

Common Sense is a model of popular journalistic brio, written to be understood by all readers, high and low. With breath-taking chutzpah, Paine singled out George as "the royal brute" responsible for all the ills of America. His attitude to monarchy in general is entertainingly severe:

> "England, since the conquest, hath known some few good monarchs, but groaned beneath a much larger number of bad ones; yet no man in his senses can say that their claim under

William the Conqueror is a very honourable one. A French
bastard landing with an armed banditti, and establishing himself
king of England against the consent of the natives, is in plain
terms a very paltry rascally original."

Nailing his colours, Paine then took the logical step of calling for war,
and for independence. "Why is it that we hesitate?" he asked. "The
sun never shined on a cause of greater worth ... For God's sake, let us
come to a final separation ... The blood of the slain, the weeping voice
of nature cries, 'tis time to part' ... The birthday of a new world is at
hand." In a few well-turned phrases, and with an eye for vivid expression, Paine transformed a previously leaden debate into pure gold:

> "I have heard it asserted by some, that as America hath flour-
> ished under her former connection with Great Britain, the same
> connection is necessary towards her future happiness, and will
> always have the same effect. Nothing can be more fallacious
> than this kind of argument. We may as well assert that because
> a child has thrived upon milk that it is never to have meat, or
> that the first 20 years of our lives is to become a precedent for
> the next 20... "

Paine never let the facts get in the way of a passionate restatement of
popular sentiment:

> "We have it in our power to begin the world over again. A
> situation, similar to the present, hath not happened since the
> days of Noah until now. The birthday of a new world is at hand,
> and a race of men, perhaps as numerous as all Europe contains,
> are to receive their portion of freedom from the event of a few
> months."

Having found his voice, Paine subsequently weighed in against slavery,
in favour of the emancipation of women, and on behalf of many other
progressive causes. In 1787, he returned to England, via revolutionary
France, and proceeded to launch a fierce attack on Edmund Burke in
The Rights of Man, for some his masterpiece.

Paine was part of a radical circle of free thinkers that included William
Blake, William Godwin and Mary Wollstonecraft. Among conservative
Britons, he was regarded with fear and hatred. His books and effigy
were regularly burned in public, and he lived a precarious life one jump

ahead of the authorities. In the American spirit, Paine was always a master of the provisional.

Paine's influential writings became a textbook for English radicalism, and widely admired on the left. His connections with both the French and the American revolutions gave him a unique position as a champion of Enlightenment politics, and his prose – more demotic and colloquial than Burke, whose "high-toned exclamation" he despised – survives as a bracing and exemplary blast of libertarian polemic.

Three to compare:
Edmund Burke: *Reflections on the Revolution in France* (1790)
Thomas Paine: *Rights of Man* (1791)
Thomas Paine: *The Age of Reason* (1793)

17. THE WEALTH OF NATIONS
BY ADAM SMITH (1776)

1776 was an *annus mirabilis* for English and American prose, a year to compare with 1859 (Darwin's *On the Origin of Species*; Dickens's *A Tale of Two Cities*; Mill's *On Liberty*). In February, Gibbon published the first volume of his *The History of the Decline and Fall of the Roman Empire*; while in March a brilliant intellectual, a star of the Scottish Enlightenment, single-handedly invented the subject of modern political economy with *An Inquiry Into the Nature and Causes of the Wealth of Nations* which swiftly became established in the minds of intelligent readers as *The Wealth of Nations*. When the first edition sold out in six months, the story went round that another celebrated Scot, the philosopher David Hume, was now joking that *The Wealth of Nations* probably required too much thought to be as popular as Gibbon's *Decline and Fall*.

Gibbon, in fact, was full of generous praise for his rival. He wrote to the Scottish historian and philosopher Adam Ferguson: "What an excellent work is that with which our common friend Mr Adam Smith has enriched the public! An extensive science in a single book, and the most profound ideas expressed in the most perspicuous language".

Smith's work, indeed, was every bit as singular as Gibbon's. Although it provided a comprehensive and magisterial treatment of its subject, it was also a work of robust common sense, intelligible to any careful reader, braiding history, philosophy, psychology, and sociology in a compelling tapestry of theory and experience. Smith, writes one commentator, was concerned to improve "the human condition in practical ways for real people". This was a book that had begun as a series of lectures delivered to audiences in Glasgow. Smith's friend Hume, joking aside, declared that the book had "depth and solidity and acuteness, and is so much illustrated by curious facts, that it must at last take the public attention".

For Smith, in a doctrine that would have been music to the ears of any energetic new Americans, a nation's labour is the source of its basic means. Moreover, Smith argued, there is an intrinsic value to the division of labour, where labour was the sole determinant of price. This simple proposition becomes complicated in more advanced societies by the intervention of wages, profit, and rent, three elements that complexify the basic economic model. Combined with Smith's wide-ranging, lucid, and profound exposition, there's also his assault on the mercantile system, an outmoded throwback that he conceived as restrictive, repressive, and inimical to individual self-expression in the marketplace.

At the heart of *The Wealth of Nations* is the provocative suggestion that self-interest is perhaps the only criterion of economic behaviour, and that the universal, unfettered pursuit of self-advantage was the only sure guarantee of general welfare. Arguably, it is the collision of Smith's ideas with the political ambitions of the American Revolution that would, eventually, make a decisive contribution to the development of western capitalism.

Crucially, for Smith, a civilised society is a trading society. There's a famous passage in book 1 where he argues for the natural place of competitive trade.

"Nobody ever saw a dog make a fair and deliberate exchange of one bone for another with another dog. Nobody ever saw one animal by its gestures and natural cries signify to another, this is mine, that yours; I am willing to give this for that ... But man has almost constant occasion for the help of his brethren, and it is in vain for him to expect it from their benevolence only. He will be more likely to prevail if he can interest their self-love in his favour..."

Accordingly, Smith's opening theme is that the regulations imposed on commerce are ill-founded and counterproductive. In Smith's day, the conventional wisdom was that gold and silver was wealth, and that countries should boost exports and resist imports in order to maximise this metallic treasure. It was Smith's transformative insight that a nation's real wealth lies in the constant traffic of goods and services thereby created – what we would call the gross national product. To maximise this, he argued, government should not restrict an individual nation's productive capacity, but set it free.

Another central theme was that such productive capacity rests on the division of labour and on the accumulation of capital that such activity makes possible. Huge efficiencies can be gained by breaking production down into a multiplicity of small tasks, each undertaken by specialists.

Smith's third theme is that a country's future income depends upon this capital accumulation. The more that is invested in better productive processes, the more wealth will be created in the future. But if people are going to build up their capital, they must be confident that it will be secure from theft. The countries that prosper are those that grow their capital, manage it well, and protect it. Smith demonstrated that this system is automatic. Where things are scarce, people are prepared to pay more for them; there is more profit in supplying them, so producers invest more capital to produce them. Where there is a glut, prices and profits will be low, and then producers switch their capital and enterprise elsewhere. Industry thus remains focused on the nation's most important needs, with no need for central direction.

For all these reasons, Smith believes that government itself must be limited. Its core functions are to maintain defence, keep order, build infrastructure and promote education. It was the duty of good government to keep the market economy open and free, and not act in ways that might distort it. Enter George Washington, Thomas Jefferson, John Adams et al. *The Wealth of Nations* was, of course, published in the year of the Declaration of Independence. This strange fact lends added significance to Smith's prediction that the Americans "will be one of the foremost nations of the world".

Three to compare:
David Hume: *The History of England* (1754-61)
Henry Thomas Buckle: *History of Civilization in England* (1857)
Karl Marx: *Capital,* Volume I (1867)

18. The History of the Decline and Fall
of the Roman Empire
by Edward Gibbon (1776-1788)

The most celebrated history book in the English language has its own famous founding myth:

"It was at Rome, on the 15th of October 1764, as I sat musing amidst the ruins of the Capitol, while the barefooted friars were singing Vespers in the temple of Jupiter, that the idea of writing the decline and fall of the City first started to my mind."

Edward Gibbon almost certainly contrived this fanciful recollection, but the scholarship that went into his *Decline and Fall* still stands, like a timeless Roman ruin: majestic, elegant and even sublime. An object of awe, Gibbon's history unfolds its narrative from the height of the Roman Empire to the fall of Byzantium. The six volumes (published between 1776 and 1788) fall into three parts: from the age of Trajan to "the subversion of the western empire" in 395 AD; from the reign of Justinian in the east to the second, Germanic empire, under Charlemagne, in the west; and from the revival of this western empire to the fall of Constantinople in 1453. In so doing, Gibbon traces the intimate and profound connection of the ancient world to his own, more modern time, linking more or less explicitly the age of the Enlightenment to the age of Rome.

Gibbon may have been an amateur historian (his life was otherwise devoted to nurturing his family's considerable wealth, and to serving in the militia), but his erudition is staggering. It was commonplace in Augustan England of the 18th century to refer to Virgil, Ovid, or Plutarch. Gibbon alludes to passages in Strabo, Sallust, Seneca, Macrobius and Longinus, among many others.

Next to his learning, there's his style, whose later devotees include both Winston Churchill, and Evelyn Waugh. "It has always been my practice," wrote Gibbon, "to cast a long paragraph in a single mould, to try it by my ear, to deposit it in my memory; but to suspend the action of the pen till I had given the last polish to my work."

Decline and Fall is a cathedral of words and opinions: sonorous, awe-inspiring and shadowy, with odd and unexpected corners of wit and irony, concealed in well-judged footnotes.

He was also happy to disavow any consequence to this immense undertaking: "History is, indeed, little more than the register of the crimes, follies, and misfortune of mankind." Gibbon also liked to season his narrative with pithy asides. For example: "Conversation enriches the understanding, but solitude is the school of genius." And again, in chapter VIII: "All taxes must, at last, fall upon agriculture." Sometimes, Gibbon is almost the equal of Tacitus in his brutal summaries of the historical process: "Corruption, the most infallible symptom of constitutional liberty."

And then there's his intellectual background, as a scholar steeped in the age of reason. Gibbon famously blamed Christianity for the disintegration of the Roman Empire. However, here and there, as in his account of Constantine's conversion, he grudgingly allows for the benefits of religion, too:

> "The sacred indolence of the monks was devoutly embraced by a servile and effeminate age; but if superstition had not afforded a decent retreat, the same vices would have tempted the unworthy Romans to desert, from baser motives, the standard of the republic. Religious precepts are easily obeyed which indulge and sanctify the natural inclinations of their votaries; but the pure and genuine influence of Christianity may be traced in its beneficial, though imperfect, effects on the barbarian proselytes of the North. If the decline of the Roman empire was hastened by the conversion of Constantine, his victorious religion broke the violence of the fall, and mollified the ferocious temper of the conquerors."

After several rewrites, with Gibbon "often tempted to throw away the labours of seven years", the first volume of his *Decline and Fall* was published on 17 February 1776, less than six months before the US Declaration of Independence, a famous climax to the revolution in the American colonies, and a more than passing coincidence. Two months after the first publication of the first volume of this colossal classic, Gibbon boasted to his stepmother about his work's reception: "It has been very well received, by men of letters, men of the world, and even by fine feathered ladies."

It is, in other words, a work of universal interest, and timeless influence, unquestionably a magnificent classic of our literature. Gibbon's own farewell to his masterpiece is almost more affecting than his celebrated account of its genesis:

"It was on the day, or rather the night, of 27 June 1787, between the hours of 11 and 12, that I wrote the last lines of the last page in a summer-house in my garden... I will not dissemble the first emotions of joy on the recovery of my freedom, and perhaps the establishment of my fame. But my pride was soon humbled, and a sober melancholy was spread over my mind by the idea that I had taken my everlasting leave of an old and agreeable companion, and that, whatsoever might be the future date of my history, the life of the historian must be short and precarious."

Three to compare:

Edward Gibbon, *Memoirs of My Life and Writings* (1796)

Winston Churchill, *A History of the English-speaking*
    Peoples (1956-58)

David Womerseley, *The Transformation of the Decline and Fall of the*
    Roman Empire (1988)

19. THE DIARY OF FANNY BURNEY (1778)
BY FANNY BURNEY

"Dear diary" is a literary commonplace. Diaries, or journals, will be

the one factual genre to which any reader can relate. Moreover, in English life and letters, which often celebrate the virtues of privacy and solitude, the diary is a quintessential national form of self-expression. Any list of great English diarists must include John Evelyn, Lord Byron, Francis Kilvert, Virginia Woolf – and Fanny Burney (1752-1840).

She was born, Frances, the third daughter of Charles Burney, a fashionable dilettante, in the reign of George II. Her life was dogged with ill health and mixed fortune, but she pioneered a career as a female writer to flourish both as a playwright (eight plays) and also as the author of some much-admired satirical fiction (four novels). Burney always described her work as "scribblings", a typically English self-deprecation. Her first novel, *Evelina*, was published anonymously in 1778, coincidentally the year in which she concluded her first set of journals. A later novel, Cecilia (1782), contained some sentences that deeply impressed the young

Jane Austen:

> "The whole of this unfortunate business," said Dr Lyster, "has
> been the result of PRIDE and PREJUDICE ... If to PRIDE
> and PREJUDICE you owe your miseries, so wonderfully is
> good and evil balanced, that to PRIDE and PREJUDICE you
> will also owe their termination."

Austen aside, Burney was also admired for her wit by some of
the foremost literary figures of her time (notably Dr Johnson, and
Edmund Burke), as well as "the bluestocking circle", David Garrick
and members of the aristocracy. Her early diaries are notable for their
first-hand account of the sensational trial of Warren Hastings and
the madness of George III, whose doctor, Francis Willis, she came to
know well, whom she characterises brilliantly:

> "Dr Willis is a man of ten thousand; open, honest, dauntless,
> light-hearted, innocent, and high-minded: I see him impressed
> with the most animated reverence and affection for his royal
> patient; but it is wholly for his character − not a whit for his
> rank."

There is not yet a satisfactory single volume anthology of Burney's
work as a diarist, but the Everyman edition (published in 1971) is a
good showcase for her gifts. Burney is sharp, observant and highly
entertaining and her satire was always laced with affection.

In 1785, thanks to her entree to metropolitan literary and court
circles, Fanny was taken on by George III and Queen Charlotte as
keeper of the robes. She became close to the queen and much courted
by members of the royal household. When the French Revolution
broke out, Burney's cosmopolitan sensibility brought her into contact
with a circle of French exiles and she subsequently married General
Alexandre d'Arblay, a hero of the uprising, in 1793. Married life was
hard, but she made ends meet with a successful novel, Camilla, or
a Picture of Youth (1796), and then followed her husband to Paris,
where he was serving in Napoleon's government.

In 1810, she began to note symptoms of breast cancer and was
treated by some of the most eminent specialists of the day. Eventually, in September 1811, she submitted to a mastectomy conducted
by "seven men in black". Burney remained conscious throughout

the operation (before the discovery of anaesthesia) and her detailed account of the procedure is a classic of reportage:

> "I mounted, therefore, unbidden, the bed stead – & M Dubois placed me upon the mattress, & spread a cambric handkerchief upon my face. It was transparent, however, & I saw, through it, that the bed stead was instantly surrounded by the seven men & my nurse. I refused to be held; but when, bright through the cambric, I saw the glitter of polished steel – I closed my eyes. I would not trust to convulsive fear the sight of the terrible incision. Yet – when the dreadful steel was plunged into the breast – cutting through veins – arteries – flesh – nerves – I needed no injunctions not to restrain my cries. I began a scream that lasted unintermittingly during the whole time of the incision – & I almost marvel that it rings not in my ears still, so excruciating was the agony. When the wound was made, & the instrument was withdrawn, the pain seemed undiminished, for the air that suddenly rushed into those delicate parts felt like a mass of minute but sharp & forked poniards, that were tearing the edges of the wound. I concluded the operation was over – Oh no! presently the terrible cutting was renewed – & worse than ever, to separate the bottom, the foundation of this dreadful gland from the parts to which it adhered – Again all description would be baffled – yet again all was not over, – Dr Larry rested but his own hand, & – Oh heaven! – I then felt the knife (rack) ling against the breast bone – scraping it!"

With the dispassionate eye of a born writer, Burney never failed to subject herself to the most searching scrutiny. In later life, having now retired to Bath, she destroyed much of her earlier diaries. Today, it is for her picture of 18th and early 19th century society that she is principally remembered. There is no definitive life, but Joyce Hemlow's *The History of Fanny Burney* (1958) is a useful starting point.

Three to compare:
Lord Byron: *Letters and Journals* (12 volumes, 1830)
Francis Kilvert: *Diaries* (three volumes, 1938–1940)
Virginia Woolf: *A Writer's Diary* (1953)

20. THE FEDERALIST PAPERS
BY 'PUBLIUS' (1788)

When the president of the United States is a corrupt and lazy, narcis

sistic clown and Alexander Hamilton has become the subject of a smash-hit hip-hop musical, you might think the game would be up for the rhetoric and idealism surrounding the birth of the American republic. In such circumstances, *The Federalist Papers*, which are so often described as "a classic in political science" unrivalled by any subsequent American writer, might seem utterly redundant, even irrelevant.

Nothing could be further from the truth. America is a society constructed of words and *The Federalist Papers* stand alongside the Declaration of Independence and the US constitution as the most sustained and deeply serious attempt to clarify what it was that the Founding Fathers had set in motion on 4 July 1776.

"Publius" – along with "Mark Twain", the only pseudonym admitted to this series – concealed the identities of three great American founding fathers: Alexander Hamilton, James Madison and John Jay who, respectively, contributed 52, 28 and five of the 85 short (approximately 1,000-1,500 word) essays that make up a document that, in the words of one critic, "lies at the very core of American governance". Indeed, the author of the Declaration of Independence, Thomas Jefferson, declared these papers to be "the best commentary on the principles of government ever written".

The Federalist Papers were composed and published very fast, in serial form, in response to an urgent, post-revolutionary crisis in which the anti-federalist movement had begun seriously to challenge "the federal union". Seventy-seven of the essays were published almost continuously in the *Independent Journal* and the *New York Packet* between October 1787 and August 1788 and collected in book form later that same year. This would be added to, and revised, in subsequent editions up to 1802. At this vital moment in the making of the United States, there was, said Hamilton, nailing the argument, only one question at stake: "Whether societies of men are really capable or not of establishing good government from reflection and choice, or whether they are for ever destined for their political constitutions on accident and force."

Addressing a debate that reverberates to the present day, Hamilton and Madison made a brilliant and powerful case for "the UNION". In essay no 9 (the words are Hamilton's) we see their breadth of wisdom and learning: "It is impossible to read the history of the petty republics of Greece and Italy without feeling sensations of horror and disgust at the distractions with which they were continually agitated, and at the rapid successions of revolutions by which they were kept in a state of perpetual vibration between the extremes of tyranny and anarchy."

To this, Jay added his own voice, in another powerful essay: "Nothing is more certain than the indispensable necessity of government; and it is equally undeniable that whenever and however it is instituted, the people must cede to it some of their natural rights, in order to vest it with requisite powers."

In such a situation, said Jay, Americans had to ask themselves the one question that would eventually morph into the debate about states' rights: "Whether it would conduce more to the interests of the people that they should be one nation, under one federal government, than that they should divide themselves into separate confederacies..."

Who knows how many Americans ever fully engaged with the complex and enthralling ideas embodied in this remarkable, and strangely passionate, text? At the time, these essays were avidly consumed by voters and readers in New York, to whom they were addressed. Hamilton seems to have encouraged the reprinting of his work in newspapers outside New York State and in several other states where the ratification debate was raging.

There were, of course, nuances of difference between the three authors behind "Publius" (Madison and Hamilton would ultimately have a bitter falling-out), but their collective support for the much-disputed US constitution is clear and unequivocal. Interestingly, in the light of the current political situation, they assigned the supreme court only a very limited role in the overall system of government. "Of the three powers above mentioned," writes Hamilton, " the JUDICIARY is next to nothing." It's an irony of history that "Publius" would have appreciated that, in the present emergency, it's precisely the judiciary that is everything.

Three to compare:
Thomas Jefferson: *Autobiography* (1821)
Benjamin Franklin: *Autobiography* (1793)
Ulysses S Grant: *Personal Memoirs* (1885)

21. The Natural History and Antiquities
of Selborne
by Gilbert White (1789)

The Rev Gilbert White was that now extinct species, the unmarried

Oxbridge don in holy orders. A lifelong curate and a fellow of Oriel College, White devoted himself to observing flora and fauna at large in the natural world, a sequence of observations for which he became world famous.

In 1755, after the death of his father, he returned to the family home in Selborne, settling for comfortable obscurity in a remote Hampshire village, an enviable career move. On the face of it, the passage of his declining years would be tranquil and serene, with no greater vicissitudes than bad weather or poor harvests.

However, around 1767, he got into correspondence, first with Thomas Pennant, a prominent zoologist, and then with Daines Barrington, another important British naturalist. His exchanges with these men would form the basis of his Natural History, a compilation published in the year of the French Revolution. There could scarcely have been a more stark contrast between the timeless, resilient stability of English country life and the bloody metropolitan dramas of France. Where Rousseau and Robespierre championed the rights of man, White celebrated the earthworm, "a small and despicable link in the chain of nature", which, if lost "would make a lamentable chasm".

It's claimed that White's *Natural History* is the fourth most-published book in the English language, after the Bible, Shakespeare and Bunyan, and it has certainly been in print since first publication, while the benign White himself is now recognised equally as a great stylist and a pioneer ecologist. His work, in literature and in nature studies, coincides with a pivotal moment in the reign of George III when zoology and botany were at the cutting edge of scientific inquiry. The young Charles Darwin would grow up with White's *Antiquities of Selborne* at his side – as a guide, philosopher and friend.

White's book reveals him to have been a man of profound general knowledge, with an appetite for medieval civilisation that was far in advance of his times. He was also a beady-eyed student of nature. As many critics have noticed, the zoology and botany of the Natural

History replaced the fabulous folklore and bizarre traditions of previous countryside writers, with White's scrupulous observations and beautifully expressed summaries:

> "The titmouse, which early in February begins to make two quaint notes, like the whetting of a saw, is the marsh titmouse: the great titmouse sings with three cheerful joyous notes, and begins about the same time."

White's letters are full of felicities, uniting into an unforgettable portrait of country life that's also the record of a new kind of zoology, scientific, precise and based on the steady accumulation of detail – the fruit of a quiet life conducted by a leisured, well-to-do, middle-aged gentleman of cultivated tastes and habits, happily cut off from the noise and irritation of urban, industrial life. As such, he is the indispensable precursor to those great Victorians who would transform our ideas about life on Earth, especially in the undergrowth – Lyell, Spencer, Huxley and Darwin.

Charm is a dangerous literary gift, but White's work is conspicuous for its philosophical equanimity and moderate spirit. As a writer, he is the reader's lovable companion, with whom it's not impossible to imagine a conversation about cobwebs, the common rush (Juncus effusus), brown owls, stinking hellebore (Helleborus foetidus) or possibly the vernal migration of the ring ouzel.

As a garrulous country parson, White is comparable in the degree of self-revelation to the infinitely more worldly (even corrupt) figure of James Boswell. He offers a similar kind of colloquial familiarity, but with this difference. Where Boswell has his eye firmly on the judgment of posterity, and on his readers' approval of his "sensibility" (a key Augustan English requirement), White wants only to celebrate the beautiful beech woods of his village, its rooks and magpies and, of course, the weather. Thus goes White's immortal summary of that revolutionary year, 1789:

> "To January 13, hard frost. To the end of the month, mild, with showers. To the end of February, frequent rain, with snow showers and heavy gales of wind. To 13th March, hard frost, with snow. To April, heavy rain, with frost and snow and sleet. To the end of April, dark, cold weather, with frequent rains. To June 9, warm spring weather, with brisk winds and frequent

showers. From June 4 to the end of July, warm, with much rain. To August 29, hot, dry, sultry weather. To September 11, mild, with frequent showers. To the end of September, fine autumnal weather, with occasional showers. To November 17, heavy rain, with violent gales of wind. To December 18, mild, dry weather, with a few showers. To the end of the year, rain and wind."

Plus ça change, plus c'est la même chose.

Three to compare:
Izaak Walton: *The Compleat Angler* (1653)
Charles Darwin: *The Voyage of the Beagle* (1839)
Richard Mabey: *The Cabaret of Plants* (2015)

22. THE INTERESTING NARRATIVE OF THE LIFE OF OLAUDAH EQUIANO BY OLAUDAH EQUIANO (1789)

Black literature begins with the slave memoirs of the 18th century. Equiano's *Interesting Narrative* is the most famous of these, especially once it was taken up by supporters of the abolition movement, but he was not the first African slave to publish a book in England, or, if we remember Dr Johnson's manservant, Francis Barber, the first to have some experience of London literary life.

In the book trade, *Letters of the Late Ignatius Sancho* (1782) were probably the first to mobilise English readers against racial discrimination and the horrors of the slave trade. During the 19th century, black literature would continue to flourish, in Britain, with Mary Seacole and, in the USA, with Frederick Douglass. In the 20th century, this tradition was sustained by largely autobiographical prose, often focusing on the imaginative reworking of the slave experience. Some outstanding recent examples include Grace Nichols: *I Is a Long Memoried Woman* (1983), Caryll Phillips: *Cambridge* (1991) and David Dabydeen: *Turner* (1994). All of these titles owe some intellectual debt to *The Interesting Narrative*.

Olaudah Equiano (c1745-1797), also known as Gustavus Vassa,

was an African writer, born in what is now the Eboe province of Nigeria, and sold into slavery aged 11. Equiano subsequently worked as the slave of a British naval officer, purchased his freedom in 1766 and went on to write his popular slave memoir. No fewer than 17 editions and reprints, and several translations, appeared between 1798 and 1827. In hindsight, *The Interesting Narrative* became an influential work that established a template for later slave life writing and subsequently an important text in the teaching of African literature. Indeed, to Henry Louis Gates Jr, Equiano is a founding figure in the making of an authentic black literary tradition.

Inevitably, perhaps, *The Interesting Narrative* has been dogged by controversy from first publication. Equiano's story was initially discredited as false (despite a preface including testimonials from white people "who knew me when I first arrived in England"). Even now, there are scholars who cast doubt on Equiano's veracity, claiming that he plagiarised his story from other sources. Whatever the truth, the surviving text of his *Interesting Narrative* is sufficiently its own, in style and character, to merit serious consideration. Equiano's story is certainly remarkable.

From the outset, he is concerned to establish his credentials as an ordinary, long-suffering African boy who has endured much and triumphed over adversity. He describes, at some length, the Eboe customs he has grown up with: circumcision, witchcraft and tribal patriarchy. As well as cataloguing his primitive beginnings, Equiano also celebrates the exotic and fabulous natural profusion of Africa, consciously playing to western fascination with the "Dark Continent": "Our land is uncommonly rich and fruitful, and produces all kinds of vegetables in great abundance. We have plenty of Indian corn, and vast quantities of cotton and tobacco. Our pine apples grow without culture; they are about the size of the largest sugar-loaf, and finely-flavoured. We have also spices of different kinds, particularly pepper; and a variety of delicious fruits which I have never seen in Europe; together with gums of various kinds, and honey in abundance."

Equiano, for all his modesty the hero of his own tale, also singles himself out for his natural eloquence. It's his strategy in the memoir to convince his readers of the injustice of slavery by writing in a tone of reason and conciliation. While he can pile on the horror of the "middle crossing", strangely, he lacks any resentment and does not castigate his white masters in print for their cruelty. His tone is nothing if not complicit: "I was named Olaudah, which, in our language signifies vicissitude or fortune; also one favoured, and having a loud voice and well-spoken."

Having established his origins, Equiano moves to describe his enslavement and transportation to the West Indies, and thence to Virginia, where he served as the slave of an officer in the Royal Navy, Michael Pascal, who renamed him "Gustavus Vassa" after the 16th century Swedish king. Equiano travelled the oceans with Pascal for eight years, during which time he was baptised and learned to read and write. Pascal then sold Equiano to a ship's captain in London, who took him to Montserrat, where he was traded with a merchant, Robert King. While working as a deckhand, valet and barber for King, Equiano earned money by negotiating on the side, accumulating enough savings to buy his freedom.

From a documentary point of view, Equiano's account of life in mid-Georgian Britain is fascinating. He gets taken up by white society and patronised by the great and the good, but he is never quite free of floggings and incarceration. Nevertheless, he does manage to save the money that will buy his freedom.

What follows are Equiano's adventures on the high seas, mixed with his conversion to Christianity. In fact, Equiano spent almost 20 years travelling the world, including trips to Turkey and the Arctic. In 1786, in London, he involved himself in the movement to abolish slavery. He was a prominent member of the "Sons of Africa", a group of a dozen black men who campaigned for abolition. After the publication of *The Interesting Narrative*, Equiano travelled widely to promote the book, whose immense popularity became integral to the abolitionist cause and made Equiano a wealthy man. In 1792, Equiano married an Englishwoman, Susanna Cullen, and they had two daughters. He died on 31 March 1797.

Three to compare:

Mary Seacole: *Wonderful Adventures of Mrs Seacole in Many Lands* (1857)

Peter Fryer: *Staying Power: The History of Black People in Britain* (1984)

Henry Louis Gates Jr: *The Signifying Monkey* (1988)

23. Reflections on the Revolution in France
by Edmund Burke (1790)

On 4 November 1789, the celebrated dissenting minister Richard

Price, whose teaching at Newington Green, north London, had exerted a profound influence on many younger writers – notably Mary Wollstonecraft – delivered a sermon in which he celebrated "the ardour for liberty" among the French people.

Price, a friend of Benjamin Franklin, was known for his support of both the French and the American revolutions, so this was hardly a surprise. But Edmund Burke – a passionate conservative – was appalled by Price's suggestion that the English king owed his position to his people, who should be at liberty to arraign him for misconduct. Price's fiery provocation stirred Burke deeply. Within a few months, he had produced this brilliant pamphlet – cast in the form of a letter "to a gentleman in Paris" – an instant bestseller, and a rhetorical *tour de force* that, in the words of the scholar Stephen Greenblatt, has become the "most eloquent statement of British conservatism favouring monarchy, aristocracy, property, hereditary succession, and the wisdom of the ages". Even now, the Irish Burke's anglophile confidence in his deeply held conservative position remains fairly breathtaking:

> "The people of England will show to the haughty potentates of the world, and to their talking sophisters, that a free, a generous, an informed nation, honours the high magistrates of its church; that it will not suffer the insolence of wealth and titles, or any other species of proud pretension, to look down with scorn upon what they look up to with reverence; nor presume to trample on that acquired personal nobility, which they intend always to be, and which is often the fruit, not the reward (for what can be the reward?), of learning, piety, and virtue."

Polemic aside, much of Burke's appeal in *the Reflections* derived from its timing. Burke was writing, in highly charged terms, at a moment when the Parisian mob's violent treatment of the French royal family was particularly shocking to English readers. The passage in the *Reflections* that's still remembered is his famous lament that "the age of chivalry is dead", followed by his fervent account of Marie Antoinette's downfall. (At the time of writing, neither she nor Louis XVI had been guillotined.) Burke's idolisation of Marie Antoinette has been widely anthologised:

> "It is now 16 or 17 years since I saw the queen of France at Versailles; and surely never lighted on this orb, which she hardly seemed to touch, a more delightful vision. I saw her just above the horizon, decorating and cheering the elevated sphere she had just begun to move in — glittering like the morning star, full of life and splendour and joy. Oh, what a revolution! And what a heart must I have, to contemplate without emotion that elevation and that fall!"

Burke has been mocked for such passages, and for the brooding melancholy of his pessimism, but his vision had one deeply original quality that sets him apart: he was passionately concerned in his writing to attempt to uncover the future development of European politics. In the age of Brexit, when all clarity of thought and argument seems lost in the fog of chaotic contemporary events, Burke's approach and method comes down to us as curiously appealing.

He opens his argument with a fierce repudiation of popular sovereignty, contrasting the inherited rights of the English establishment he favoured with "the rights of man" demanded by French revolutionaries. Such claims, Burke decides, are based on "extravagant and presumptuous speculations" that must be at odds with an ordered and civilised society, and will inevitably lead to poverty and chaos. Burke loves order. "Good order is the foundation of all good things." And he loves any social contract that underpins domestic stability:

> "Society is indeed a contract … it becomes a partnership not only between those who are living, but between those who are living, those who are dead, and those who are to be born."

Burke believed in gradualism, not armies, as the surest and best agency of social change. He revered tradition, and he had a deep respect for stable government. In another famous passage, he drew on nature to contrast the hectic fever of revolutionary France with the tranquil stability of England:

"Because half a dozen grasshoppers under a fern make the field ring with their importunate chink, whilst thousands of great cattle, reposed beneath the shadow of the British oak, chew the cud and are silent, pray do not imagine that those who make the noise are the only inhabitants of the field."

He wanted government to articulate the sum of man's reason:

"Government is a contrivance of human wisdom to provide for human wants. Men have a right that these wants should be provided for by this wisdom."

To him, therefore, this French revolution in Paris was anathema. As he saw it, such revolution was harsh, brutal and profoundly inhumane. Overthrow the monarchy and you entered a barbarous wasteland. Against such excesses, Burke contrasts the English system, evolved through the ages, "placed in symmetry with the world."

Finally, Burke's conclusion – that the defective institutions of the old regime should have been repaired, not destroyed – is predictable enough from the pen of such a philosophical politician. To Burke, "a perfect democracy is the most shameless thing in the world".

At the end, he reveals himself, with some modesty, to be fearful of change and simply wanting to contribute to a better society, struggling "for the liberty of others". When, as he puts it, "the equipoise of the vessel in which he sails, may be endangered", he was merely "desirous of carrying the small weight of his reasons to that which may preserve its equipoise".

Nevertheless, in the evolution of conservative thinking, his Reflections is a landmark as well as a masterpiece of Augustan English prose, an object of reverence among later generations, especially among writers such as Benjamin Disraeli, Thomas Carlyle and Walter Bagehot.

Three to compare:
Mary Wollstonecraft: *A Vindication of the Rights of Men* (1790)
Tom Paine: *Rights of Man* (1791)
Edmund Burke: *Letters on a Regicide Peace* (1796)

24. THE LIFE OF SAMUEL JOHNSON LLD
BY JAMES BOSWELL (1791)

Like some of the greatest titles in this list, James Boswell's life of Dr Johnson, the most famous biography in the English language, had a protracted, tortuous and tortured gestation. Boswell first advised his friend and mentor of his intention to write his life in 1772, when Johnson was 62, and the would-be biographer 31. He had, however, been making notes and gathering materials for his "presumptuous task" since their first encounter in 1763.

After Johnson's death in 1784, Boswell settled down to organise a "prodigious multiplicity of materials", a labour that, he admitted after five years of struggle, was costing him acute labour, perplexity and vexation. Moreover, he was being overtaken by rival lives (A potboiling "biographical sketch" by Thomas Tyers had appeared in 1784; Hester Thrale's *Anecdotes of the Late Samuel Johnson* in 1786; then *A Life of Samuel Johnson* by his friend and executor, Sir John Hawkins, came out in 1787). Worse, he was becoming a figure of pity and contempt in Grub Street, the self-appointed biographer who had both missed the bus and simultaneously failed his own life's mission.

However, when it was published in 1791, Boswell's *Life* was soon recognised as a masterpiece, a fitting monument to a great English writer and an extraordinary work of art in its own right. Inevitably, there was the usual sniping. During the course of a life in Grub Street, Boswell had acquired many enemies. The main objections to his work fall under three heads: first, as the work of an acolyte, it's plainly not a conventional biography; second, even by that standard, it fails – Boswell only knew Johnson in the latter half of his life and sometimes took outrageous liberties with his material; third, as an exercise in "life-writing", it falls short, being scarcely more than a loosely linked string of scenes from a life. To which the obvious riposte is: open the book, forget about the narrow academic critique and read one of the most original works of English prose, as much a mirror to its author as to it subject.

Boswell never makes much secret of the fact that he and his subject have been friends and associates. For some 250 pages in my Everyman edition, he supplies a faithful, almost mundane, account of Johnson's early years in Lichfield and his move to London.

When the 22-year-old Boswell finally meets Johnson, who was then aged 53, *Life* catches fire. Boswell, who has longed for this introduction and who confides to his own journal that he will "cultivate this acquaintance", describes himself as "much agitated" at the prospect of meeting the great man. A roguish companion, present at the meeting, knowing the doctor's famous dislike of the Scots, interjects that Boswell comes from Scotland. At this, the future biographer protests:

> "Mr Johnson, (said I) I do indeed come from Scotland, but I cannot help it." I am willing to flatter myself that I meant this as a light pleasantry to soothe and conciliate him, and not as an humiliating abasement at the expence [sic] of my country, but this speech was unlucky. With the quickness of wit for which he was so remarkable, he seized the expression 'come from Scotland' ... and retorted, 'That, Sir, I find, is what a very great many of your countrymen cannot help.'"

Boswell's nerves are jangling, but a sympathetic onlooker advises him: "Don't be uneasy. I can see he likes you very well."

What follows is the blossoming of the strangest literary friendship on record. Young Boswell was a libertine, a flatterer and a self-important voyeur. On his own account, he is at once humble, vainglorious, creepy, complacent and sentimental. But Johnson, the pugnacious Tory, lifelong stoic and fierce Augustan intellectual, was not only charmed by Boswell's devotion, he seemed to have been motivated by it too, perhaps because he identified an ulterior motive in Boswell's excessive note-taking. "One would think," he told his confidante Thrale, that "the man had been hired to spy upon me". Perhaps Johnson was even inspired by his new audience. His conversation and opinions take wing, becoming progressively more Johnsonian.

Although it was 10 years before Boswell found the courage to confess he was writing his *Life*, there were some clues to his ultimate intention. One turning point occurred with the pair's celebrated tour of Scotland. In August 1773, 10 years after first meeting Boswell, Johnson set out with his young friend on *A Journey to the Western Islands of Scotland*, as his (1775) account of their travels expressed it. Boswell's rival account, his *Journal of a Tour to the Hebrides* (1785) became a first draft of a biographical approach to his mentor. This trial run for *Life* was a success. Now Boswell started working on the "vast treasure of his conversations at different times" that he had recorded in his journals.

Boswell may have been responsible for creating the image of Johnson as a critic who loved to hold forth ("Depend upon it, Sir …"), but he also records a lot of merriment, banter and jollity. The bookseller Tom Davies declares that "Johnson laughs like a rhinocerous". The conversation, fuelled with quantities of port, ranges promiscuously across all manner of topics: printers, adultery, birds, primogeniture, marriage, crowds, booksellers, Americans, the plays of Sheridan, bad poets (especially Thomas Gray), bears, fame, Whigs, warfare and cookery books. Life is also a book of table talk, overheard conversations and literary repartee.

Johnson's circle included bishops, academics, booksellers, even George III, whose meeting with Johnson is a high point of Boswell's first volume (there were two).

It's almost impossible to do this book the justice it deserves by selective quotation. Boswell probably needed an editor, but his obsessive note-taking and occasional banality make for compulsive reading. As a biographer, he is both a voyeur and a provocateur, a ringmaster, a social climber and sycophantic stooge. How self-aware is he? It's hard to say. But when, in the final pages, Johnson's life draws to a close – he was mortally afraid of dying – the reader had lost both a friend (Johnson) and a great friendship (Boswell and Johnson). The subject of this classic biography, who died in 1784, was immediately buried at Westminster Abbey, revered as one of the greatest Englishmen. Simultaneously, Boswell's health began to fail through a combination of alcoholism and VD. He died in London in 1795 and was buried in the crypt of the family mausoleum in Auchinleck, Ayrshire.

Three to compare:
W Jackson Bate: *Samuel Johnson* (1977)
Richard Holmes: *Dr Johnson and Mr Savage* (1993)
Adam Sisman: *Boswell's Presumptuous Task* (2000)

25. A VINDICATION OF THE RIGHTS OF WOMAN
BY MARY WOLLSTONECRAFT (1792)

The term "feminism" did not exist when Mary Wollstonecraft wrote

this short book (just 98pp in my Vintage Classics edition) and some critics have resisted its author's identification with the movement. In hindsight, however, we can now see that its assault on "mistaken notions of female excellence" was the first great expression of feminist ideas. Although she does not insist on the equality of the sexes, you'll still find, articulated in thrilling clarity, the essence of Woll-stonecraft's argument for the education of women, and for an increased female participation in everyday society. This little book, which declared that "from the tyranny of man, the greater number of female follies proceed", set off the first ripples of what would eventually become the worldwide movement for women's rights. A classic of post-revolutionary thought, shaped by the Enlightenment, Wollstonecraft's *Vindication* changed life for women the world over.

Wollstonecraft began her career in 1787 with *Thoughts on the Education of Daughters* and then spent several years writing reviews, pamphlets, *Mary* (a novel), and her first foray into pre-feminist polemic, *A Vindication of the Rights of Men* (1790), which was a passionate response to Edmund Burke's *Reflections on the Revolution in France*. This, one of dozens of pamphlets inspired by Burke, was, in Wollstonecraft's words, an "effusion of the moment", attacking "the grand principles at which he [Burke] has levelled many ingenious arguments in a very specious garb".

Wollstonecraft's *Rights of Men* attracted plenty of attention and brought her into the circle of the radical philosopher William Godwin, whom she would ultimately marry.

In 1792, however, she visited revolutionary Paris, where she fell wildly in love with an American, Gilbert Ismay, with whom she had a daughter, Fanny. Caught up in the ferment of the revolution, she became enraged by Talleyrand's recommendation to the National Assembly that women should only have "domestic education". She had already begun to consider the subjection of women in society; now she found an occasion for her arguments. Accordingly, Wollstonecraft's *Vindication* carries a dedication to Talleyrand, a respectful appeal "to reconsider the subject, and maturely weigh what I have advanced respecting the rights of woman and national education".

Written in 1791 and published in 1792, with a second edition appearing that same year, *Vindication* was sold as the first volume of a work that, in Wollstonecraft's mind, would be "divided into three parts". There were, she wrote at the outset, "many subjects, cursorily alluded to" that would "furnish ample matter for a second volume, which in due time will be published." In the event, Wollstonecraft wouldn't write any subsequent volumes.

Before this date, there had been books that argued for the reform of female education, often for moral reasons or to better befit women for their role as companions for men. In contrast, in her introduction, Wollstonecraft criticises women's education thus: "I attribute [these problems] to a false system of education, gathered from the books written on this subject by men, who, considering females rather as women than human creatures, have been more anxious to make them alluring mistresses than affectionate wives and rational mothers ... the civilised women of this present century, with a few exceptions, are only anxious to inspire love, when they ought to cherish a nobler ambition, and by their abilities and virtues exact respect."

She goes on to say, with revolutionary ardour, that "I shall first consider women in the grand light of human creatures, who, in common with men, are placed on this earth to unfold their faculties".

But *Vindication* soon became more than a reassertion of women's educational rights and, instead, a full-blown demand for men and women to enjoy the benefits of reason. Within a very few pages, she had plunged into her bold analysis of men's "sexual character", following this with an assault on Rousseau for the false distinctions he makes in his approach to the sexes in Emile.

As Wollstonecraft's voice finds its polemical register, *Vindication* acquires its distinct character, at once passionate and idiosyncratic. With thrilling candour, she freely admits: "A wild wish has just flown from my heart to my head, and I will not stifle it, though it may excite a horse-laugh. I do earnestly wish to see the distinction of sex confounded in society, unless where love animates the behaviour. For this distinction is, I am firmly persuaded, the foundation of the weakness of character ascribed to women; is the cause why the understanding is neglected, whilst accomplishments are acquired with sedulous care; and the same cause accounts for their preferring the graceful before the heroic virtues."

Such a "wild wish" aside, an important part of Wollstonecraft's purpose is to unfold an unambiguous argument: "From the tyranny of man, I firmly believe, the greater number of female follies proceed; and the cunning, which I allow makes at present a part of their character, I likewise have repeatedly endeavoured to prove, is produced by oppression."

It's here that Wollstonecraft gets drawn into a discussion on women's character, opposing "sensibility" to "reason". She herself has a strong preference for "modesty", and struggles with the issue of sexuality: "Were I to name the graces that ought to adorn beauty, I should instantly exclaim cleanliness, neatness and personal reserve. It is obvious, I suppose, that the reserve I mean has nothing sexual in it, and that I think it equally necessary in both sexes."

This is a rare, almost glancing, reference to the equality of the sexes. As quickly becomes apparent to every reader, and as many commentators have noted with dismay, she nowhere says unequivocally that men and women have equal rights. She is also prone to statements that must have made later feminists shudder: "As a sex, women are habitually indolent; and everything tends to make them so." This, to modern readers, must inevitably diminish her finer moments of abstract, philosophical analysis: "Asserting the rights which women in common with men ought to contend for, I have not attempted to extenuate their faults; but to prove them to be the natural consequence of their education and station in society. If so, it is reasonable to suppose that they will change their character, and correct their vices and follies, when they are allowed to be free in a physical, moral and civil sense."

Still, having made this concession, Wollstonecraft returns to the high ground of her argument: "Let woman share the rights, and she will emulate the virtues of man; for she must grow more perfect when emancipated, or justify the authority that chains such a weak being to her duty."

Many subsequent feminist writers would take issue with the idea of "the weaker vessel". Wollstonecraft, a pioneer, struggled to break free from the tyranny of that notion. Indeed, some of the best passages in *Vindication* flow directly from unresolved feelings about what it means to be a mother, a lover, even a wife, within a patriarchal male society, and how to assert women's rights in such circumstances.

Vindication is an important book, but it's not faultless. From its first publication, it has enjoyed a mixed press. Horace Walpole denounced her as "a hyena in petticoats". In hindsight, the fate of the *Vindication* has become intimately braided with its author's own story, her troubled relations with the opposite sex, and her attempted suicide. For many, from Virginia Woolf on, Wollstonecraft's tragic, short life is now seen as just as important as her writing in the forging of a feminist critique of society. Indeed, Woolf described Wollstonecraft – her writing, arguments and "experiments in living" – as immortal: "She is alive and active, she argues and experiments, we hear her voice and trace her influence even now among the living."

Her relationship with the proto-anarchist William Godwin was unconventional. She married him after becoming pregnant. In August 1797, Wollstonecraft gave birth to a second daughter, who would grow up to be Mary Shelley, author of *Frankenstein*. The birth was followed by the agonising complications of puerperal fever. Mary Wollstonecraft died 11 days later. She was 38.

Three to compare:
Mary Wollstonecraft: *A Vindication of the Rights of Men* (1790)
JS Mill: *The Subjection of Women* (1869)
Virginia Woolf: *A Room of One's Own* (1929)

26. THE AUTOBIOGRAPHY
OF BENJAMIN FRANKLIN (1793)

Benjamin Franklin's face – on banknotes, letterheads and civic documents – is an ageless icon of the American revolution, at once benign but cunning, projecting a mood that's universal and accessible. In life, he was a great inventor (of stoves, lightning rods and bifocals); in literature, a great self-inventor. In all these guises (icon, innovator, self-advertiser), he is a true founding father, and 100% American. His *Autobiography* is perhaps his finest creation, what the critic Jay Parini has called "a foundational book for Americans" that offers "a template for self-invention".

The book itself is quite short, having been published in an abbreviated form after his death, but the tale it tells – a boy who makes his way in the world without connections, wealth or education, essentially living off his wits – is an archetypal portrait of "the founding fathers' founding father". There's also a revolutionary strand running through the text that makes it an ABC of democratic revolt as well as a canny self-portrait of a robust and rather enthralling radical, a lover of life, of women, and of simple pleasures, with an apparently uncomplicated delight in the world around him. His can-do enthusiasm and practical, folksy approach to the issues of the day is – dare one say? – quintessentially American. In other manifestations, it surfaces again in the lives and careers of US presidents such as Teddy Roosevelt, Harry Truman and Ronald Reagan.

Franklin was a man always boiling over with ideas and opinions, a man of print and paper. Long before his *Autobiography* he had become famous for his *Almanack* (published under the pseudonym "Poor Richard"), and its pithy sayings: "Fish and visitors stink in three days"; "No gains without pains"; "Make haste slowly"; and, most ironic and American, "God helps those who help themselves".

His *Autobiography* was the culmination of a life devoted to the break with a colonial "tyranny". In the making of the American republic, Franklin had a hand in three crucial founding documents: the Declaration of Independence, the wartime alliance with France; and the peace treaty with the Britain of George III. Breaking free of protocol and decorum, his Autobiography became the inimitable personal statement of a patriot who had long subordinated himself to a struggle for political and national liberty.

A printer by profession, Franklin was also a newspaper proprietor and a publisher. He had the ink of revolution in his veins. The *Autobiography*, unfinished at his death in 1793, was compiled from four separate and unfinished manuscripts: first, a memorable opening, Franklin's letter to his son that establishes a blueprint for the American dream: "Before I enter upon my public appearance, it may be well to let you know the then state of my mind with regard to my principles and morals, that you may see how far those influenc'd the future events of my life. My parents had early given me religious impressions, and brought me through my childhood piously in the Dissenting way."

Franklin never failed to promote himself as a gregarious seeker after truth: "I began now to have some acquaintance with the young

People of the Town that were Lovers of Reading with whom I spent my evenings very pleasantly; and gaining Money by my Industry and Frugality, I lived very agreeably..."

The afterlife of the Autobiography provoked reactions from writers as varied as Keats, Melville and Emerson whose essay on "self-reliance" refers to the founding father as frugal and "inoffensive". Franklin himself would have been just as delighted to know that, according to legend, *The Autobiography* was one of the few books that Davy Crockett kept to hand during the final siege at the Alamo. A beacon of sturdy reassurance and common sense, it remains a great book in a crisis.

Three to compare:
Benjamin Franklin: *Poor Richard's Almanack* (1732)
DH Lawrence: *Studies in Classic American Literature* (1923)
F Scott Fitzgerald: *The Great Gatsby* (1925)

27. TRAVELS IN THE INTERIOR DISTRICTS OF AFRICA BY MUNGO PARK (1799)

Mungo Park's *Travels* is a classic of English exploration literature – a contemporary bestseller whose influence lingered throughout the next century, and into the 20th, inspiring a remarkable variety of writers, from Wordsworth and Melville, to Conrad and Hemingway.

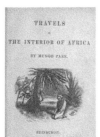

A solitary, quiet, young Scot with itchy feet, Park had ventured alone into the African interior in search of the Niger river at the age of 24. He was equipped with a horse, an umbrella, a change of clothes, a compass, a pistol – and a hat. When he emerged 18 months later, he was in rags, but carrying a fistful of notes and his hat. He was greeted as one who had risen from the dead, and soon after his remarkable escape he began to commit the story of his adventures to paper.

Park's matter-of-fact, but well-observed narrative style, occasionally adorned with flourishes of dry wit, owes something to Defoe, but soon becomes quite compulsively original:

"This place [Jillifree, in the kingdom of Barra, the Gambia] is much resorted to by Europeans, on account of the great quantities of bees-wax which are brought hither for sale: the wax is collected in the woods by the Feloops, a wild and unsociable race of people: their country, which is of considerable extent, abounds in rice; and the natives supply the traders, both on the Gambia, and Cassamansa rivers, with that article, and also with goats and poultry, on very reasonable terms."

Park was not just a hero-explorer of "the Dark Continent", he was also fiercely engaged in the contemporary debate about slavery and its longed-for abolition. This makes him modern; and so does his prose, which is not only a thrilling tale of adventure and survival, but also (in his confrontations with the practice of the slave trade) an eye-witness's argument against a humanitarian catastrophe.

First, the adventures: in his solitude, he was often the victim of violent theft, was once left for dead, and is almost always finding himself in some kind of jeopardy. Park usually travelled with native guides, or on his own, with not much idea of where he was going, apart from what he could pick up from local people. Inter alia, he was captured by Moors, but escaped. On his travels again, he had to bang on village gates to avoid being eaten by lions. He was chronically unwell, often with malaria, but also from the side-effects of malnutrition (he nearly starved to death during a famine).

Throughout his *Travels*, Park the quiet man reports an extraordinary, heart-stopping tale with equanimity and good humour. For instance, having been robbed of "horse and apparel", he reports:

The little raiment upon me could neither protect me from the sun by day, nor the dews and musketoes [sic] by night: indeed, my shirt was not only worn thin, like a piece of muslin, but withal was so very dirty, that I was happy to embrace an opportunity of washing it; which, having done, and spread it upon a bush, I sat down naked, in the shade, until it was dry.

Park always exhibits the dry humour of the witty Scot. For example, he notes that it is always a good idea to submit to a lion when, as an explorer, you are in range of its paw. As a writer who achieves an extraordinary detachment from the privations he experienced, Park made a deep impression on Joseph Conrad. who writes (in Geography and Some Explorers):

"Western Sudan means for me an episode in Mungo Park's life. It means for me the vision of a young, emaciated, fair-haired man, clad simply in a tattered shirt and worn-out breeches, gasping painfully for breath and lying on the ground in the shade of an enormous African tree (species unknown)…"

The purpose of Park's journey was to achieve an eyewitness proof (an "oracular demonstration") that the river Niger flowed east, and would thus be congenial for trade and commerce. But he was a highly sensitive reporter. His "*Observations concerning the State and Sources of Slavery in Africa*" are not merely authoritative, they are also devastating. Park identifies captivity, famine, insolvency and crime as the four principal causes of slavery.

Towards the conclusion of his travels, Park falls in with a "slave coffle" on the way to market. His account of the death of a slave girl (Nealee) is a classic of reportage: "The sad fate of this wretched woman," he writes, "made a strong impression on the minds of the whole coffle, and the schoolmaster fasted the whole of the ensuing day in consequence of it. We proceeded in deep silence …"

Well received in his own time, and consistently rediscovered by subsequent generations, Park's *Travels* has never quite achieved the broader recognition as a classic that it deserves. The explorer's own life was similarly overtaken by oblivion. On a second mission to the Niger, he and his party are reported to have met their deaths in the depths of their quest for its source. Park was just 34.

Three to compare:
HM Stanley: *Through the Dark Continent* (1878)
Earnest Hemingway: *The Green Hills of Africa* (1935)
T Coraghessan Boyle: *Water Music* (1981)

28. TALES FROM SHAKESPEARE
BY CHARLES AND MARY LAMB (1807)

In the autumn of 1796, at the age of 21, Charles Lamb, a city clerk

with a lifelong stutter, came home from his desk at the East India Company to find that his sister, Mary, had stabbed their mother to death in a mad seizure. He described the events of 22 September in a letter to a friend:

"I will only give you the outlines. My poor dear dearest sister in a fit of insanity has been the death of her own mother. I was at hand with only time enough to snatch the knife out of her grasp. She is at present in a madhouse, from whence I fear she must be moved to a hospital. God has preserved to me my senses – I eat and drink and sleep, and have my judgment I believe very sound. My poor father was slightly wounded, and I am left to take care of him and my aunt."

Young Charles Lamb had to persuade the parish to let him take responsibility for his sister for the rest of her days. Mary's madness would recur briefly almost every year until her death in 1847. However, there remained enough good reason in her for brother and sister to collaborate on literary projects, possibly as a sort of therapy. Besides, from all accounts, Charles Lamb was exceptionally kind, extraordinarily free from affectation and blessed with an innate good humour. It seems that he accepted his fraternal duty without complaint, and channelled his own and his sister's imaginative energies into literature, in particular the highly popular *Tales from Shakespeare,* a bestselling book throughout the 19th century.

Lamb had already launched a precocious career when, in 1794, he and close friend Samuel Taylor Coleridge published a number of poems in the Morning Post. In 1796, he had four sonnets in Coleridge's volume, *Poems on Various Subjects,* and still more verse in the second edition, published the following year. Lamb also became friends with Hazlitt and Wordsworth, whose fame rubbed off on him. Combined with the delights of his prose, more than his poetry, and the glamour of this gifted circle, Lamb slowly acquired what one critic has called "the status of cultural teddy bear in the Victorian establishment".

Tales from Shakespeare epitomises the best of Lamb: his qualities of clarity, readability and charm, literary gifts that would reach their highest expression in Essays of Elia, published in the influential *London Magazine* during 1820. A forerunner of Lamb's mature later work, his Tales have a personal and sometimes conversational tone that won generations of readers. It was from this point that Lamb's reputation as "the most delightful of English essayists" began to be formed.

Lamb and his Mary took the often-dark complexity of Shakespeare's stage plots and simplified them for younger readers, paraphrasing and bowdlerising where necessary. You will, for instance, look in vain here for a prose rendering of the relentless horrors in *Titus Andronicus* or the bloody and violent revenges in *Timon of Athens*. The Lambs do not want to go near the popular political message of *Coriolanus* and they make no attempt to produce a schoolroom version of *Henry the Fourth, Henry the Fifth* or *Richard the Third*.

Ever since the actor David Garrick had (belatedly) celebrated Shakespeare's bicentenary with an extravagant Stratford pageant in 1769, there had been a steady deification of "the bard" that would reach a climax during the 19th century. Charles and Mary Lamb anticipated this and their work is part of the *zeitgeist*. As they write in their preface: "What these tales shall have been to the young readers, that and much more it is the writers' wish that the true plays of Shakespeare may prove to them in older years – enrichers of the fancy, strengtheners of virtue, a withdrawing from all selfish and mercenary thoughts, a lesson of all sweet and honourable thoughts and actions, to teach courtesy, benignity, generosity, humanity: for of examples, teaching these virtues, his pages are full."

Lamb was already a champion of the – to us – perverse idea that Shakespeare plays better on the page than the stage. His essay, *On the Tragedies of Shakespeare Considered with Reference to their Fitness for Stage Representation*, is a classic Romantic dismissal of the theatre. In that essay, Lamb argues that Shakespeare should be read, rather than staged, in order to protect his genius from vulgar commercial performances, a critique derived from the excesses of contemporary theatre practice.

Besides contributing to the burgeoning myth of the bard, *Tales from Shakespeare* shaped a century of literary responses to England's national poet. Some of these *Tales* read oddly today. Here, for instance, is the Lambs' introduction to *Measure for Measure*, one of Shakespeare's darkest plays: "In the city of Vienna, there once reigned a duke of such a mild and gentle temper that he suffered his subjects to neglect the laws with impunity; and there was in particular one law, the existence of which was almost forgotten … a law dooming any man to the punishment of death who should live with a woman that was not his wife…"

Nevertheless, *Tales from Shakespeare* was a key text in the 19th century English library. Its influence lingers, too, in latterday "retellings" of Shakespeare by writers such as Margaret Atwood and Anne Tyler.

Three to compare:
Charles Lamb: *Essays of Elia* (1823)
Charles Lamb, Adam Phillips (ed): *Selected Prose* (1985)
Jane Smiley: *A Thousand Acres* (1991)

29. Confessions of an English Opium-Eater by Thomas De Quincey (1822)

Ever since Alexander Pope's liberating declaration that "the proper

study of mankind is man", there's been a strong thread of intimate life-writing braided into the catalogue of English prose. Today, no bookshop is complete without its table of memoirs, reminiscences or confessional autobiographies, each owing something to Rousseau *(Les Confessions)* and, possibly, to Goethe *(Dichtung* und *Wahrheit)*, but perhaps most immediately, above all, to De Quincey.

There is something so wonderfully modern and provisional about Thomas De Quincey that, of all the 19th century writers in this series, he's a figure you could imagine seeing – but perhaps not conversing with – in Covent Garden (where much of *Confessions* was written) or on a stagecoach to London (he was incurably nomadic). The back-story to this classic memoir is simple enough.

De Quincey was always a drop-out and a drifter. He ran away from school in his teens, wandered homelessly in Wales and London, somehow got to Oxford, where he acquired the taste for opium, and began to discover his *raison d'etre*:

"From my birth, I was made an intellectual creature; and intellectual in the highest sense my pursuits and pleasures have been, even from my schoolboy days. If opium-eating be a sensual pleasure, it is no less true that I have struggled against this fascination with a fervent zeal, and have at length untwisted, almost to its final links, the chain which fettered me. Such self-conquest may be set off in counterbalance to any degree of self-indulgence".

There's little doubt that, to De Quincey, there was probably no one quite as interesting as himself. But he was not just an obsessive narcissicist; he could be a good companion, too. He certainly seems gifted with an instinctive sympathy for his literary contemporaries. After Oxford, having met Coleridge and Wordsworth, and subsequently flourishing as their admirer and friend, he settled in the Lake District, at Grasmere. Here, he fell under the spell of the Lake Poets to become a full-blown and in some senses archetypal Romantic. By 1812, he was also fully addicted to opium; then he married a wealthy farmer's daughter, ran through her money and, finally, turned to journalism to make ends meet.

Confessions of an Opium-Eater, first published anonymously (to some metropolitan sensation) in the *London Magazine* in 1821, appeared in book form in 1822, and secured De Quincey's reputation. He was 38. For the next 30 years, he would live precariously, in the more marginal purlieus of Grub Street, as the author of this increasingly famous memoir.

De Quincey's rather majestic, classically learned and singular style inspires every page of his writing. His *Confessions* guarantees him a place in this series as a writer whose life and writing were equally expressive of an unquenchable originality of thought and behaviour.

Consider, for instance, his acknowledgement of the drug whose symptoms were "as though rats were gnawing at the coats of one's stomach". Taking inspiration from Walter Raleigh's *History of the World* (1614), De Quincey salutes his drug as Raleigh had once saluted death:

"Oh! Just, subtle, and mighty opium! That to the hearts of poor and rich alike, for the wounds that will never heal, and for "the pangs that tempt the spirit to rebel", bringest an assuaging balm; eloquent opium! That with thy potent rhetoric stealest away the purposes of wrath; and to the guilty man, for one night givest back the hopes of his youth, and hands washed pure of blood; O just and righteous opium! That to the chancery of dreams summonest, for the triumphs of despairing innocence, false witnesses…"

De Quincey, on the evidence of his own narrative, appears to have had the constitution of a thoroughbred. Certainly, in his mature years, he was ingesting enough opium to kill a horse, apparently, between 8,000 and 12,000 drops a day. He writes:

"My daily ration was eight thousand drops [which later fell] spontaneously from a varying quantity of eight, ten, or twelve thousand drops of laudanum to about three hundred".

By middle age, he had got his addiction pretty much under control, but he was still afflicted with his former nightmares:

"My dreams are not calm; the dread swell and agitation of the storm have not wholly subsided; my sleep is still tumultuous; and, like the gates of Paradise to our first parents when looking back from afar, it is still (in the tremendous line of Milton) "With dreadful faces thronged and fiery arms".

All things considered, the self-controlled equanimity of this classic volume is little short of miraculous.

It is never less than a pleasure to be in De Quincey's company. The reader never quite knows what he's going to say next, but it's always diverting, never dull, and as full of Romantic enchantment as you'd expect from a lifelong friend of the incomparable Coleridge.

Three to compare:
Thomas De Quincey: *On Murder Considered as One of the Fine Arts* (1827)
Edgar Allan Poe: *Tales of the Grotesque and Arabesque* (1840)
Frances Wilson: Guilty Thing: *A Life of Thomas De Quincey* (2016)

30. An American Dictionary
of the English Language
by Noah Webster (1828)

On 23 July 1788, a curious procession marched through New York City. The occasion was the ratification of the new American constitution. The demonstrators included all sorts – professional men, tradespeople and labourers. "In the procession," recalled one of the participants, "an association of young men, of which the writer was one, called the Philological Society, carried through the streets of New York, a book inscribed Federal Language."

These words are Noah Webster's, celebrating a now forgotten side of US linguistic nationalism. The most famous of all American lexicographers, an indefatigable champion of American English (sometimes referred to as "federal language"), Webster was as influential in the making of American English as George Washington was in the prosecution of the American Revolution. From his youthful *Dissertation on the English Language* (1789) to his great monument of 1828, now simply referred to as *Webster's*, this great American patriot's work, like Samuel Johnson's in England, is a landmark.

Webster was born in Hartford, Connecticut in 1758 and, like many young revolutionaries, turned from law to teaching as a means of livelihood. It was a self-defining career move. The 13 colonies were at war with Britain and schoolbooks, traditionally imported from London, were in short supply. In the can-do spirit of the New World, Webster set about filling the gap. Between 1783 and 1785, Webster published three elementary English textbooks: a speller, a grammar and a classroom reader, to which he attached the grandiose title *A Grammatical Institute of the English Language"*.

Above all, it was the blue-backed, immensely practical *American Speller* that became the runaway bestseller, shifting more than 80m copies in Webster's lifetime. It was his intention, as he put it, "to introduce uniformity and accuracy of pronunciation into common schools".

The success of the *American Speller* gave Webster, on a royalty of one cent per copy, more than enough to live on. He now devoted the rest of his life to championing the new, and distinctive "American language". In his dissertation of 1789, he had already declared his commitment to the separation of American English from its parent:

> "Several circumstances render a future separation of the American tongue from the English necessary and unavoidable … Numerous local causes, such as a new country, new associations of people, new combinations of ideas in arts and sciences, and some intercourse with tribes wholly unknown in Europe, will introduce new words into the American language."

This, Webster predicted, would produce a language in North America as different from British English as Dutch, Danish or Swedish. It was not enough to let history take its course. Americans had to act. "Our honour," Webster wrote, "requires us to have a system of our own, in language as well as government." In 1806, taking the next step in his programme to standardise America's national language, Webster published his first dictionary ("a compendious dictionary of the English language"), and continued to call for a "detachment" from English literary models: "There is nothing which so debases the genius and character of my countrymen as the implicit confidence they place in English authors, and their unhesitating submission to their opinions."

The culmination of Webster's lexicographical revolution came in 1828 with the publication of his *American Dictionary of the English Language*.

Webster's classic volume was larger than Dr Johnson's by about a third, and contained not only more entries (70,000) than ever before, but also countless examples of American usage. However, a lifetime of struggle, and perhaps a year spent in England, had mellowed the old warrior. In the preface to this, his lasting monument, he conceded, with uncharacteristic mildness: "The body of the language is the same as in England, and it is desirable to perpetuate that sameness." But he never ceased to be an American patriot:

The United States commenced their existence under circumstances wholly novel and unexampled in the history of nations. They commenced with civilization, with learning, with science, with constitutions of free government, and with that best gift of God to man, the Christian religion. Their population is now equal to that of England; in arts and sciences, our citizens are very little behind the most enlightened people on earth; in some respects, they have no superiors; and our language, within two centuries, will be spoken by more people in this country, than any other language on earth, except the Chinese, in Asia, and even that may not be an exception.

Despite its now honoured place in the history of American English, the first edition of Webster's sold only 2,500 copies. He was forced to mortgage his home to bring out a second printing, and the rest of his life was dogged by debt. Webster died in New Haven, Connecticut in 1843 with much of his achievement unrecognised and unapplauded.

But his dictionary had become a pillar of American culture. So much so that, when "Webster's Third" (*Webster's Third New International Dictionary of the English Language*, unabridged), published in 1961, appeared to turn its back on its own traditions, replacing a rigorous "prescriptive" approach for a more permissive "descriptive" method, there was a national outcry. The dictionary's treatment of "ain't" aroused special fury among language conservatives, for seeming to reject a previously universal hostility in the classroom to such usage.

Since 1961, Webster's has been reprinted successively with minor changes. An addenda section was added in 1966, to cope with the constant influx of new words. This was expanded in 1971, 1976, 1981, 1986, 1993 and 2002. Now, like all dictionaries the world over, Webster's has a new online existence, reaching a global audience that Noah Webster could only have dreamed about.

Three to compare:
Dr Samuel Johnson: *A Dictionary of the English Language* (1755)
HL Mencken: *The American Language* (1919)
Strunk and White: *The Elements of Style* (1959)

31. DOMESTIC MANNERS OF THE AMERICANS
BY FRANCES TROLLOPE (1832)

By the 1830s, the young American republic, almost three generations

after the war of independence, was beginning to attract the attention of visitors from its former British and French colonial masters. Two contrasting volumes capture this new fascination: *Domestic Manners of the Americans* by Anthony Trollope's mother, Fanny; and *Democracy in America* by Alexis de Tocqueville (1835). Rarely have gossip and grandeur been so juxtaposed.

Where the great French social scientist was inspired by the disappointments of the French Revolution, and his own Gallic passion for *liberté*, addressing his subject in the spirit of the Enlightenment, Mrs Trollope wrote, as the creature of misfortune, to pay the family bills. On a whim, her husband, a failed barrister, had decided to open a fancy goods store in Cincinnati, an act of commercial lunacy that was such a spectacular disaster it became known locally as "Trollope's Folly". But Frances, undaunted by bankruptcy, and galvanised by adversity, responded with inspired energy. In the words of her descendant, the bestselling novelist Joanna: "She sat down with her travel diary amid the debris of her efforts and began *Domestic Manners of the Americans*."

Frances Trollope was neither "literary", nor especially well educated, but she had a wonderful natural curiosity towards the world about her, a strong sense of humour, some vivid conservative opinions, and a nose for "hypocrisy". Above all, a vital quality, she lacked inhibitions: she was not afraid to describe what she found in front of her, and every word she wrote was based on the truth, as she saw it, of her observation. For Mrs Trollope, American "domestic manners" were, not to mince words, ghastly.

She singled out the Yankee dinner table for her special scorn, assaulting: "the strange uncouth phrases and pronunciation; the loathsome spitting ... the frightful manner of feeding with their knives ... and the still more frightful manner of cleaning the teeth afterwards with a pocket-knife..."

Mrs Trollope wrote without a backward glance, or much regret. Her attitudes might now seem shocking, but her eye for detail was impeccable. The reportage in *Domestic Manners* is invaluable. Still, there were some things she got badly wrong. Later, more seriously, when she was famous for *Domestic Manners*, she admitted: "Had I again to travel through the Union with a view to giving an account of what I saw, I should certainly devote a much larger portion of my attention to the great national feature – negro slavery."

She is in good company. Even today, some commentators on US society are still underestimating the race question. Mrs Trollope's account of her travels, from New Orleans, up the Mississippi to Cincinnati, to Washington, to Philadelphia, New York, and thence to Canada, before returning home to London, describes a society whose national character is still, in its shadowy outlines, visible today.

Domestic Manners of the Americans is both a classic travelogue and an anglocentric rant. Trollope was all too quick to observe her neighbours' lack of culture, noting that, in America, Shakespeare was judged obscene and Chaucer redundant. And the language – my dear, the language!

> "I very seldom, during my whole stay in the country, heard a sentence elegantly turned, and correctly pronounced from the lips of an American. There is always something either in the expression or the accent that jars the feelings and shocks the taste."

Like Dickens a decade later, Mrs T deplored the American habit of spitting. Her neighbours' behaviour was a disgusting mix of the vulgar and the prudish. She could not abide the endless handshaking, and raucous geniality. American architecture was crude and tasteless; its roads impassable; and its shopkeepers dishonest. What really got her goat was American hypocrisy: "They inveigh against the governments of Europe, because … they favour the powerful and oppress the weak. You may hear this declaimed upon in Congress, roared out in taverns, discussed in every drawing-room, satirised upon the stage, nay, even anathematised from the pulpit: listen to it, and then look at them at home; you will see them with one hand hoisting the cap of liberty, and with the other flogging their slaves.

What she rather snobbishly saw as an immigrant culture, she patronised as crude and deficient, a British reaction to American life not unknown today. Finally, her travels were over. Her concluding summary reflects much of the confusion that persists between the

Old and New Worlds: "A single word indicative of doubt, that any thing, or every thing, in that country is not the very best in the world, produces an effect which must be seen and felt to be understood. If the citizens of the United States were indeed the devoted patriots they call themselves, they would surely not thus encrust themselves in the hard, dry, stubborn persuasion, that they are the first and best of the human race, that nothing is to be learnt, but what they are able to teach, and that nothing is worth having, which they do not possess."

Three to compare:
Alexis de Tocqueville: *Democracy in America* (1835)
Charles Dickens: *American Notes* (1842)
Robert Louis Stevenson: *The Amateur Emigrant* (1895)

32. ESSAYS
BY RW EMERSON (1841)

Ralph Waldo Emerson burst on to the American literary scene in

the autumn of 1836, as the protegé of Thomas Carlyle, under whose spell he had fallen during a visit to England in 1833. On his return to America, duly inspired, the 30-year-old Emerson embarked on a brilliant career as an acclaimed public lecturer, a programme of self-enlightenment through which he would evolve his post-Romantic and quasi-religious idea of transcendentalism. This ecstatic concept, typical of the American mind at its more fervent and mystical, was first expressed in a lecture entitled Nature that Emerson gave at Harvard on 5 November 1836 in which he articulated his belief that "Nature is the symbol of spirit". This, according to the critic Jay Parini, would influence "generations of poets and nature writers" for whom this call to arms became "a major source of ideas".

"Nature," Emerson declared, in a self-conscious echo of the Romantic ideal, "is the incarnation of thought." He added, with thrilling opacity, that "The world is the mind precipitated." In explication of these mysteries, he argued that to experience the "wholeness" with nature for which we are naturally suited, we must be separate from the quotidian distractions imposed by society. For Emerson, it was "solitude" that would be the singular mechanism through which the questing individual might become fully engaged in the world of nature.

He instructed, in words which soon resonated among an emerging generation of Americans: "To go into solitude, a man needs to retire as much from his chamber as from society. I am not solitary whilst I read and write, though nobody is with me. But if a man would be alone, let him look at the stars."

When a person experiences true solitude, in nature, it "takes him away", elevating him to a new level of consciousness. Society, Emerson said, destroys wholeness, whereas "Nature, in its ministry to man, is not only the material, but is also the process and the result. All the parts incessantly work into each other's hands for the profit of man. The wind sows the seed; the sun evaporates the sea; the wind blows the vapour to the field; the ice, on the other side of the planet, condenses rain on this; the rain feeds the plant; the plant feeds the animal; and thus the endless circulations of the divine charity nourish man."

From this kind of exalted secular piety, it's a short step to Emerson's definition of a spiritual relationship with nature through which the individual can discover the "spirit of nature", and accept it as the Universal Being: "Nature is not fixed but fluid; to a pure spirit, nature is everything."

Like all the great American intellectual salesmen, Emerson was intent on establishing himself as the chief explicator of nature's special language – a unique means of communication, offered exclusively to his followers: "Nature is a language and every new fact one learns is a new word; but it is not a language taken to pieces and dead in the dictionary, but the language put together into a most significant and universal sense. I wish to learn this language, not that I may know a new grammar, but that I may read the great book that is written in that tongue."

This was heady stuff in straitlaced, post-revolutionary New England. Other invitations followed and on 31 August 1837, now speaking within the precincts of Harvard, Emerson gave his now-famous Phi Beta Kappa "Oration", which would become known as The American Scholar, described by Oliver Wendell Holmes as America's "intellectual eclaration of independence".

After this, Emerson never looked back. He became the Sage of Concord, Massachusetts whose *Essays* approached the status of holy writ. The first volume of these was published in 1841; its influence would reverberate down the remaining decades of the century.

Some of Emerson, stripped of its high-mindedness, is a passionate American frontier howl which, strangely, can also morph into unvarnished Trumpism: "No law can be sacred to me but that of my nature. Good and bad are but names very readily transferable to that or this; the only right is what is after my constitution; the only wrong what is against it … The doctrine of hatred must be preached as the counteraction of the doctrine of love when that pules and whines. I shun father and mother and wife and brother, when my genius calls me. I would write on the lintels of the doorpost, Whim."

"A foolish consistency," Emerson remarks soon after this, "is the hobgoblin of little minds."

Emerson, one of the most influential writers in the United States during the 19th century, is central to American Romanticism. His essays and lectures had a profound influence on the thinkers, writers and poets who came after him. Once, when asked to sum up his work, he said he believed in the "infinitude" of the private individual. Emerson is also renowned as a mentor and friend of Henry David Thoreau whose *Walden* owes him a deep debt.

Three to compare:
Henry David Thoreau: *Walden* (1854)
Dale Carnegie: *How to Win Friends and Influence People* (1936)
Robert Macfarlane: *The Wild Places* (2007)

33. NARRATIVE OF THE LIFE OF FREDERICK DOUGLASS, AN AMERICAN SLAVE
BY FREDERICK DOUGLASS (1845)

If there is one African American who can make the strongest claim

to be the godfather of the literature derived from the black American experience, it must be Frederick Douglass (1818-1895). To some critics, he remains "the most influential African American of the 19th century".

Throughout his long career, Douglass cut an imposing figure, renowned as an impassioned abolitionist, a fiery writer and newspaper editor. He was a great public speaker, who became a one-man crusade for black liberation, part of it conducted in collaboration with Abraham Lincoln, the president who would secure the end of slavery. As a spokesman for his people, Douglass distilled his fortunes into a sequence of vivid personal narratives – this memoir would be followed by two further autobiographies – which, at a time when very few slaves could read or write, captured the imagination of the American reading public.

According to many accounts, the determination from his earliest years to escape bondage set Douglass apart. He was born into slavery in the Chesapeake shore, Maryland. At first, he sought to liberate himself through education and self-improvement, but came to recognise that he would have to become a fugitive from the south, like so many others. In fact, Douglass made two escape attempts before he was assisted in a successful route to the free states by Anna Murray, a free black woman in Baltimore with whom he had fallen in love.

In September 1838, Douglass boarded a train to north-east Maryland. Murray had provided him with some of her savings and a sailor's uniform. He also carried identification papers obtained from a free black seaman. Within 24 hours, Douglass was able to make his way to the safe house of an abolitionist in New York.

Once securely in the north, he sent for Murray to meet him in New York, where they married, before settling in New Bedford, Massachusetts, a thriving free black community. Douglass joined a black church and attended abolitionist meetings. He also became associated with *The Liberator,* an anti-slavery newspaper whose editor, William Lloyd

Garrison, was impressed with Douglass's strength and rhetorical skill. Among the obiter dicta handed down from this stage of Douglass's career, we find: "If there is no struggle, there is no progress", and: "it is easier to build strong children than to repair broken men".

Soon after this decisive public breakthrough, Douglass delivered his first speech at the Anti-Slavery Society's annual convention. His fame grew, a quasi-modern celebrity that was followed by the first instalment of his autobiography, a "massively resonant" account of the darkest aspect of American life that deeply shocked its first readers, as Douglass doubtless intended.

> "I speak advisedly when I say this – that killing a slave, or any coloured person, in Talbot county, Maryland, is not treated as a crime, either by the courts or the community," he wrote. "Mr Thomas Lanman of St Michael's killed two slaves, one of whom he killed with a hatchet, by knocking his brains out. He used to boast of the commission of the awful and bloody deed. I have heard him do so laughingly, saying, among other things that when others would do as much as he had done, we should be relieved of "the d----d niggers".

In addition to this kind of rhetorical assault on white supremacy, in 1848, Douglass served as a key delegate at the Seneca Falls Convention, where women and African Americans came together in quest of the right to vote. Douglass, meanwhile, continued to write powerfully about the routine degradation of the slave community:

> "We [the slaves] were all ranked together at the valuation. Men and women, old and young, married and single, were ranked with horses, sheep, and swine. Horses and men, cattle and women, pigs and children – all held the same rank in the scale of being, and were all subjected to the same narrow examination, the same indelicate inspection. At this moment, I saw more clearly than ever the brutalising effects of slavery upon both slave and slaveholder."

By the middle of the century, Douglass had become the most celebrated African American in the United States.

When President Obama opened the National Museum of African American History and Culture in Washington, he said: "Yes, African Americans have felt the cold weight of shackles and the stinging lash of the field whip. But we've also dared to run north and sing songs from Harriet Tubman's hymnal. We've buttoned up our Union Blues to join the fight for our freedom. We've railed against injustice for decade upon decade, a lifetime of struggle and progress and enlightenment that we see etched in Frederick Douglass's mighty, leonine gaze."

Douglass devoted his career to "agitating the American conscience". In his time, he addressed many reform causes, from women's rights and temperance, to land reform, free public education, and the abolition of capital punishment. But his priority was his ceaseless campaign to end slavery and secure equal rights for African Americans. Even at the end of his long life, he continued to encourage young black Americans to "Agitate!" He once said, presciently, that "Power concedes nothing without a demand. It never did and it never will."

As a towering public figure, Douglass wrote three main versions of his autobiography, but the first − his *Narrative of the Life of Frederick Douglass, an American Slave* − was the one that caught American public attention. Vivid and shocking, the book became a bestseller, was picked up by Henry Thoreau in *Walden* and became highly influential in the fight for abolition. For Thoreau, the plight of black Americans exposed a deep existential anxiety that we are somehow all slaves, and ultimately led to his own anti-slavery writing.

Douglass's original *Narrative* was followed by *My Bondage and My Freedom* (1855), which in turn was superseded by the *Life and Times of Frederick Douglass*, his last autobiography, published in 1881 and covering events during the civil war.

In 2017, thanks to the vicissitudes of US politics, the legacy of Frederick Douglass has been taken up by President Trump, who, at the beginning of Black History Month, made some characteristically bizarre comments:

> "Frederick Douglass is an example of somebody who's done an amazing job and is getting recognised more and more, I notice. Harriet Tubman, Rosa Parks, and millions more black Americans who made America what it is today. Big impact."

Three to compare:
WFB Du Bois: *The Souls of Black Folk* (1903)
Richard Wright: *Black Boy* (1945)
Barack Obama: *Dreams from my Father* (1995)

34. HOUSEHOLD EDUCATION
BY HARRIET MARTINEAU (1848)

Harriet Martineau's story offers the parable of a certain kind of

literary endeavour that's never far from the experience of quite a few writers in this list, ie contemporary success, and short-term celebrity, followed by a more prolonged oblivion, punctuated by moments of renewal and rediscovery.

Martineau came to prominence aged 21 with her first published work, *Devotional Exercises* (1823), partly inspired by her Unitarian upbringing. Thereafter, she would be an indefatigable writer for the rest of her life, making a career in which she supported herself through her pen, a considerable achievement for a woman in Victorian England. Martineau wrote numerous books and essays from a sociological, religious, reforming and even a feminist perspective. For some commentators, she is a pioneer sociologist both in her own right as the author of books such *as Society in America* (1837) and also as the translator of Auguste Comte. In the former, she articulated a passionate critique of women's prospects in the new world: "The intellect of women is confined by an unjustifiable restriction of education... As women have none of the objects in life for which an enlarged education is considered requisite, the education is not given... The choice is to either be ill-educated, passive and subservient or well-educated, vigorous and free only upon sufferance."

Martineau got taken up by Malthus, Carlyle, Dickens and JS Mill, among many. The young Princess Victoria was a fan. In her work, Martineau had a clearly stated method that was relatively new for its time: "When one studies a society, one must focus on all its aspects, including key political, religious and social institutions." She believed that only through a complete analysis of society could she truly understand women's status among men.

As part of the rising generation of "Victorians", she became friends with Charles Darwin, whose brother, Erasmus, suffered unrequited love for her, and it's the author *of On the Origin of Species* who provides the best portrait of Martineau in her prime. After one meeting, he wrote: "She was very agreeable and managed to talk on a most wonderful number of subjects, considering the limited time. She is overwhelmed with her own projects, her own thoughts and own abilities." Later, he described her as "a wonderful woman", although he was plainly intimidated by her formidable exterior.

Household Education, one of her most popular books, appeared in 1848, as a protest against the abysmal state of women's education. Her opinions, quite radical at the time, now seem antiquated. Martineau held that women had a natural inclination to motherhood and believed that domestic work went hand in hand with learning for a proper, well-rounded education.

She divided the child's education into the influence of Nature, the influence of the parents and the influence of conscience, "the greatest and noblest" moral power of man. From here, she moved to the training of "the intellect". Throughout her writing, there's a quasi-ecstatic tone, striking a note of moral earnestness that characterises much Victorian prose. For example: "Intellectual and moral beauty are so blended, it would be impossible for the one to exist without the other. It is just so in the human character – the intellect of a human being cannot be of a high order if the moral nature is low; and the moral state cannot be a lofty one where the intellect is torpid."

It is for such passages that Martineau's work has dated so badly and fallen out of favour. And yet, in her time, she was doing what countless parenting and educational bestsellers have done since.

"I go further than most persons..." she wrote, "in desiring thorough practice in domestic occupations, from an early age, for young girls." But she also proposed that freedom and rationality, rather than command and obedience, are the most effectual instruments of education. In some moods, Martineau can be almost fiery: "Every woman ought to have that justice done to her faculties that she may possess herself in all the strength and clearness of an exercised and enlightened mind and may have at command, for her subsistence, as much intellectual power and as many resources as education can furnish her with. Let us hear nothing of her being shut out, because she is a woman, from any study that she is capable of pursuing; and if one kind of cultivation is more carefully attended to than another, let it be the discipline and exercise of the reasoning faculties."

Suffering persistent ill health, Martineau withdrew from the fray. When *On the Origin of Species* was published in 1859, Erasmus Darwin sent a copy to his old flame. In late middle age, she was still reviewing books from her home in the Lake District. Martineau returned her thanks, praising "the quality and conduct of your brother's mind. It is," she went on, recognising in Darwin something of her own method-ology, "an unspeakable satisfaction to see here the full manifestation of its earnestness and simplicity, its sagacity, its industry, and the patient power by which it has collected such a mass of facts, to transmute them by such sagacious treatment into such portentous knowledge. I should much like to know how large a proportion of our scientific men believe he has found a sound road."

True to her free-thinking credo, Martineau supported Darwin precisely because his theory was not based in theology. For Martineau, the abolition of church and religion was her goal: "In the present state of the religious world, Secularism ought to flourish. What an amount of sin and woe might and would then be extinguished."

Martineau, a creature of her time, was in no doubt of her contri-bution to Victorian culture and society. Her own, posthumously published, appraisal of herself was made in a frank autobiographical sketch, published by the *Daily News*:

> "Her original power was nothing more than was due to earnestness and intellectual clearness within a certain range. With small imaginative and suggestive powers, and therefore nothing approaching to genius, she could see clearly what she did see, and give a clear expression to what she had to say. In short, she could popularise while she could neither discover nor invent."

Three to compare:
Isabella Beeton: *Mrs Beeton's Book of Household Management* (1861)
JS Mill: *The Subjection of Women* (1869)
Dr Benjamin Spock: *The Common Sense Book of Baby and Child Care* (1946)

35. London Labour and the London Poor
by Henry Mayhew (1851)

The Victorians were fascinated by the world around them, perhaps because the marriage of imagination and technology seemed to make it, for the first time, so accessible. Empire and industry had created immense wonders at home and abroad. For some, a trip to the East End was as thrilling and exotic as a riverboat journey up the Congo. Writers and journalists of all kinds, writing for an astonishing range of publications, were drawn to this new material as moths to a flame, weaving a strand of English prose – a mix of philanthropic criticism, travelogue, sociology and reportage – that persists to the present. From Mayhew we get Jack London, who begat George Orwell, who begat EP Thompson, and whose influence possibly lingers in the nonfiction of John Berger, Iain Sinclair and Will Self, among many others.

Henry Mayhew, the founding father of this tradition, is as hard to describe as much of the work he produced. Was he a journalist, a writer, a radical commentator or a crusading reformer? In some ways, he was all of these and then something else: a detached but compassionate observer who never allowed prejudice, snobbery or surprise to cloud his judgment.

Perhaps, in the absence of much information about the man himself, there are some clues to Mayhew's polyvalent tastes and character in his biography. The son of a London solicitor, he ran away from school (Westminster) and briefly worked for his father before striking out on his own as a dramatist and journalist. Some of his plays and farces were very successful and in 1841, he became co-founder and editor of *Punch*. At the same time, as a jack of all trades, he was also involved in setting up the *Illustrated London News,* a feature of British journalism that survived long into the 20th century.

Towards the end of the 1840s, after a career devoted to novels and stories, as well as books on science, religion and travel, Mayhew turned to "philanthropic journalism", at first a series of 82 articles, conceived as "letters", published in the *Morning Chronicle,* and later collected in book form. If he was moved by the plight of the London poor uncovered in these reports and the extent to which a desperate underclass was suffering starvation, disease and homelessness, Mayhew rarely let his feelings distort his plain but harrowing descriptions, often reported as first-person accounts from the individuals to whom he spoke.

On his own account, Mayhew's main purpose was simply to educate his uncaring, indifferent and materialist society. He writes: "... supplying information concerning a large body of persons of whom the public had less knowledge than of the most distant tribes of the earth ... the traveller in the undiscovered country of the poor must ... be content to lie under the imputation of telling such tales, as travellers are generally supposed to delight in."

The book inspired by Mayhew's credo, *London Labour and the London Poor*, is a masterpiece of reportage and social observation. Researched and written around the time of the Great Exhibition – that majestic monument of Victorian self-advertisement – it explores the marginal life of the greatest metropolis in the world, painting a vivid portrait of a teeming, voluble city, especially the speech, habits, demeanour and diversions of the labouring poor at mid century.

Mayhew influenced Dickens, inevitably, but Dickens's London was in many ways Georgian. Later in the century, Conan Doyle's and Wilde's London was becoming quasi-Edwardian. Mayhew, on the other hand, gives us a picture of Victorian city life at its most durable and dynamic, replete with chaos, cruelty, dirt, disease, heartbreak, death and dying.

The joy of Mayhew is his obsession with detail. For scope and depth, he has no equal and George Orwell, among many, learned some important lessons here. On every page, Mayhew is inspired by a reporter's curiosity, an artist's imagination and a novelist's attention to the minutiae of everyday life. Here is a typical, oft-quoted, description of a metropolitan street market from the first volume of London Labour:

"The pavement and the road are crowded with purchasers and street-sellers. The housewife in her thick shawl, with the market-basket on her arm, walks slowly on, stopping now to look at the stall of caps, and now to cheapen a bunch of greens. Little boys, holding three or four onions in their hand, creep between the people, wriggling their way through every interstice, and asking for custom in whining tones, as if seeking charity. Then the tumult of the thousand different cries of the eager dealers, all shouting at the top of their voices, at one and the same time, is almost bewildering. 'So-old again,' roars one. 'Chestnuts all 'ot, a penny a score,' bawls another. 'An 'aypenny a skin, blacking,' squeaks a boy. 'Buy, buy, buy, buy, buy bu-u-uy!' cries the butcher. 'Half-quire of paper for a penny,' bellows the street stationer. 'An 'aypenny a lot ing-uns.' 'Twopence a pound grapes.' 'Three a penny Yarmouth bloaters.' 'Who'll buy a bonnet for fourpence?' 'Pick 'em out cheap here! three pair for a halfpenny, bootlaces.' 'Now's your time! beautiful whelks, a penny a lot.'

This passage precisely answers Mayhew's own criteria for his work, set out in the preface to the final edition of a four-volume work. He is concerned, he says, to complete "a cyclopedia of the industry, the want, and the vice of the great metropolis". More than that, writes Mayhew: "I shall consider the whole of the metropolitan poor under three separate phases, according as they will work, they can't work, and they won't work." To this end, he interviewed beggars, Punch and Judy men, market traders, prostitutes, labourers and sweatshop workers. Moreover, in a lasting lesson to all journalists, Mayhew was not afraid to get his feet dirty. He visited the famous "mudlarks" who scavenged in the stinking mud of the Thames bank and even tracked down the "pure finders" who collected dogshit for tanners and cobblers. He described their clothes, how and where they lived, their entertainments and customs and made detailed estimates of the numbers practising each trade, plus the money they made. "Follow the money" is just one of many lessons he taught. And from all this investigation, Mayhew hardly needed to draw the obvious conclusion. His work demonstrated to a shocking degree how marginal and precarious many Londoners' lives were, in the richest city in the world.

Occasionally, his reporter's mask will slip. At the end of his preface, Mayhew writes: "My earnest hope is that this book may serve to give the rich a more intimate knowledge of the sufferings ... of the poor whose misery, ignorance and vice ... is, to say the very least, a national disgrace to us."

Where is Henry Mayhew today?

Three to compare:
Friedrich Engels: *The Condition of the Working Class in England* (1845)
Jack London: *The People of the Abyss* (1903)
George Orwell: *Down and Out in Paris and London* (1933)

36. THESAURUS
BY DR PETER MARK ROGET (1852)

Like the striations in a Mesozoic rock, the accumulated word-hoard

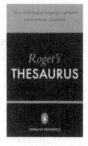

of English reflects successive upheavals: Roman invasion, seasonal Danish incursion, varieties of Anglo-Saxon terror, and finally Norman conquest. The result is a massive vocabulary that dwarfs all rivals. Where French has about 100,000 words, and German approximately 185,000, English boasts some 500,000 words (in the OED), with a further 400,000 technical terms not even listed. Above all, and as a result of these successive accretions, English is rich in synonyms, making the language a pecu-

liarly subtle medium for the expression of countless fine shades of meaning. In *The English People* (1947), Orwell addresses this quality.

He writes: "English vocabulary is made much larger than it appears by the practice of turning one part of speech into another. For example, almost any noun can be used as a verb; this in effect gives an extra range of verbs, so that you have knife as well as stab, school as well as teach, fire as well as burn, and so on ... English is also a borrowing language. It readily takes over any foreign word that seems to fill a need. A recent example is the word blitz."

To the creative mind, this incredible versatility represents a wonderful polyphony; to the rational mind, chaos; to an inquiring Victorian scientist, the opportunity for a taxonomic field day. The unique upshot: the English writer's beloved thesaurus, a volume we now take for granted as the indispensable companion to any dictionary; an extraordinary and remarkable invention whose author was first and foremost a scientist.

In his own time, Dr Peter Mark Roget was most renowned for a now forgotten volume, *Animal and Vegetable Physiology Considered With Reference to Natural Theology* (1834), one of several works commissioned by the Earl of Bridgewater to celebrate "the power, wisdom and goodness of God, as manifested in the creation". As such, Roget had a strong personal investment in the power and importance of language, the "word of God". However, to engage with this mystery, Roget believed mankind should have appropriate equipment.

"Every workman in the exercise of his art should be provided with proper implements," he wrote in 1852, expressing the sober and profes-sional spirit of his age. "The writer employs for the accomplishment of his purposes the instrumentality of words. It is therefore essential to his success that he be provided with a copious vocabulary." More than just fortunate recipients of great linguistic forces, all writers should possess perfect field intelligence, "an entire command of all the resources and appliances of his language", to make each of them an emperor of words.

Behind this grand theme was the larger Victorian purpose of successfully administering an ordered world. Roget knows that, with language, everything is at stake: "Strict accuracy should regulate our use of language." Otherwise, false logic might sway "the unthinking multitude". Worse, he writes, "a misnomer can turn the tide of popular opinion; an artful watchword, thrown among combustible material, has kindled the flame of deadly warfare, and changed the destiny of an empire."

Roget was a distinguished scientist and mathematician, as well as an eminent Victorian. All his life, he had carried a notebook in which he jotted lists of related words and phrases with which to improve his self-expression. Finally, in retirement, aged 71, he set about turning these lists into a system that would regulate the unruly chaos of his adopted tongue (the Roget family had been French émigrés).

As the child of refugees, coming late to English, Roget has no interest in obsolete terms and is strikingly hospitable to foreign borrowings, sometimes a matter of contention in lexicographical circles.

The first edition of *Roget's Thesaurus* of English words and phrases was constructed around six primary categories, partly based on Aris-totle, which survive in a modified form into the latest version: abstract relations; space; the material world; the intellect; volition; and sentient and moral powers.

Each of these, like branches stemming from a tree, were further divided into sub-categories (known as "heads"). In the Longman's edition of May 1852, there were just 1,000 "heads". Abstract relations, for instance, divided into existence; relation; quantity; etc – and exis-tence divided into existence; non-existence; substantiality; insubstanti-ality; intrinsicality; extrinsicality, and so on.

For all his taxonomic zeal, Roget's "treasure house", whose purpose was to exhibit with scientific precision the relations between words and their meanings, together with their logical opposition, quickly became both a hall of mirrors and a cacophonous echo-chamber in which the astounding and magical variety of the English language took over in accumulating arpeggios of antonym and synonym.

There was also the more popular, and often overlooked, dimension of Roget's work: his was a new kind of lexicon that acknowledged colloquialisms and — horrors — slang, for example, "wassail", "swig", "soak", "souse", "booze", and "guzzle". His became a sober-minded book with many unintended and wayward outcomes. For instance, without Roget's entry for "extinct" (no more, dead and gone, defunct, etc) there might have been no Monty Python parrot sketch:

> "'E's not pining [for the fjords]! 'E's passed on! This parrot is no more! He has ceased to be! 'E's expired and gone to meet 'is maker! 'E's a stiff! Bereft of life, 'e rests in peace! If you hadn't nailed 'im to the perch 'e'd be pushing up the daisies! 'Is metabolic processes are now 'istory! 'E's off the twig! 'E's kicked the bucket, 'e's shuffled off 'is mortal coil, run down the curtain and joined the bleedin' choir invisible!! THIS IS AN EX-PARROT!!"

As a true Victorian, Roget himself had bigger ambitions than the liberation of the free mind. He saw his thesaurus as the building block in a grander project, the construction of a universal language, for the realisation of "a golden age of union and harmony" among nations. What we, his inheritors, got is something much better, and more useful: an indispensable guide (explanation, clarification, commentary, glossary, lexicon) to the mysteries (form, order, practice, functioning, performance) of a language now used more widely across the world (earth, planet, geosphere, sphere, home of man) than any other.

Three to compare:
Dr Samuel Johnson: *A Dictionary of the English Language* (1755)
James Murray (ed): *A New English Dictionary on Historical Principles* (1884)
HW Fowler: *A Dictionary of Modern English Usage* (1926)

37. WALDEN
BY HENRY DAVID THOREAU (1854)

On Independence Day 1845, an idealistic young American (Thoreau was just 28) turned his back on what he saw as his country's depressing materialism, its commercial and industrial soullessness and took himself off to a life of solitude in a country cabin near Walden Pond, just outside Concord, Massachusetts. In his famous account of this experiment, Thoreau later wrote:

"I went to the woods because I wished to live deliberately, to front only the essential facts of life, and see if I could not learn what it had to teach, and not, when I came to die, discover that I had not lived. I did not wish to live what was not life, living is so dear; nor did I wish to practise resignation, unless it was quite necessary. I wanted to live deep and suck the marrow out of life, to live so sturdily and Spartan-like as to put to rout all that was not life, to cut a broad swath and shave close, to drive life into a corner, and reduce it to its lowest terms, and, if it proved to be mean, why then to get the whole and genuine meanness of it, and publish its meanness to the world; or if it were sublime, to know it by experience, and be able to give a true account of it in my next excursion."

These were not just any old woods, but property owned by Ralph Waldo Emerson, the great transcendentalist and intellectual guru to some of the most creative minds of mid 19th century America and himself a passionate advocate of "solitude". Whatever the influences on Thoreau, his account of his two-year stay on the northern shore of the pond has become the classic American statement of personal liberation, an ecstatic rendering of spiritual individuality and a hymn to the natural world: "If a man does not keep pace with his companions, perhaps it is because he hears a different drummer. Let him step to the music which he hears, however measured or far away." As the critic Jay Parini has written: "Thoreau defines American independence."

Thoreau shared with his fellow transcendentalists (who, as well as Emerson, included Amos Bronson Alcott, George Ripley, Elizabeth Peabody, Theodore Parker and Jones Very) a deep concern for the decline of "integrity" in American society. For these seekers after truth, "the woods" became, like "the greenwood" in Merrie England, the place where an individual could truly savour the mysteries of life, free from the restricting conformities of church and state. Where most of his American neighbours were striving to acquire things, Thoreau wanted to dispossess them:

> "I see young men, my townsmen, whose misfortune is to have inherited farms, houses, barns, cattle, and farming tools; for these are more easily acquired than got rid of."

Having left behind a world in which, famously, he had witnessed so many men and women leading "lives of quiet desperation", Thoreau was determined to live "deliberately" for himself. In *Walden*, he takes the 26 months he spent on Walden Pond and constructs a narrative of his ennobling solitude, in chapters such as Economy, Where I Lived, and What I Lived For, The Bean Field, The Ponds and House Warming.

However, the uncompromising transcendental message of these first chapters gets rather blurred in the middle of the book. For instance, in Visitors, it's clear that Thoreau in the woods has become, locally, an object of great curiosity. His solitary cabin boasted just three chairs, but he writes:

> "I have had 25 or 30 souls, with their bodies, at once under my roof, and yet we often parted without being aware that we had come very near one another."

Faced with such distractions, Thoreau developed an effective means of diverting gawkers and thrill-seekers from his cabin:

> "Many a traveller came out of his way to see me and the inside of my house, and, as an excuse for calling, asked for a glass of water. I told them that I drank at the pond, and pointed thither, offering to lend them a dipper."

At the end of this chapter, in one enigmatic paragraph raising as many questions as answers, he describes his most "cheering visitors":

> "Children come a-berrying, railroad men taking a Sunday morning walk in clean shirts, fishermen and hunters, poets and

philosophers, in short, all honest pilgrims, who came out to the woods for freedom's sake, and really left the village behind, I was ready to greet with, – "Welcome, Englishmen! Welcome, Englishmen!" for I had had communication with that race."

Walden also conceals a dramatic interlude, on which Thoreau chooses not to elaborate: his arrest for non-payment of poll tax, an episode alluded to in the chapter entitled The Village. As a result of this, he composed a lecture entitled The Relation of the Individual to the State, which eventually became his essay *Civil Disobedience*. This is a strong contender for the most celebrated essay in American prose, especially since Gandhi used it to support non-violent resistance in India and Africa and Martin Luther King quoted its arguments during the civil rights movement of the 1960s.

This strange outcome of Thoreau's self-sequestration in the Concord woods is just one of the many unintended consequences derived from the great tradition of Anglo-American literature devoted to the questions of freedom and individuality. Elsewhere, as John Updike noted, *Walden* became imprisoned in its reputation as a classic: "Such a totem of the back-to-nature, preservationist, anti-business, civil-disobedience mindset, and Thoreau so vivid a protester, so perfect a crank and hermit saint, that the book risks being as revered and unread as the Bible."

Three to compare:
Edward Abbey: *Desert Solitaire: A Season in the Wilderness* (1968)
Annie Dillard: *Pilgrim At Tinker Creek* (1974)
Peter Matthiessen: *The Snow Leopard* (1978)

38. The Life of Charlotte Brontë
by Elizabeth Gaskell (1857)

Charlotte Brontë, who died in 1855 aged 38, might almost have been

an Elizabeth Gaskell heroine. Like Margaret Hale in *North and South* (1855), or Molly Gibson in *Wives and Daughters* (1864), she'd had to look after a widowed and cantankerous father in very difficult circumstances, facing the grim realities of sickness and death. Perhaps it was this that inspired an extraordinary friendship between two great Victorian writers, which would ultimately blossom into one of the most remarkable literary biographies in English prose.

The two novelists first met in the Lake District in the summer of 1850. They were, in many respects, polar opposites. Gaskell was beautiful, worldly and dizzyingly public: a mother of four; familiar with Florence Nightingale, Ruskin, Thomas Carlyle, and even Dickens, with whom she did not get on ("If I were Mr G," exclaimed Dickens, "oh heaven, how I would beat her"). By contrast, Brontë (pseudonymously hiding behind "Currer Bell") was a sickly, self-effacing, reclusive woman, appalled by children, who hardly ever ventured into literary London. Yet each was fascinated by the other.

Brontë had soon invited Mrs Gaskell to Haworth, a rare honour, and Gaskell was also deeply impressed by her new friend. "Such a life as Miss Brontë's I have never heard of before," she marvelled to one correspondent.

Within five years of this first meeting, however, Brontë was dead. Barely 10 weeks after her death, her grieving father, Patrick, made the first overture to Mrs Gaskell to write his daughter's life. Two days later, Gaskell was telling Brontë's publisher, George Smith, how anxious she was "to perform this grave duty laid upon me well and fully".

The whole project has a confident, predestined air of Victorian certainty. The biographer embarked on her "grave duty" quite settled in the conviction that her version would define her friend's posterity: "the more fully she – Charlotte Brontë – the friend, the daughter, the sister, the wife, is known … the more highly she will be appreciated," she wrote.

Unlike most contemporary biographers, Gaskell set out on her research with an explicit mission: to set down the facts, as she saw them, of a "wild, sad life and the beautiful character that grew out of it".

From the first, her account would be coloured by her devotion to her friend, even if she could admit that her version was partisan: "The difficulty that presented itself most strongly to me when I first had the honour of being requested to write this biography," she wrote, "was how I could show what a noble, true, and tender woman Charlotte Brontë really was, without mingling up with her life too much of the personal history of her nearest and most intimate friends. After much consideration of this point, I came to the resolution of writing truly, if I wrote at all; of withholding nothing, though some things, from their very nature, could not be spoken of so fully as others."

Her discretion would have one set of consequences; her industry another. The alacrity with which Gaskell completed her task must leave most modern biographers gasping in astonishment. This was a commission executed at warp speed, barely 18 months from start to finish. A book of some 500 pages, begun in the summer of 1855, was sent to the printer in the spring of 1857, and published on 25 March the same year.

The portrait of "Miss Brontë" – partly based on extensive quotation from Charlotte's letters – that Gaskell presented to the mid-Victorian reader caused an immediate stir, stoking a controversy that lingers today. If she was fairly scrupulous in the portrait of her subject, which is never more than a point of mild contention, Gaskell gave her novelistic instincts free rein in her treatment of Brontë's brother, Branwell, and their father, Patrick. *Vis à vis* Branwell, she describes the young man's downfall and premature death as the result of a passionate affair with his employer's wife, who in the first edition Gaskell libelled to such a degree that first and second printings had to be withdrawn, revised and corrected.

What, you might ask, has any of this to do with Charlotte Brontë? Gaskell was determined to present her subject's sufferings at home as part of the intolerable burdens that shaped her life and art, and to do this she used all the evidence she could find. In any event, her account of Branwell's destruction at the hands of Lydia Robinson is nothing compared to her portrait of Patrick Brontë. Again, Gaskell is frank about the difficulties she faced as a biographer. Of Brontë père, she writes: "But I do not pretend to be able to harmonize points of character, and account for them, and bring them all in to one consistent and intelligible whole. The family with whom I have now to do shot their roots down deeper than I can penetrate. I cannot measure them, much less is it for me to judge them. I have named these instances of eccentricity in the father because I hold the knowledge of them to be necessary for a right understanding of the life of his daughter."

As one critic has written: "The father of the Brontës was certainly aware of his own eccentricities, and, while there can be no doubt that Mrs Gaskell exaggerated them in order to indicate the pressures under which Charlotte suffered during her childhood, his own protests were mild in comparison with the praise he had for the Life when it first appeared."

For some, Patrick Brontë was irredeemably tarnished by Gaskell's portrait, although much of her picture of the Brontës' home life seems highly circumspect: "The sisters [Anne, Emily and Charlotte] had kept the knowledge of their literary ventures from their father, fearing to increase their own anxieties and disappointment by witnessing his; for he took an acute interest in all that befell his children, and his own tendency had been towards literature in the days when he was young and hopeful."

This is certainly tactful; elsewhere, she strays closer to hagiography. To a degree that no 21st century biographer would emulate, Gaskell suppressed a number of inconvenient truths. During her years in Belgium, Charlotte had fallen in love with her teacher, Constantin Héger, a married man. Although both *The Professor* (1857) and *Villette* (1853) convey graphically her state of mind during this affair, Gaskell decided it was too delicate a matter for Victorian sensibilities. In a number of other areas, she was frank enough, but Gaskell also omitted any reference to Charlotte's relationship with George Smith, her publisher, who also published the *Life*.

Gaskell is much more comfortable at Haworth than in literary London, and she paints an unforgettable portrait of the home life of the sisters in general, and Charlotte in particular. Her use of the letters of Ellen Nussey, a family friend, illustrates her determination to present an overall picture of the artist growing up in an emotionally starved, and tortured domestic society that remains both fascinating and appalling. Gaskell's account of Haworth was both the making of the *Life*, and the source of an ongoing controversy. The facts remain that the terrible sequence of the deaths of Branwell, Emily and Anne, braided with a life overshadowed by the tyrannical "eccentricities" of their father, placed an almost unimaginable burden on the mind of a deeply sensitive and thoughtful novelist.

Gaskell herself was certain she had done her best. She wrote to Nussey that "I weighed every line with my whole power and heart" to fulfil the biographer's "great purpose of making her known". For some, indeed, Gaskell's *Life* is her best book.

Three to compare:
James Boswell: *The Life of Samuel Johnson* (1791)
John Forster: *The Life of Charles Dickens* (1874)
Jenny Uglow: *Elizabeth Gaskell – A Habit of Stories* (1993)

39. THE WONDERFUL ADVENTURES OF
MRS SEACOLE IN MANY LANDS
BY MARY SEACOLE (1857)

In Britain, mainly for historical reasons, there is distressingly little

black prose of consequence to be found in the English canon before the 20th century. Mary Seacole stands out as a gloriously entertaining exception, a Caribbean witness to the black experience in the Victorian age who deserves to be much better known. Hers, indeed, is the first autobiography by a black woman in Britain, and it describes a remarkable life story.

She was born Mary Jane Grant in Jamaica in 1805 during slavery, but teasingly declares at the outset that "as a female and a widow", she may be excused from "giving the precise date of this important event". What's not in doubt is that she died in England in fairly comfortable circumstances on 14 May 1881 and was buried in St Mary's Roman Catholic cemetery in Kensal Green, London. In her lifetime, she was a much-loved and widely revered black woman who was especially renowned throughout the empire for her work with the sick and wounded of the Crimean war. In fact, although she is sometimes described as "the black Florence Nightingale", Seacole always called herself "a Creole", with mixed-race ancestry.

Seacole was the daughter of James Grant, a Scots lieutenant with the British army, and a free Jamaican woman. "I have good Scotch blood coursing in my veins," she writes. Her mother was a "doctress", a healer who used Caribbean and African herbal remedies, from whom young Mary acquired her nursing skills.

The structure of Seacole's *Wonderful Adventures* was probably shaped by commercial considerations: she had to captalise on her fame as a veteran nurse from the Crimean war, a conflict that captured the mid century British imagination to a remarkable degree. Accordingly, she cuts to the chase, disposing of her first 40 years, during which she visited relatives in England ("I am not going to bore the reader with my first impressions of London"), in a single chapter. Then, once she has moved to Cruces, in Panama, she uses several chapters to get into her stride as a mature woman, before focusing on her career in the Crimea, drawn to the experience, she writes, by the heady "pomp, pride and circumstance of glorious war".

But first she had to overcome many obstacles to fulfil her ambition "to join my old friends of the 97th, 48th, and other regiments [encountered in the Caribbean], battling with worse foes than yellow fever or cholera... " On the face of it, her ambitions were too "visionary".

"To persuade the British public that an unknown Creole woman would be useful to their army before the walls of Sebastopol was too improbable an achievement to be thought of for an instant." In the end, however, the terrible conditions in the Crimea came to her assistance. After the battles of Balaclava and Inkerman, public opinion swung decisively behind missions of mercy to the hospitals in Scutari. Seacole was on her way. Denied official support, she went out to the Crimea using her own resources, to open an establishment, the "British hotel", near Balaclava, which would offer "a mess-table and comfortable quarters for sick and convalescent officers". Ever resourceful, she arrived in Scutari with a letter of introduction to Florence Nightingale, whom she describes as "a slight figure with a pale, gentle and firm face".

Seacole seems to have had the kind of indomitable energy (and extravagant costume) we now associate with Camila Batmanghelidjh. Arriving in the Crimea, she talks her way into meeting Nightingale at the Barrack hospital in Scutari. She reports that the "lady with the lamp" was friendly: "What do you want, Mrs Seacole? Anything we can do for you? If it lies in my power, I shall be very happy."

Seacole's "hotel" was a great success, supplying British military personnel with food, drink and domestic comforts. "Mother Seacole", as she was known, was never afraid to roll up her sleeves and get involved, even serving as a chef: "Whenever I had a few leisure moments, I used to wash my hands, and roll out pastry."When called to "dispense medications," she did so with aplomb, as well as dispensing frequent glasses of champagne.

In addition to her mission to the forces, Seacole also catered for spectators at the battles, in which she inevitably got mixed up. She was, wrote Russell, "both a Miss Nightingale and a chef", who was always visible in her brightly coloured and conspicuous outfits – bright blue, or yellow, with ribbons in contrasting colours. Seacole's mission was idiosyncratic: "If I had nothing else to be proud of, I think my rice puddings, made without milk, upon the high road to Sebastopol, would have gained me a reputation. What a shout there used to be when I came out of my little caboose, hot and curried, and called out, 'Rice pudding day, my sons."

And then there was also the influence of Mother Seacole's renowned baking, especially her cakes:

> "I declare I never heard or read of an army so partial to pastry as that British army before Sebastopol. I had a reputation for my sponge cakes that any pastry cook in London might have been proud of."

When the war ended, Seacole returned to Britain, but the strain of war had taken its toll. She was destitute and unwell. However, she was greeted as a celebrity from the conflict, attending a celebratory dinner in August 1856, at which Florence Nightingale was the guest of honour. The Times described huge enthusiasm, with "burly" sergeants protecting her from the pressure of the crowd. Her financial difficulties did not go away, with the creditors who had supplied the "British hotel" in hot pursuit. Eventually, in circumstances not described in *Wonderful Adventures*, she landed up in the bankruptcy court in November 1856.

The closing pages of her short conclusion deal with her return to England. She was perhaps too modest to describe how she became the toast of London society, friends with the Princess of Wales, for whom she worked as a masseuse, and an exotic late-Victorian celebrity, loved for quirky humour and robust, slightly raffish, joie de vivre.

Seacole's *Wonderful Adventures*, a bestseller in its day, was dedicated to a veteran of the Crimea, Major General Lord Rokeby, commander of the 1st Division, which indicates Seacole's debt to the conflict. Russell contributed a preface in which he described Seacole's memoir as "unique in literature". He characterised Seacole as "a plain truth-speaking woman who has lived an adventurous life amid scenes which have never yet found a historian".

Russell certainly bears some responsibility for creating the "myth" of Mary Seacole. In 1855, one of his reports in the Times probably strayed rather too close to rhapsodic hyperbole: "I have seen her nurse, under fire, our wounded men. A more tender or skilful hand about a wound or a broken limb could not be found among our best surgeons. I saw her at the fall of Sebastopol, laden not with plunder (good old soul), but with wine, bandages, and food for the wounded and the prisoners."

There's no doubt that this "good old soul" plainly captivated those around her, and her autobiography (which was possibly dictated to a publisher's "ghost") perfectly captures her personal magnetism.

Three to compare:
WEB Du Bois: *The Souls of Black Folk* (1903)
Richard Wright: *Black Boy* (1945)
Malcolm X (with Alex Haley): *The Autobiography of Malcolm X* (1965)

40. ON LIBERTY
BY JOHN STUART MILL (1859)

"Freedom", in the Anglo-American literary tradition, is a word that

excites a visceral response. From Magna Carta to the Declaration of Independence, the idea of "liberty" has inspired reverence, passion, and eloquence. It is a touchstone, with dangerous even revolutionary connotations, as Shakespeare understood. In Act II, scene II of *The Tempest*, there's a moment when Caliban, almost rapping, expresses a wild inarticulate desire for liberation:

'Ban 'Ban Ca–Caliban
Has a new master – Get a new man!
Freedom, high-day! High-day, freedom! Freedom, high-day,
    freedom!

And so, when John Stuart Mill addressed the idea of the free and sovereign individual in *On Liberty*, he was plugging into a current of English thought with deep and ancient connections. More immediately, he was picking up from Tom Paine, Adam Smith and William Godwin. But he had a different philosophical agenda from his predecessors. Those traditions, the popular and the radical, celebrated something perilously close to a state of nature. Mill's more sober purpose was to transform the idea of liberty into a philosophically respectable theory and express it in a form that could co-exist with Victorian culture and society, animating the body politic, but not upsetting it:

> "The subject of this essay is not the so-called 'liberty of the will', so unfortunately opposed to the misnamed doctrine of philosophical necessity; but civil, or social liberty: the nature and limits of the power which can be legitimately exercised by society over the individual."

There was no one better suited to this challenge than JS Mill. After the extraordinary education described in his *Autobiography*, he had emerged as the widely respected and leading philosopher/economist of his age. Years later, looking back, the Tory prime minister Arthur Balfour recalled that, during his student days at Cambridge, "Mill possessed an authority in the English universities comparable to that wielded in the Middle Ages by Aristotle."

On Liberty was also inspired by Mill's peculiar personal situation. Rejecting the father who had subjected him to a bizarre upbringing, the subject of his *Autobiography*, he had formed "a perfect friendship" with Harriet Taylor, a married woman with advanced "bohemian" ideas about love, marriage and divorce. For 20 years, until Mr Taylor died in 1849, Mill and his mistress could not marry. Once they were free to tie the knot, they withdrew to the suburbs to commune with a life of intense privacy, cut off from convention and conformity, and increasingly obsessed with intimations of mortality. Mill was explicit about these thoughts as an inspiration for *On Liberty*: "We have got a power of which we must try to make good use during the few years of life we have left. The more I think of the plan of a volume on Liberty, the more likely it seems to me that it will be read and make a sensation."

He was pitching the idea of the book at an exalted level, and even claimed, in a nod to Gibbon's account of his decision to write *The Decline and Fall of the Roman Empire,* that he had first conceived it as he was "mounting the steps of the Capitol". In the end, however, it was indeed overshadowed by mortality. Harriet Taylor died in 1858. Within weeks of her death, Mill overcame the anxieties he nurtured about so great a subject, delivered his manuscript to the publisher, and the book appeared the following February, as both a memorial and an intellectual landmark.

In the English literary tradition, 1859 is an *annus mirabilis*. As well as *On the Origin of Species*, this was the year that saw the publication of that Victorian classic, *Self-Help* by Samuel Smiles, and *A Tale of Two Cities* by Charles Dickens. *On Liberty* joins these titles as a work of exquisite prose (Mill is a fine, lucid writer) advancing "one very simple principle", an idea he expresses thus:

> "That principle is, that the sole end for which mankind is warranted, individually or collectively, in interfering with the liberty of action of any of their number, is self-protection. That the only purpose for which power can be rightfully exercised over any member of a civilised community, against his will, is to prevent harm to others."

What follows is a complex elaboration of this "very simple principle" in various spheres – thought, discussion, action – in which Mill establishes that the liberty of the individual should be absolute so long as he or she does not interfere with other individuals:

> "That the only purpose for which power can be rightfully exercised over any member of a civilized community, against his will, is to prevent harm to others. His own good, either physical or moral, is not a sufficient warrant . . . Over himself, over his body and mind, the individual is sovereign."

This freedom, inevitably, has to be qualified, to preserve civil concord. At the same, as a profound individualist, Mill never ceases to champion the sovereignty of the free man, who must never become a wage-slave, or mere cog in an industrial machine:

> "It really is of importance, not only what men do, but also what manner of men they are that do it. Among the works of man, which human life is rightly employed in perfecting and beautifying, the first in importance surely is man himself. Supposing it were possible to get houses built, corn grown, battles

fought, causes tried, and even churches erected and prayers said, by machinery – by automatons in human form – it would be a considerable loss to exchange for these automatons even the men and women who at present inhabit the more civilised parts of the world, and who assuredly are but starved specimens of what nature can and will produce."

On Liberty articulates Mill's adamant belief in the importance of humanity:

"Human nature is not a machine to be built after a model, and set to do exactly the work prescribed for it, but a tree, which requires to grow and develop itself on all sides, according to the tendency of the inward forces which make it a living thing."

All of this leads to Mill's concluding summary: a classic British statement about the role of the state.

"The worth of a State, in the long run, is the worth of the individuals composing it; and a State which postpones the interests of their mental expansion and elevation to a little more of administrative skill, or of that semblance of it which practice gives, in the details of business; a State which dwarfs its men, in order that they may be more docile instruments in its hands even for beneficial purposes – will find that with small men no great thing can really be accomplished; and that the perfection of machinery to which it has sacrificed everything will in the end avail it nothing."

A decade after the appearance of *On Liberty*, Matthew Arnold published *Culture and Anarchy* which some have seen as "a powerful indictment" of Mill's doctrine. Arnold querulously suggested that "doing as one likes" was a charter for the Englishman's right "to march where he likes, enter where he likes, hoot as he likes, threaten as he likes, smash as he likes." This was the beginning of a Victorian backlash to Mill's spirited and measured assertion of the English individual's rights. It's an argument that continues, in very different language, to this day.

Three to compare:
John Locke: *A Letter Concerning Toleration* (1689)
Jeremy Bentham: *Chrestomathia* (1816)
John Stuart Mill: *Autobiography* (1873)

41. ON THE ORIGIN OF SPECIES
BY CHARLES DARWIN (1859)

When Charles Darwin first *saw On the Origin of Species by means of Natural Selection, or The Preservation of Favoured Races in the Struggle for Life* in book form, he is said to have remarked that he found it tough going. Actually, the book, composed in a hurry to forestall his rivals, after 20 years of research, and aimed at that mythical beast "the educated general reader", is extraordinarily accessible, sometimes even moving, in its lucid simplicity. That's all the more remarkable for a revolutionary work of scientific theory, arguably the most important book published in the English language during the 19th century.

From a 21st century perspective, Darwin's *Origin* has two roles in this list. First, it is a profoundly influential work of biology, argued in astonishing and compelling detail. For example, one famous passage (too long to quote in full) describes the ecological benefits to "a large and extremely barren heath" derived from the planting of Scotch fir:

> "I went to several points of view, whence I could examine hundreds of acres of the unenclosed heath, and literally I could not see a single Scotch fir, except the old planted clumps. But on looking closely between the stems of the heath, I found a multitude of seedlings and little trees, which had been perpetually browsed down by the cattle. In one square yard ... I counted 32 little trees; and one of them, judging from the rings of growth, had during 26 years tried to raise its head above the stems of the heath, and had failed. No wonder that, as soon as the land was enclosed, it became thickly clothed with vigorously growing young firs."
> [pp 123-24]

Second, *The Origin of Species* was also a controversial and popular title that caught the imagination of the mid-Victorian public, transformed attitudes to Christianity and the human race, and would become a source book for generations of capitalists, communists and, ultimately, the Nazis. As the author of radical thought, grounded in profound observation, Darwin was described as "the most dangerous man in England", whose account of natural selection challenged the "truth" of the Bible, the automatic authority of God in nature, and the privileged position of the human animal at the centre of creation.

Darwin's plan had always been to write a much longer book about the vulnerability of the species. When his friend and colleague Alfred Russel Wallace sent him a paper setting out the theory of natural selection, an idea inspired by a reading of Thomas Malthus on population growth, Darwin was immediately provoked into getting a lifetime of work and speculation into print before any rival established a competitive version.

As it turned out, Darwin had no need to worry. Although John Murray, his publisher, was unsure about the market, and initially printed just 1,250 copies, this edition (now incredibly rare) sold out on the first day. The question of survival in Victorian society was highly topical, and Darwin's account of natural selection caught the public mood. He himself was quite tentative about his new theory, and always stressed the length of time involved in the process of species adaptation: "Its action depends on there being places in the polity of nature, which can be better occupied by some of the inhabitants of the country undergoing modification of some kind … The action of natural selection will probably still oftener depend on some of the inhabitants becoming slowly modified; the mutual relations of many of the other habitants being thus disturbed."

Darwin goes on: "Owing to this struggle for life, any variation, however slight and from whatever cause proceeding, if it be in any degree profitable to an individual of any species, in its infinitely complex relations to other organic beings and to external nature, will tend to the preservation of that individual, and will generally be inherited by its offspring … I have called this principle, by which each slight variation, if useful, is preserved, by the term of Natural Selection, in order to mark its relation to man's power of selection."

As many critics have noted, *The Origin* is a polemical book written in a mild, sometimes defensive, and uncontentious way by a passionate, life-long naturalist with a deep reverence for nature. Darwin's dithyrambic conclusion is celebrated: "It is interesting to contemplate an entangled bank, clothed with many plants of many kinds, with birds singing on the bushes, with various insects flitting about, and with worms crawling through the damp earth, and to reflect that these elaborately constructed forms, so different from each other, and dependent on each other in so complex a manner, have all been produced by laws acting around us …

Thus, from the war of nature, from famine and death, the most exalted object which we are capable of conceiving, namely, the production of the higher animals, directly follows. There is grandeur in this view of life, with its several powers, having been originally breathed into a few forms or into one; and that, whilst this planet has gone cycling on according to the fixed law of gravity, from so simple a beginning endless forms most beautiful and most wonderful have been, and are being, evolved."

This is a side of *The Origin* rooted in Darwin's love of the English countryside. In Victorian society, there were many harsher aspects. For Marx and Engels, Darwinism was the biological equivalent of class war. For some Americans, such as Andrew Carnegie and Teddy Roosevelt, his ideas explained the dynamics of capitalism. To the imperial powers who were drifting towards war in the 1900s, war – some said – was a "biological necessity". Many of Darwin's apologists have given his ideas a bad name. But, at its humane and deeply reflective heart, this pioneering book is a secular hymn to the countryside, the place in which Darwin himself was always happiest.

Three to compare:
Gilbert White: *The Natural History and Antiquities of Selborne* (1789)
Thomas Malthus: *An Essay on the Principle of Population* (1798)
Charles Darwin: *The Voyage of the Beagle* (1839)

42. CULTURE AND ANARCHY
BY MATTHEW ARNOLD (1869)

In 1848, a year of European revolutions, Matthew Arnold, the eldest son of a celebrated Victorian headmaster, voiced fears about his society that still seem hauntingly prescient and topical. "I see a wave of more than American vulgarity, moral, intellectual, and social, preparing to break over us," he wrote. Arnold was also a poet, critic and educationist of great distinction. In Dover Beach, his finest poem, he expressed similar anxieties in some famous lines:

"And we are here as on a darkling plain
Swept with confused alarms of struggle and flight,
Where ignorant armies clash by night."

Arnold was acutely conscious of the threat of "ignorant armies" during 1866-69, the years in which he incubated this classic of social and literary criticism. Like many Victorian masterpieces, *Culture and Anarchy* began as a magazine series, and an important part of its appeal is as a tour de force of magazine journalism, a genre Arnold himself defined as "literature in a hurry".

The two great events, foreign and domestic, that shaped the writing of Arnold's passionate argument for self-improvement through culture were, first, the European revolutions of 1866-70, especially the rise of Prussia; and second, the Great Reform Bill of 1867, together with the London riots that preceded it.

Initially, however, this is a book inspired by, and dedicated to, literature. Arnold was his father's son, a passionate advocate for the civilising effect of words and ideas, after the classical example of Greece and Rome. Arnold was also influenced by JH Newman's *The Idea of a University*, and was inspired to define culture as the essential means by which the provincial stupidity and boorishness of English life could be neutralised on behalf of progress. Arnold's disdain for what passed as "culture" in Victorian times, is evident from his opening page:

> "The culture which is supposed to plume itself on a smattering of Greek and Latin is a culture which is begotten by nothing so intellectual as curiosity; it is valued out of sheer vanity and ignorance, or else as an engine of social and class distinction, separating its holder, like a badge or title, from other people who have not got it."

"True" culture, as Arnold defines it, with reference to the glorious Hellenic past, is simply "the study of perfection", the harmonious expansion of all the powers of human nature. In sentiments that would later be developed and enriched by the more feverish imagination of Oscar Wilde, for whom "culture" was at once sacrosanct and sublime, Arnold believed that a full apprehension of its virtues must be attained by a knowledge of the best that has been said and thought in the world, by the free play of the mind over the facts of life, and by a sympathetic attitude towards all that is beautiful. In one typical passage, he expresses his argument thus:

> "I have been trying to show that culture is, or ought to be, the study and pursuit of perfection; and that of perfection, as

pursued by culture, beauty and intelligence, or, in other words, sweetness and light, are the main characters."

Arnold's famous borrowing from Jonathan Swift – "Sweetness and light" – expresses culture as a dynamic concept: "sweetness" as a mature sense of beauty, and "light" as the exercise of an alert and active intelligence. Although the overall expression of this belief reeks of Victorian high-mindedness, Arnold gave both purpose and direction to an articulate critique of industrial society.

Culture & Anarchy appeared in book form just one year before Forster's all-important Education Act of 1870 and it posed questions that still perplex us today: what kind of life should individuals in mass societies be encouraged to lead? How do such societies best ensure that our quality of life is not impoverished? How to preserve an elevated and exclusive freedom of thought in an age of democratic fervour?

Opposed to this exalted assertion of an ideal version of "the good life", there was the vulgarity, vigour and vehemence of Victorian England at its zenith. This, Arnold argues, was a heedless and exuberant individualism (replete with prejudice, greed, xenophobia, racism, intolerance and aggression) that would lead to anarchy. He nails this claim by showing how Victorian barbarism affected all strata of national life.

In some of his wittiest and most entertaining passages, Arnold divided English society into three classes – the Barbarians, the Philistines, and the Populace. (With an almost audible sigh, he complains: "It is awkward and tiresome to be always saying the aristocratic class, the middle class, the working class.") The Barbarians or aristocracy, he says, have a superficial "sweetness and light", but are too concerned with the maintenance and enjoyment of their privileges to attain a true sense of beauty and a true liberation of thought:

> "The Barbarians had the passion for field-sports; as of the passion for asserting one's personal liberty ... The care of the Barbarians for the body, and for all manly exercises; the chivalry of the Barbarians, with its characteristics of high spirit, choice manners, and distinguished bearing – what is this but the politeness of our aristocratic class?"
> The Philistines or middle classes are devoted to money-making and a narrow form of religion; they are indifferent or hostile to beauty; and they are 'the enemy of the children of light', or servants of the idea."

Finally, the rowdy Populace are violent in their prejudices and brutal in their pleasures. But all three groups are agreed that "doing as one likes" is the chief end of man, and all are self-satisfied. As a magazine writer of genius, Arnold dazzles his readers with entrancing contemporary detail: for instance, the case of the Mr Smith who "feared he would come to poverty and be eternally lost", to the great Reform crises, and to the commercial values to which working people had become enslaved. There are also many topical jokes in the text (nicely explicated in the Cambridge University Press edition of *Culture and Anarchy*, edited by J Dover Wilson), which indicate Arnold's wry and subtle sense of humour. He comes across as the kind of man you'd be happily stuck with on a wet afternoon in the country. His sensibility is supremely English; exquisitely well read; and exceedingly sophisticated.

By its wit, its pithy definitions and its potent charm, *Culture and Anarchy* caught the public mood and aroused in its Victorian readers a mid-season bout of self-analysis, even self-criticism, whose influence lingered for decades. As one later commentator observed, "The evils of English society it attacks and the remedies it proposes are by no means out of date".

Arnold might be surprised by that verdict. In his closing paragraph, he notes, ironically, that "now we go the way the human race is going, while they [the Liberals] abolish the Irish Church by the power of the Nonconformists' antipathy to establishments, or they enable a man to marry his deceased wife's sister."

Three to compare:
John Henry Newman: *The Idea of a University* (1852/1858)
Charles Darwin: *The Origin of Species* (1859)
John Stuart Mill: *On Liberty* (1859)

43. NONSENSE SONGS
BY EDWARD LEAR (1871)

In the English literary tradition, to have a name like "Lear" is to

 embody profound, pre-modern connotations of madness. But Edward Lear, who was born in 1812 in Holloway, north London, one of 21 children, to middle-class parents, was not mad. Nonetheless, he would come to represent almost singlehandedly a tradition of literary dementia that stretches back to Merrie England. According to Noel Malcolm, in *The Origins of English Nonsense*, this important genre braids the oral "Mother Goose" tradition with the

verbal games of court poets and playful scholars. For Lear, his identity as "the laureate of nonsense" was also shaped by his experience as a sufferer of epilepsy, as well as asthma and bronchitis, and afflicted by many querulous aversions: noise, crowds, hustle, gaiety, fools and bores…

"Mister Lear" was certainly eccentric. A nomadic artist, a lifelong solitary of homosexual inclinations, the one-time art master to Queen Victoria, he burst on to the literary scene in 1846 with *A Book of Nonsense*, a collection of some 115 limericks, beginning with:

> "There was an old man with a beard
> Who said, 'It is just as I feared!–
> Two Owls and a Hen, four Larks and a Wren,
> Have all built their nests in my beard."

A Book of Nonsense was an overnight bestseller, and made Lear famous, but it did not make him happy. He spent the next several years travelling and painting, doodling odd verses, and perfecting his mature persona as a lovable but dotty "old cove", who countered boredom with globetrotting, and sketching. Of his art, a bizarre marriage of strange words and stranger cartoons, he liked to say that he was walking in the "dusty twilight of the incomprehensible …"

Lear's nonsense, an antidote to discomfort and irritation, opened up a whole new world of infectious wordplay, childish fantasy and surreal adventure. Like several later Victorian writers, notably JM Barrie, RL Stevenson and Kenneth Grahame, he was, according to one critic, "invincibly boyish, and almost childlike", a Peter Pan who did not want to grow up. An innovative versifier, the last thing he wanted was to remain like Swift's fantasy creatures, the Struldbrugs, "cut and dried for life..."

When it came to life itself, both Lear and his contemporary Lewis Carroll enjoyed their alter egos – the latter as an Oxford don, the former as an itinerant artist. For both, "nonsense" was an escape into a more vivid, imaginative reality. Their most sublime nonsense is simultaneously age-old and childish. No catalogue of English and American prose is complete without *Nonsense*. This sub-genre flourishes in the nonfiction tradition like a wild and multicoloured weed in a knot garden.

As a younger man, in mid century, Lear freely admitted he was "a queer beast" who was always sketching, and who lived to draw and paint. His watercolours remain highly collectable to this day, but nonsense was his forte – the self-expression of a wanderer, a whimsical humorist, a grumbler and an eternal child. In 1863, he described himself as wanting to be a "Lord High Bosh and Nonsense Producer", and tried through contacts to become a "Grand Peripatetic Ass and Bosh-producing Luminary" to the Greek Court, a scheme that came to nothing.

Instead, he found the freedom to complete his masterpiece, *Nonsense Songs, Stories, Botany and Alphabets*, first published in 1871, a potent compendium of verbal delirium and lexicographical fantasy. It's one of the extraordinary coincidences of our literature that this title, with its Quangle-Wangle, "runcible spoon" and the "Dong with a Luminous Nose" should appear in the same year as Carroll's nonsense masterpiece Jabberwocky (from *Alice's Adventures Through The Looking-Glass*).

In this vein, it's a short step from the Lear of *Nonsense Songs* to the James Joyce of *Finnegans Wake*. It was Lear not Joyce who wrote "sufficient unto the day is the weevil thereof". Long before some of the experiments of modernism, *Nonsense Songs* contains such poems as The Owl and the Pussycat and The Jumblies, nonsense classics that express a haunting and melancholy obsession with finding happiness in faraway lands where a lonely pig will marry an unlikely avian/feline couple in an offbeat ceremony, or where a bunch of intrepid blue-fingered travellers in a leaky vessel could find comfort and joy by whistling and warbling "a moony song/To the echoing sound of a coppery gong."

The Jumblies (for it is they) cry "Timballo!" and, improbably, "live in a Sieve and a crockery-jar". They have not a care in the world, and drink a home brew called "Ring-Bo-Ree". Lear's vision of the Jumblies is a hypnotic, even enchanting, mash-up of schoolboy truancy, piratical gallivanting, and imperial fantasy:

> "They sailed to the Western Sea, they did,
> To a land all covered with trees,
> And they bought an Owl, and a useful Cart,
> And a pound of Rice, and a Cranberry Tart,
> And a hive of silvery Bees.
> And they bought a Pig, and some green Jack-daws,
> And a lovely Monkey with lollipop paws,
> And 40 bottles of Ring-Bo-Ree,
> And no end of Stilton Cheese."

In Lear's imagination, the Jumblies' overseas adventures are benign: they are enriched and matured by their travels. When they return home, the voyagers are widely admired for their courage and determination in the exploration of the exotic. Their tale is magical, and nonsense in the English (and American) tradition is magical, hovering in the margins of many, much more sober, texts to provide a frisson of imaginative transgression. It probably does not do to analyse this genre too closely, but without this "laureate of nonsense", we would not have: Pink Floyd, James Joyce, Flann O'Brien, Dr Seuss, John Lennon, Woody Allen, JRR Tolkien, Spike Milligan, Norton Juster, Terry Pratchett, Carl Sandburg, Bob Dylan, David Byrne, Julia Donaldson or even the incomparably unhinged Glen Baxter.

Three to compare:
Lewis Carroll: *The Hunting of the Snark* (1876)
Harry Graham: *Ruthless Rhymes for Heartless Homes* (1898)
Julia Donaldson: *The Gruffalo* (1999)

44. TRAVELS WITH A DONKEY IN THE CÉVENNES BY ROBERT LOUIS STEVENSON (1879)

Robert Louis Stevenson offers the very rare example of a great writer

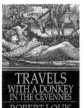

who excelled in nonfiction as much as fiction. Contemporary critics also puzzled over the character of his greatness. Would Stevenson, asked one in 1892, "take his definite and final place in English literature as a writer of essays or novels?"

Today, the answer to that question might seem obvious. *Treasure Island, Kidnapped* and *Dr Jekyll and Mr Hyde* remain imperishably popular – timeless and universal. At the same time, Stevenson's travel writing, a small part of his nonfiction output, is as outstanding and influential as his fiction. What's less often acknowledged is the fact that it was Stevenson's poor health that drove him to travel abroad: he was always in search of relief for his chronic bronchial condition (possibly tuberculosis) and the frequent haemorrhages that dogged his short life.

Graham Greene, Robert Byron and Bruce Chatwin (among many) all owe a debt to *An Inland Voyage* and *The Amateur Emigrant*. However, from a short list, *Travels With a Donkey in the Cévennes* remains Stevenson's masterpiece, a "little book" that describes a wayward, inconsequential journey and a strange love affair (with a donkey) in which, as in all the best journeys, the author finds himself renewed, refreshed and, returning from his travels, once more ready for the fray.

The brilliance of *Travels With a Donkey* is to keep the reader always suspended in the moment, through a combination of wry and exquisite observation and an undercurrent of delight in the pleasures of the human comedy. Here, Stevenson introduces Modestine, his celebrated donkey:

> "Father Adam had a cart, and to draw the cart a diminutive she-ass, not much bigger than a dog, the colour of a mouse, with a kindly eye and a determined under-jaw. There was something neat and high-bred, a quaker-ish elegance, about the rogue that hit my fancy on the spot."

And so RLS and Modestine set off – at her own pace...

"What that pace was, there is no word mean enough to describe; it was something as much slower than a walk as a walk is slower than a run; it kept me hanging on each foot for an incredible length of time; in five minutes it exhausted the spirit and set up a fever in all the muscles of the leg."

However, help is at hand in the shape of a peasant saviour, a *deus ex machina* who, before he left Stevenson's company, gave him "some excellent, if inhumane, advice". This, in conjunction with "a switch" was "the true cry or masonic word of donkey-drivers, 'Proot!'"

Sadly, the efficacy of this "true cry" was limited:

"I hurried over my mid-day meal, and was early forth again. But, alas, as we climbed the interminable hill upon the other side, 'Proot!' seemed to have lost its virtue. I prooted like a lion, I prooted mellifluously like a sucking-dove; but Modestine would be neither softened nor intimidated."

So Stevenson would travel the Cévennes at Modestine's pace, which possibly explains why his 12-day journey (something of a pilgrimage for latterday Stevenson fans) covers just 120 miles in 12 days.

It was a solitary trip, but it comes to life through the traveller's interplay with his stubborn companion, a relationship that quickly starts to resemble a love affair:

"By the whiteness of the pack-saddle, I could see Modestine walking round and round at the length of her tether; I could hear her steadily munching at the sward; but there was not another sound, save the indescribable quiet talk of the runnel over the stones."

His farewell to his travels is also his farewell to his donkey:

"As for her, poor soul! She had come to regard me as a god. She loved to eat out of my hand. She was patient, elegant in form, the colour of an ideal mouse, and inimitably small. Her faults were those of her race and sex; her virtues were her own. Farewell, and if for ever –"

Inwardly, as a writer, he was always razor-sharp; tougher than tungsten; indestructible; immortal.

Three to compare:
Graham Greene: *Journey Without Maps* (1936)
Robert Byron: *The Road to Oxiana* (1937)
Bruce Chatwin: *In Patagonia* (1977)

45. LIFE ON THE MISSISSIPPI
BY MARK TWAIN (1883)

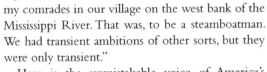

"When I was a boy, there was but one permanent ambition among my comrades in our village on the west bank of the Mississippi River. That was, to be a steamboatman. We had transient ambitions of other sorts, but they were only transient."

Here is the unmistakable voice of America's greatest and most original, prose writer describing the childhood that would inspire his masterpiece, *The Adventures of Huckleberry Finn* (1884).

Life on the Mississippi is not just the brilliant sketch that precedes the vaster and more colourful canvas of a celebrated novel, it expresses the heart and soul of Samuel Clemens, the alter ego of Mark Twain. Alongside *The Innocents Abroad* (1869) and *Roughing It* (1872), this *tour de force* of unreliable reportage, spliced with travel, history and memoir, provides a deep insight into *Huckleberry Finn* as well as a key to its author and his outrageous originality. As his most recent biographer, Ron Powers, has put it: "Twain's way of seeing and hearing things changed America's way of seeing and hearing things. He was the Lincoln of American literature."

Clemens was a steamboat pilot from 1857 until the civil war closed the Mississippi in 1861. This great river flowed so deeply through his mind and art that he would eventually extract his final pseudonym from its waters (having flirted with, and rejected, Thomas Jefferson Snodgrass, W Epaminondas Adrastus Blab and Sergeant Fathom). In the end, Clemens took his pseudonym from the language of the river he loved. "Mark twain" – mark two, a depth of 12ft, safe water – was the leadsman's cry and it has inspired no end of psychobabble about the significance of "the most recognised alias in the history of aliases". Twain had no truck with any of that. At the height of his fame, he told a fan: "I have been an author for 20 years, and an ass for 55." In *Life on the Mississippi*, he makes light of his alter ego:

> "[Captain Isaiah Sellers] was not of literary turn or capacity,
> but he used to jot down brief paragraphs of plain practical
> information about the river, and sign them 'Mark Twain', and
> give them to the New Orleans Picayune … At the time that the
> telegraph brought the news of his death, I was on the Pacific
> coast. I was a fresh new journalist, and needed a nom de guerre;
> so I confiscated the ancient mariner's discarded one, and have
> done my best to make it remain what it was in his hands – a sign
> and symbol and warrant that whatever is found in its company
> may be gambled on as being the petrified truth."

"Petrified truth" might be an apt synonym for young Sam Clemens's
brand of nonfiction. In the making of Mark Twain, the great American writer, *Life on the Mississippi* follows two other crucial volumes
of literary self-invention. In *The Innocents Abroad*, Clemens had established himself as the voice of his generation:

> "This book is a record of a pleasure trip. If it were a record of
> a solemn scientific expedition it would have about it the gravity,
> that profundity, and that impressive incomprehensibility which
> are so proper to works of that kind, and withal so attractive …
> It is only a record of a picnic."

Next, in *Roughing It*, his hilarious account of his adventures in the
Nevada silver mines, he transformed this voice into an instrument for
narrating the authentic American experience in a language that would
resonate throughout the United States. Finally, in *Life on the Mississippi*, working from sketches 'Old Times on the Mississippi' already
published in the *Atlantic Monthly* in 1875, he not only completed
the making of Mark Twain, he also located his future subject: the
Mississippi childhood that would lead directly to *The Adventures of
Tom Sawyer* (1876) and *Huckleberry Finn*.

In this teeming nonfiction preamble to his great novels, Mark Twain
and the mighty Mississippi become equally mythic. As one critic has
put it, he becomes "that river's attendant spirit", and like the ever-
changing current on which young Samuel Clemens learned his trade
as a riverboat pilot, so the ever-changing vision of the writer Mark
Twain takes wing in these magical pages through a succession of tall
tales, boyhood reminiscences, scraps of history, outrageous "stretchers"

(aka, alternative facts), and the crusty wisdom of the immortal Horace Bixby, whose role in these pages is to instruct the cub pilot in the mysteries of the steamboat business. That is, of course, if he can hold his temper despite the intolerable provocations of his pupil:

> "This [Twain's impertinence] was a red rag to a bull. He [Bixby] raged and stormed so that I judge it made him blind, because he ran over the steering-oar of a trading-scow. Of course the traders sent up a volley of red-hot profanity. Never was a man so grateful as Mr Bixby was: because he was brim full, and here were subjects who would talk back. He threw open a window, thrust his head out, and such an irruption followed as I never had heard before ... When he closed the window he was empty. You could have drawn a seine through his system and not caught curses enough to disturb your mother with."

Twain does more than engage in the merciless teasing of "Mr Bixby", he celebrates his calling:

> "We had a fine company of these river inspectors along this trip ... Two or three of them wore polished silk hats, elaborate shirt-fronts, diamond breast-pins, kid gloves, and patent leather boots. They were choice in their English, and bore themselves with a dignity proper to men of prodigious reputations as pilots."

"If I have seemed to love my subject," writes Twain, catching himself getting carried away, "it is no surprising thing, for I loved the profession far better than any I have followed since, and I took a measureless pride in it. The reason is plain: a pilot, in those days, was the only unfettered and entirely independent human being that lived on Earth."

You might think that a writer such as Mark Twain would always feel "unfettered" (he certainly presents himself thus on the page), but there you would be wrong. "Writers of all kinds," he continues, "are manacled servants of the public. We write frankly and fearlessly, but then we 'modify' before we print."

In hindsight, this passage possibly foreshadows the immense 10-year struggle Twain had in the writing of *Huckleberry Finn*. Here, in *Life on the Mississippi*, perhaps for the last time, he was free to be himself – in two happily "unfettered" personas.

Three to compare:

Mark Twain: *The Innocents Abroad* (1869)

Mark Twain: *Roughing It* (1872)

Mark Twain: *The Adventures of Huckleberry Finn* (1884)

46. PERSONAL MEMOIRS
BY ULYSSES S GRANT (1885)

According to Mark Twain, these are "the best [memoirs] of any general's since Caesar", but we have to take that verdict with a pinch of salt: Twain was also Grant's publisher. As a one-time Confederate soldier, Twain liked to joke that it was General Grant's prowess on behalf of the Union cause that had persuaded him to desert the colours and become a journalist.

Twain had first invited the retired president to write his autobiography in 1881, but Grant had declined the offer. A modest man, he had replied, "No one is interested in me", referring to two books about him which had recently flopped. But when, in 1884, he was swindled out of his savings, and desperate for money, Twain's offer seemed much more tempting. Now, writing in pencil, or dictating to a secretary, he began to compose the book that many commentators agree sets the gold standard for presidential memoirs.

For the critic Edmund Wilson, who put Grant in the exalted literary company of Walt Whitman and Henry Thoreau, this powerful autobiography is "a unique expression of the national character. [Grant] has conveyed the suspense which was felt by himself and his army and by all who believed in the Union cause. The reader finds himself on edge to know how the civil war is coming out."

Grant's memoirs are all the more remarkable for having been completed under duress. When he began to write, he had begun to suffer the agonising pain of throat cancer. It was only his inflexible determination, the quality that had made him a great general, that mastered the torments of ill-health – sleepless nights, fear of dying – to articulate his account for a devoted American audience. By many accounts, Grant's memoirs fully capture the man himself: they are well observed, often humorous, invariably charming, penetrating and lucid.

Throughout this very substantial autobiography, like the great man he was, Grant is supremely generous to his enemies, loyal to his friends and associates, and always devoted to another civil war hero, his president, Abraham Lincoln. On every page, his narrative has the simple directness of the finest English prose, inspired by the King James Bible on which he had been raised. The overall effect is both intimate and majestic.

When Grant finished the manuscript in July 1885, it was rushed into galley proof. On 23 July, having completed his final corrections, Grant died in his summer cottage on the slopes of Mount McGregor, in New York state. His *Personal Memoirs*, published a few months later, were at once acclaimed as a masterpiece. One contemporary critic wrote that "no other American president has told his story as powerfully as Ulysses S Grant. The book is one of the most unflinching studies of war in our literature." More than a century later, Gore Vidal added his own assessment: "It is simply not possible to read Grant's memoirs without realising that the author is a man of first-rate intelligence."

Personal Memoirs immediately sold more than 300,000 copies. It has remained in print ever since.

Three to compare:
Abraham Lincoln: *Speeches and Writings* 1832–1858
Omar Bradley: *A General's Story* (1951)
Bill Clinton: *My Life* (2004)

47. Brief Lives
by John Aubrey
(edited by Andrew Clark, 1898)

Posterity in books is fickle. For the odd and unpredictable afterlives of

some English classics, consider the case of John Aubrey. This gossipy gentleman-scholar, antiquarian and pioneer biographer died in 1697, after a life brushed by the wings of history. At the time of his death, his chances of being remembered must have seemed vanishingly slim. The only title published in his lifetime Miscellanies: *A Collection of Hermetick Philosophy* (1696) was deemed "mad". Slowly, however, his numerous manuscripts were rediscovered, although a really substantial portion of *Brief Lives* did not appear in print until 1813. Finally, two centuries after Aubrey's death, in 1898, a Church of England rector and scholar, the Rev Andrew Clark, edited a transcript of *Brief Lives* in a bowdlerised edition that finally established Aubrey's name in the English canon.

Thereafter, in the 20th century, his reputation took off. Anthony Powell published *John Aubrey and His Friends* in 1948. A year later, Oliver Lawson Dick published the first complete scholarly edition, which alphabetised the *Lives* and modernised the text. Paradoxically, this updating helped revive Aubrey's reputation once and for all, and eventually inspired Patrick Garland's one-man play, eventually performed by Roy Dotrice, a show that ran for 40 years on both sides of the Atlantic. In 2015, Kate Bennett published a new and complete scholarly edition (*Brief Lives With an Apparatus for the Lives of Our English Mathematical Writers*) with OUP; in the same year, Ruth Scurr's brilliantly imaginative John Aubrey, *My Own Life* came out in celebration of a national treasure – an ingenious literary man, and a writer of originality, wit and wisdom who had constructed "a paper museum" of timeless fascination.

Brief Lives began as a collaboration with the Oxford antiquarian Anthony Wood. When Aubrey was asked to write the life of the great philosopher Thomas Hobbes, he became inspired to follow the classical example of, for example, Plutarch, and compiled a list of some 55 lives, mainly drawn from contemporary English society.

Aubrey's *Brief Lives* are mostly pen portraits of distinguished

17th century Englishmen: writers (Shakespeare, Sir Walter Raleigh, Andrew Marvell, John Milton), scientists (William Harvey, Robert Boyle), mathematicians (Henry Briggs, Edmund Gunter), doctors (Thomas Vaughan), theologians (John Hales), astrologers (John Dee), soldiers (Charles Danvers, Robert Moray, Thomas Morgan), sailors (Sir Kenelm Digby), lawyers (John Hoskins, Edward Coke), philosophers (Robert Hooke), Church of England divines (Thomas Goffe, William Holder) and many others.

Aubrey's highly entertaining brief life of Sir Walter Raleigh has been widely anthologised:

> "He loved a wench well; and one time getting up one of the Mayds of Honour up against a tree in a Wood ('twas his first lady) who seemed at first boarding to be something fearful of her Honour, and modest, she cryed, Sweet Sir Walter, what do you me ask? Will you undoe me? Nay, sweet Sir Walter! Sweet Sir Walter! Sir Walter! At last, as the danger and the pleasure at the same time grew higher, she cryed in the extasey, Swisser Swatter Swisser Swatter. She proved with child, and I doubt not but this Hero took care of them both, as also that the Product was more than an ordinary mortal."

Aubrey's treatment of women is typical of his age, as was his attitude to outsiders. *Brief Lives* has almost no foreigners (Colbert, Descartes and Erasmus) and very few independent women.

Aubrey, a self-effacing, modest man, was a brilliant oral historian, who treasured the minutiae of everyday life and took care to exclude himself from his biographical research. Scurr says, "he knew he was inventing the modern genre of biography", and his obsession with what he took to be the truth makes him a very modern figure. He said he was after "the naked and plaine trueth, which is here exposed so bare, that the very pudenda are not covered, and affords many passages that would raise a blush in a young virgin's cheeke". He was sometimes criticised for being "too minute" (trivial), but Aubrey's answer was that "a hundred yeare hence that minutenesse will be gratefull." He was a man who trusted in posterity – and thus posterity rewards him.

Three to compare:

48. THE VARIETIES OF RELIGIOUS EXPERIENCE
BY WILLIAM JAMES (1902)

The United States is a society, first described in Thomas Jefferson's

revolutionary words in 1776, that constantly rewrites its narrative – in law, philosophy, economics and belief, as well as through poetry, drama and fiction. In moments of change, its finest writers have often found new forms of expression and ideas that both illuminate the American story and help to redefine it.

William James, brother of the more famous Henry, was a classic American intellectual, a brilliant New Englander and renowned pragmatist – a celebrity in his time who coined the phrase "stream of consciousness". He responded to the cultural and social ferment of the late 19th century with the Gifford lectures, given in Edinburgh during 1900-02. When he turned these talks into a book, James, a Harvard psychologist and the author of *The Principles of Psychology,* placed himself at the crossroads of psychology and religion to articulate an approach to religious experience that would help liberate the American mind at the beginning of the 20th century from its puritan restrictions by advancing a pluralistic view of belief inspired by American traditions of tolerance. Like his brother, he was obsessed by the problem of expressing individual consciousness through language; this is just one of the principal themes of *The Varieties of Religious Experience.*

Psychology aside, this is an odd book in many ways, especially for its unorthodox approach to the precepts of organised religion. One commentator has described it as "a classic that is too psychological to have shaped most religious inquiry and too religious to have influenced much psychological research". And yet, in the words of *Psychology Today*, it remains "the most notable of all books in the field of the psychology of religion and probably destined to be the most influential book written on religion in the 20th century."

In his approach to religious experience, William James writes that he had to face a hard problem: "first, to defend 'experience' against 'philosophy' as the real backbone of the world's religious life; and second, to make the reader believe that [the life of religion] … is mankind's most important function."

James begins his argument with the assertion that religion answers basic human needs. From here, he separates belief from its tribal origins. Religion, he says, has become a consumer item for individuals. His only concern about religion is what it tells us about "what goes on in the single private man". Then he comes up with a famous definition:

> "Religion … shall mean for us the feelings, acts, and experiences of individual men in their solitude, so far as they apprehend themselves to stand in relation to whatever they may consider the divine."

Using potted biographies of well-known writers and thinkers, including Tolstoy and John Bunyan, William James concludes a long and fascinating exploration of the "healthy mind", the "sick soul", and the "divided self", with closing chapters on mysticism, saintliness, atonement and conversion. Here, too, he presented an account of God as a finite being, inextricably caught up in world affairs, and linked to human activity and ambitions. He closes with a witty question: "Who knows whether the faithfulness of individuals here below to their own poor over-beliefs may not actually help God in turn to be more effectively faithful to his own greater tasks?"

Three to compare:
William James: *The Principles of Psychology* (1890)
William James: Pragmatism: *A New Name for Some Old Ways of Thinking* (1907)
Louis Menand: *The Metaphysical Club: A Story of Ideas in America* (2001)

49. DE PROFUNDIS
BY OSCAR WILDE (1905)

In life and death, Oscar Wilde possessed a unique self-mythologising genius. Long before he secured his place in Britain's pantheon of great dramatists, he had established himself as the witty icon of an aesthetic ideal. By the spring of 1882, when he went to America declaring his "genius", he was doubly celebrated in both the United States and England (where Gilbert & Sullivan had just satirised Wilde's aesthetic move-ment in the character of the poet Bunthorne in Patience), as much for himself as for his writing. For a tantalisingly brief period, until the summer of 1894, when he wrote *The Importance of Being Earnest* in three weeks, Wilde blazed like a meteor across Victorian London before crashing and burning at his Old Bailey trial (after the disaster of the Queensberry libel case) in May 1895. A lesser artist might have been broken by that fall, but Wilde was ultimately inspired by it.

In his cell, between January and March 1897, in preparation for his release from Reading jail in April, Oscar Wilde began to write an extraordinary letter. He wanted to address his notorious relation-ship with Lord Alfred Douglas, the *fin-de-siècle* romance that had swiftly become a fatal tragedy. "Bosie" had remained aloof from his former lover throughout the two years of Wilde's sentence ("with hard labour"), and the 80 pages of manuscript written on 20 folios of thin blue prison paper became Wilde's tormented bid for some kind of rapprochement. What began as an act of would-be reconciliation blossomed into an excruciating, and utterly compelling, chapter of autobiography, an aesthetic apologia (Epistola: In Carcere et Vinculis – "Letter: from Prison and in Chains"), and finally a *tour de force* of prose by a late-Victorian writer of genius.

Wilde was always a master of disguises and personas. *The Impor-tance of Being Earnest* is all about double lives. In *De Profundis* (its title, "from the depths", is taken from Psalm 130), he puts on the mask of the disgraced, and penitent, prisoner to review his affair with Bosie, to attempt a kind of confession and then, suitably purged, to assert "a fresh mode of self-realisation". More than a century after its first appearance (Wilde's friend Robert Ross both gave the manuscript its final title, and arranged for its publication), the ruthless and often self-lacerating candour with which Wilde lays himself bare is still shocking.

At first, he addresses the heyday of his affair, its carefree and irresponsible passion, and his reckless indulging of the younger man:

> "From the very first there was too wide a gap between us. You had been idle at your school, worse than idle at your university. You did not realise that an artist requires for the development of his art the companionship of ideas, an intellectual atmosphere, quiet, peace and solitude."

As Wilde's realisation of his self-destruction sinks in, he rehearses the terrible sequence of events that would lead to his downfall, disgrace, and imprisonment: "Everything about my tragedy has been hideous. Our very dress [as convicts] makes us grotesques. We are the zanies of sorrow…"

A famous passage recalls the prisoner's transfer from London to Reading, by train, on 13 November 1895:

> "From two o'clock till half-past two on that day I had to stand on the centre platform of Clapham Junction, in convict dress and handcuffed, for the world to look at. Of all possible objects I was the most grotesque. When people saw me they laughed. Each train as it came up swelled the audience. For half an hour I stood there in the grey November rain surrounded by a jeering mob. For a year after that was done to me, I wept every day at the same hour and for the same space of time."

This episode sees Wilde at one of his worst and lowest depths. Thereafter, *De Profundis* gains vigour and confidence as the prisoner charts his brilliant career as "a man who stood in symbolic relations to the art and culture of his age". He contrasts the high moments of his art and its astonishing success with the humiliation of bankruptcy and jail. Somehow, he must come to terms with the great "Oscar" becoming a drab prison number "C.3.3.", a cipher. Other parts of *De Profundis* hint at Wilde's subsequent campaign for prison reform ("the prison system is absolutely and entirely wrong"), and the fate of the system's inmates, an obsession that culminated in *The Ballad of Reading Gaol*, his lyrical masterpiece.

Thus emboldened, and with his artistic muscles recovering some of their old potency, Wilde begins to make a comparison between his life as an artist and the life of Christ, a theme that runs fitfully through his earlier prose writing, especially *The Critic as Artist* (1890) and *The Soul of Man Under Socialism* (1891). For Wilde, the noble artist, the figure of Christ is the supreme archetype of the suffering creator, as well as the ultimate individualist. In the degradation and shame of his 1895 trial, Wilde finds the glimmerings of his role as a martyr, a role he is happy to share with the son of God.

Never let it be said that Oscar Wilde was short of self-belief. "All of this", he writes, "is foreshadowed and prefigured in my art ... A great deal of it is hidden away in the note of Doom that like a purple thread runs through the gold cloth of Dorian Gray."

> "I now see that Sorrow is at once the type and test of all great Art. What the artist is always looking for is that mode of existence in which soul and body are one and indivisible: in which the outward is expressive of the inward: in which Form reveals...
>
> To the artist, expression is the only mode under which he can conceive life at all. To him what is dumb is dead. But to Christ it was not so..."

Having made this grandiose connection, the letter descends into a sustained rebuke of Bosie's character and behaviour, in which his "horrible habit of writing offensive letters" comes across as perhaps the least troubling quality in a young man whose vanity, greed, treachery and vicious self-centredness dragged Wilde down.

And yet, remarkably, Wilde concludes with instructions for their joint future conduct once he has been released, and ends on a note of reconciliation:

> "You came to me to learn the Pleasure of Life and the Pleasure of Art. Perhaps I am chosen to teach you something much more wonderful, the meaning of Sorrow, and its beauty. Your affectionate friend. Oscar Wilde."

It's hard not to conclude that the thrilling majesty of Wilde's prose was wasted on Bosie. Within three and a half years of completing this extraordinary document, Wilde was dead. He was 46.

Three to compare:
Cardinal Newman: *Apologia Pro Vita Sua* (1864)
John Stuart Mill: *Autobiography* (1873)
Oscar Wilde: *The Picture of Dorian Gray* (1891)

50. THE SOULS OF BLACK FOLKS
BY WEB DU BOIS (1903)

Just as Barack Obama, "the skinny kid with a funny name", seemed to spring from nowhere in the summer of 2004 with his electrifying keynote speech in Boston to the Democratic convention, so – on the printed page – did William Edward Burghardt Du Bois (1868-1963) burst into American life in April 1903 as the passionate spokesperson for African Americans. Of mixed French, Dutch and African parents, Du Bois is emblematic of America's complex relationship to slavery.

The Souls of Black Folk is a loosely linked collection of essays that explored in highly personal terms Du Bois's prophetic assertion that "the problem of the 20th century is the problem of the colour line". It became an almost immediate hit.

Du Bois believed that African Americans must always see themselves as they are perceived by whites "through a veil".

The young man who would become one of the most famous African Americans of his day had already had a brilliant career at Harvard, where his tutors included Henry James's brother William, and George Santayana. In 1895, after a stint in Berlin, Du Bois became the first black American to be awarded a Harvard doctorate. He went on to publish pioneering research into the condition of "Negroes in America", culminating in 1899 with *The Philadelphia Negro*.

Du Bois, following the example of America's first great black leader Frederick Douglass, used the essay as a genre in which to address the race question. By 1903, he had accumulated enough material for the volume that would become, in the words of one commentator, "the political bible of the Negro race".

The Souls of Black Folk might appear to be a collection of essays (each chapter also has a musical epigraph derived from "10 master songs" from the Negro tradition) but it has a powerfully coherent inner structure. Three opening chapters explore the slave history of black America. These are followed by six chapters of sociology, Du Bois's scholarly forte. To give the book the rhetorical shape of a debate – thesis, antithesis, synthesis – Du Bois concludes with five chapters of "spirituality", culminating in a cry of freedom.

Within *The Souls of Black Folk* Du Bois explores the dominant metaphor of "the veil". In simple terms, Du Bois believed that African Americans possess "no true self-consciousness" but rather a "double consciousness" and must always see themselves as they are perceived by whites "through a veil".

Du Bois expressed his ideas about this "sensation" as follows: "It is a peculiar sensation, this double-consciousness, this sense of always looking at oneself through the eyes of others, of measuring one's soul by the tape of a world that looks on in amused contempt and pity. One ever feels his two-ness – an American, a Negro; two souls, two thoughts, two unreconciled strivings; two warring ideals in one dark body, whose dogged strength alone keeps it from being torn asunder."

This concept of African American duality is – writes Henry Louis Gates Jr – Du Bois's "most important gift to the black literary tradition".

In turn, the veil metaphor alludes to St Paul's famous phrase (1 Corinthians 13: 12) about seeing ourselves "through a glass, darkly". Much of the rhetorical power of *The Souls of Black Folk* comes from a writer steeped in the language and cadences of the King James Bible.

At times, *The Souls of Black Folk* aspires to a kind of poetry. In chapter 14, Of the Sorrow Songs, Du Bois addresses the Negro spiritual, those "weird old songs in which the soul of the black slave spoke to men". Growing passionate, he asks "Would America have been America without her Negro people?" He concludes with a passage that leads directly to Martin Luther King: "If somewhere in this whirl and chaos of things there dwells Eternal Good, pitiful yet masterful, then anon in His good time, America shall rend the Veil and the prisoned shall go free. Free, free as the sunshine trickling down the morning into these high windows of mine, free as yonder fresh young voices welling up to me from the caverns of brick and mortar below – swelling with song, instinct with life, tremulous treble and darkening bass."

Three to compare:
Ralph Ellison: *Invisible Man* (1952)
James Baldwin: *The Fire Next Time* (1963)
Barack Obama: *Dreams from My Father* (1995)

51. EMINENT VICTORIANS
BY LYTTON STRACHEY (1918)

Lytton Strachey's partisan, often inaccurate but brilliant demolitions of four great 19th century Britons did much to usher in the modern era.

Eminent Victorians is often seen as an oedipal massacre of discredited father figures – an assault on the Victorian establishment from which Strachey, the son of a general, had sprung. But its chronology says that it was really inspired by the First World War, with the gestation of the manuscript, from 1912-18, shaped by the apocalypse in Flanders.

Strachey originally planned a rogues' gallery of many famous Victorians that included Darwin, Carlyle, John Stuart Mill and Ellen Terry. In the event, he settled on four brief lives – each chosen to illustrate the psychology of four neurotic careerists who typified a society tormented by sex and religion.

He began with Cardinal Manning, a miniature portrait of a Victorian divine at the heart of a complex discussion of the place of Rome in the church. This was followed by a study of Florence Nightingale during the crucial years of her service in Crimea. Similarly, with Thomas Arnold, the famous headmaster of Rugby, mythologised in the Victorian classic *Tom Brown's School Days,* he concentrated on his 14 years at the school, culminating in his premature death. Finally, his study of General Gordon focused on the general's last dramatic days in Khartoum. Strachey implied in several brilliant passages that Gordon was unhinged, a suggestion that he had only hinted at in his previous portraits of his other Victorians:

"Gordon's fatalism ... led him to dally with omens, to search for prophetic texts, and to append, in brackets, the apotropaic initials DV [Deo volente – God willing] after every statement in his letters implying futurity, led him also to envisage his moods and his desires, his passing reckless whims and his deep unconscious instincts, as the mysterious manifestations of the indwelling God."

As an acolyte of Bloomsbury, Strachey knew all about Freud. He was determined to find a sexual explanation for his chosen quartet's monstrous ambitions.

Strachey's biographer Michael Holroyd has suggested that the four portraits shadowed the movements of a symphony, or a string quartet. Cardinal Manning: allegro vivace; Florence Nightingale: andante; Dr Arnold: scherzo; and General Gordon: rondo.

What is not in doubt is that the four sections of *Eminent Victorians* correspond to the passage of the First World War. "Manning" was written in 1912-14, the most exuberant phase of hostilities. "Nightingale" was completed in 1915, when the parallels between the Crimean hospitals and British military field hospitals were strongest. "Arnold" was done from 1915-16; and "Gordon" was completed in the worst year of the war, 1917. The whole book itself was published in May 1918, several months before the armistice, and caught the public mood of rejection of those who had in some way contributed to a national catastrophe.

Strachey would sacrifice anything for his art. His portraits of these 19th century imperial icons are brilliant but unreliable, coruscating but partisan, and enthralling but frequently derivative. As critics never cease from pointing out, Strachey worked exclusively from secondary sources. Moreover, he would sacrifice anything, especially facts, for effect. His character assassination of General Gordon, based on at least one known forgery, is particularly egregious. The first line of "Cardinal Manning" mistakes his birth date. Strachey did not care, declaring with grandeur that it is "as difficult to write a good life as to live one".

On publication, Strachey was acclaimed and denounced in equal measure. The main thing, as he saw it, was that *Eminent Victorians* was discussed all over, from the prime minister downwards. Strachey went on to publish *Queen Victoria* in 1921, *Elizabeth and Essex* in 1928, and died from cancer in 1932. But this remains the classic that brought down the curtain on the Victorian age. With Woolf, Eliot and Keynes, Strachey had ushered in the 20th century.

Three to compare:

TE Lawrence: *Seven Pillars of Wisdom* (1922)

Virginia Woolf: *To the Lighthouse* (1927)

Michael Holroyd: *Lytton Strachey – A Critical Biography*,
    2 vols (1967, 1968)

52. THE AMERICAN LANGUAGE
BY HL MENCKEN (1919)

The American century began in 1917 when President Wilson declared war on Germany and shipped more than a million troops to France. Two years later, a pugnacious columnist from Baltimore, who was obsessed with language, boldly made the decisive assertion of linguistic independence that had been implicit in American life and letters since 1776.

HL Mencken's *The American Language* is a creature of its time, a flexing of American cultural muscles, but it also signalled an important new chapter in English language prose. After Mencken, in the words of the critic Edmund Wilson, "American writers were finally able to take flight from the old tree and to trust for the first time their own dialect".

The writer who made this crucial break with tradition was an inveterate controversialist and patriot, a witty master of American prose. The martini, he once declared, was the only American invention "as perfect as the sonnet". In his day, Mencken was as influential in the US as George Bernard Shaw in Britain. A lifelong contributor to the *Baltimore Sun*, a scourge of office-holders and frauds, Mencken would anatomise and dissect just about anything that took his fancy, from "the average man" to "the immortality of the soul" – two pieces chosen at random from his own selection, *Chrestomathy,* a word (he claimed) that means "a collection of choice passages from an author or authors".

That word was a typical Mencken discovery. He was fascinated by the dynamic interplay of American society and the English language and wrote prodigiously about it. Once, reflecting on the American frontier, he wrote that the wild west marked "the gothic age of American drinking as of American word-making". Alistair Cooke, in an interview I had with him in the 1980s, recalled Mencken proudly advising him about the English equivalents for American cuts of meat: rump for sirloin and best end for rib chops. Such examples, he had said at the beginning of *The American Language*, refuted the "absurd efforts" made to prove "that no such thing as an American variety of English existed – that the differences I constantly encountered in English, and that my English friends encountered in American, were chiefly imaginary".

In the first edition, echoing Noah Webster, he declared that British English and American English were on divergent paths. In the fourth edition, after many modifications, he was still beating the drum for linguistic independence. Mencken had always loathed "marshmallow gentility":

> "The American of today is much more honestly English, in any sense that Shakespeare would have understood, than the so-called standard English of England. It still shows all the characteristics that marked the common tongue in the days of Elizabeth I, and it [*American English*] continues to resist stoutly the policing that ironed out standard English in the 17th and 18th centuries."

Mencken's nationalist pride was also single-minded. He paid almost no attention to the other independent varieties of English that were coming to maturity after the First World War. The index to my edition of *The American Language*, for instance, has only a handful of references to Australia and none to New Zealand. As an early 20th century snapshot of American prose – the teeming variety of spoken American inevitably defeated even Mencken, as he freely admitted – *The American Language* remains a masterpiece of advocacy and entertainment. Much has changed in the last 100 years, but Mencken's conclusion to his closing chapter, "the future of the language", remains as resonant as ever:

> "In all human beings, if only understanding be brought to the business, dignity will be found, and that dignity cannot fail to reveal itself, soon or late, in the words and phrases with which they make known their high hopes and aspirations and cry out against the intolerable meaninglessness of life."

Three to compare:

Noah Webster: *American Dictionary of the English Language* (1828)

HW Fowler: *The King's English* (1908)

AC Baugh and Thomas Cable: *A History of the English
    Language* (1935)

53. THE ECONOMIC CONSEQUENCES OF THE PEACE
BY JOHN MAYNARD KEYNES (1919)

The Economic Consequences of the Peace is one of those rare books
that seem to exude brilliance, power and polemical
passion from the opening page, propelled by the
urgency and consequence of the subject. Unlike
some other rhetorical classics in this list, it executes
its argument with a rapier not a blunderbuss, using
the clinical ferocity of hammered steel not wild,
explosive irruptions of outrage.

Reading Keynes in 2017, nearly a hundred years
after first publication, you don't have to know the
diplomatic minutiae of the Versailles peace treaty,
a notorious historical disaster, to appreciate that here is a brilliant
writer (who would subsequently become a great economist) flexing
his intellectual muscles for the first time on the world stage. Uniquely,
too, this is a book whose subject is economics but whose message is
geopolitical. It's a book, moreover, suffused with a deep and compelling sense of imminent catastrophe: "In Paris, where those connected
with the Supreme Economic Council received almost hourly the
reports of the misery, disorder and decaying organisation of all central
and eastern Europe, allied and enemy alike, and learned from the lips
of the financial representatives of Germany and Austria unanswerable
evidence of the terrible exhaustion of their countries, an occasional
visit to the hot, dry room in the president's house, where the Four
fulfilled their destinies in empty and arid intrigue, only added to the
sense of nightmare."

Keynes's arguments for a more generous settlement were prescient.
Above all, he saw with unique clarity the geopolitical tenor and
perspective expressed by the Big Four, a combination of grandeur,

vanity and vengeance that would shape Europe after the Great War and send it spiralling towards an even bigger catastrophe.

Keynes was so disturbed by what he saw that ultimately he resigned out of the conviction that the great powers were hell-bent on drafting an unjust settlement with immeasurably terrible consequences.

His essay immediately became a worldwide bestseller. It rapidly became the source of conventional left-liberal wisdom on the treaty. In its mature form, this was the widespread opinion that the final document imposed on the defeated Germans at Versailles on 28 June 1919 (exactly five years after the assassination of Archduke Ferdinand) was a recklessly punitive, "Carthaginian" settlement.

Another international consequence of Keynes's work was that his book helped to consolidate American public opinion against the treaty. Woodrow Wilson never got the treaty ratified by Congress, and the failure of his vision for a new world soured the rest of his presidency, and possibly contributed to his stroke. As a result, America's commitment to, and involvement in, the League of Nations was never more than half-hearted. In a real sense this would shape the allies' interwar response to a resurgent Germany under the Nazis. In turn, the perception among the British public that Germany had been treated unfairly would fuel the 1930s policy of "appeasement", a policy that would, in the end, lead to the outbreak of the Second World War.

The Economic Consequences of the Peace made JM Keynes internationally famous, and established his reputation as a provocative and leading economist, a reputation that would be consolidated by the publication of his masterpiece, *The General Theory of Employment, Interest and Money* (1936).

And yet, for the general reader who wants to engage with the mind of Keynes at its most accessible, and entertaining, *The Economic Consequences of the Peace* makes perfect reading. Moreover, it is one of those very rare titles whose influence lasted long into the future. After the end of the Second World War, when Keynes became a key player in establishing the Bretton Woods agreements of 1944, he remembered the lessons from Versailles as well as the depression of the 1930s. As is often pointed out, it was the Marshall plan of 1945 that came most closely to resemble the ideas of systematic reconciliation first proposed by Keynes in *The Economic Consequences of the Peace*.

Three to compare:

Harold Nicolson: *Peacemaking*, 1919 (1933)

JM Keynes: *The General Theory of Employment, Interest and Money* (1936)

Robert Skidelsky: *John Maynard Keynes, 1883-1946: Economist, Philosopher, Statesman* (2004)

54. TEN DAYS THAT SHOOK THE WORLD
BY JOHN REED (1919)

After the First World War, the Bolshevik revolution of 1917 was the next great event of the 20th century to capture the literary imagination. Russia, for so long an enigma, became the focus of every kind of fantastic speculation that, in the long term, would morph into many shelves of biography and history, novels of espionage, and finally, George Orwell's *Animal Farm*.

At first, however, the Russian Revolution was simply a sensational item of world news. What could be more thrilling than the fall of the tsar, or more arresting than the triumph of the proletariat (a word now fallen into disuse)? The revolution was all the more intoxicating, because its leaders, especially Lenin and Trotsky, were brilliant newspaper copy – passionate intellectuals and articulate middle-class revolutionaries who seemed to be men of action committed to translating communist theory into their vision of a new society.

British and American journalists flocked to Petrograd (now St Petersburg), the epicentre of the earthquake that was toppling the old autocracy, among them a young socialist from Portland, Oregon, named John ("Jack") Reed, who had recently graduated from Harvard with a passion for socialism.

Reed later wrote that Harvard had made him, and many others, "realise that there was something going on in the dull outside world more thrilling than college activities", whereupon he and his fellows turned their attention to the writings of innovative minds such as HG Wells.

From Harvard, Reed had moved to New York to try his luck as a journalist. In 1913, he joined the staff of *the Masses*, edited by Max

Eastman, becoming part of a journalistic milieu that included Lincoln Steffens, Ida Tarbell, John Dos Passos, Emma Goldman, and the radical playwright Eugene O'Neill, as well as the feminist and journalist Louise Bryant, whom he married in 1916.

On *The Masses*, Reed's modus operandi, as a reporter, was to get arrested, which he regularly did, while looking for trouble. Soon, weary of provoking the US authorities, he broadened his horizons to take in the ferment in the old world as well as the new. In 1917, appalled by Woodrow Wilson's declaration of war against Germany, the newlyweds set off for Europe, and wound up in St Petersburg at the beginning of the revolution. Reed saw at once that this was his great opportunity. Where previously he had written and published poetry and flirted with the Mexican revolution, now his prose caught fire at the prospect of a worldwide socialist catharsis. Reed was exhilarated by what he was witnessing:

The last month of the Kerensky regime was marked first by the falling off of the bread supply from two pounds a day to one pound, to half a pound, to a quarter of a pound, and, in the final week, no bread at all. Hold-ups and crime increased to such an extent that you could hardly walk down the streets. Not only had the government broken down, but the municipal government had absolutely broken down.

After this first, thrilling encounter with revolution (Reed also met both Lenin and Trotsky), Reed and Bryant returned to the US, and became trapped in a succession of bruising lawsuits inspired by the American authorities' fear of Bolshevism. Reed's life at this time was every bit as dramatic as the world from which he had just returned. All his papers from his Russian trip were confiscated, and would not be returned for seven months. At this juncture, Reed seized his moment, not least because his wife (Louise Bryant) was about to publish her own version, *Six Red Months in Russia*. His editor, Max Eastman, recalls a meeting with his correspondent during the period of time when Reed shut himself away to write his account of the revolution in, he claimed, 10 days:

"He was gaunt, unshaven, greasy skinned, a stark, sleepless, half-crazy look on his slightly potato-like face. He had come down after a night's work for a cup of coffee.

" 'Max, don't tell anybody where I am. I'm writing the Russian revolution in a book. I've got all the placards and papers up there in a little room and a Russian dictionary, and

I'm working all day and all night. I haven't shut my eyes for 36 hours. I'll finish the whole thing in two weeks. And I've got a name for it too – Ten Days That Shook the World. Goodbye, I've got to go get some coffee. Don't, for God's sake, tell anybody where I am!' "

Since March 1917, when the roaring torrents of workmen and soldiers beating upon the Tauride Palace compelled the reluctant imperial Duma to assume the supreme power in Russia, it was the masses of the people, workers, soldiers and peasants that forced every change in the course of the revolution. They hurled the Miliukov ministry down; it was their soviet that proclaimed to the world the Russian peace terms–"No annexations, no indemnities, and the right of self-determination of peoples"; and again, in July, it was the spontaneous rising of the unorganised proletariat who once more stormed the Tauride Palace, to demand that the soviets take over the government of Russia.

Reed's account of what he saw continues to shape many subsequent versions of the Russian Revolution. The great film director Sergei Eisenstein based his film *October (Ten Days That Shook the World)* on the American reporter's work. Reed's account was romantic, partisan and intensely personal:

"More potent still, [the Bolsheviks] took the crude, simple desires of the workers, soldiers and peasants, and from them built their immediate programme. And so, while the Mensheviks and socialist revolutionaries involved themselves in compromise with the bourgeoisie, the Bolsheviks rapidly captured the Russian masses. In July they were hunted and despised; by September the metropolitan workmen, the sailors of the Baltic fleet, and the soldiers, had been won almost entirely to their cause. The September municipal elections in the large cities were significant; only 18% of the returns were Menshevik and socialist revolutionary, against more than 70% in June ..."

Reed's work is edged with tragedy, too. On his first return to America after the October revolution, he got bogged down in a debilitating series of trials for sedition as a communist. His penchant for trouble-seeking told on his mental and physical health, and he began to suffer from insomnia and depression. By the time he set off back to Russia to participate in the second congress of the Comintern, he was visibly deteriorating from scurvy and malnutrition.

Already the revolution was disintegrating into faction fighting. Reed, always prey to the appeal of a good story, allowed himself to be seconded, on behalf of the Comintern, to another congress in Baku. The journey wrecked his health and, by the time he returned to Moscow, he was suffering from typhus. He died on 17 October 1920, was given a hero's funeral, and buried in the Kremlin Wall, a unique honour.

It is part of the myth of *Ten Days* that Reed should die so soon after publication, as a martyr to a great cause. In 1922, his book was republished with an encomium from Lenin himself.

Ten Days That Shook the World is neither history nor polemic, but a bit of both – a rhetorical act of witness that is both authentic and unputdownable. It remains one of the great texts of American journalism: ironically, it gains an extra and paradoxical credibility from being un-fact-checked and unmediated. With all its many flaws, both ideological and literary, it remains a masterpiece of reportage.

Three to compare:
Louise Bryant: *Six Red Months in Russia* (1918)
Arthur Ransome: *Six Weeks in Russia* (1919)
George Orwell: *Animal Farm* (1945)

55. THE WASTE LAND
BY TS ELIOT (1922)

The Great War was a mass slaughter. It also became the catalyst for a

social and cultural earthquake. But not until a young American poet began, in 1919, to address the desolate aftermath of this Armageddon did the interwar years begin to acquire the character we now associate with the 1920s, and also become explicable to the survivors of an apocalypse.

The Waste Land has attracted many labels, from the quintessential work of "modernism" to the "poetical equivalent to Stravinsky's Rite of Spring". It was also one of those very rare works that both embody and articulate the spirit of the age. As such, it would be adored, vilified, parodied, disparaged, obsessed over, canonised and endlessly recited.

A generation after its publication, Evelyn Waugh would conjure the mood of interwar Oxford, and Charles Ryder's initiation into university life in *Brideshead Revisited*, by having Anthony Blanche declaim *The Waste Land* at the top of his voice from Sebastian Flyte's balcony.

TS Eliot first announced "a long poem I have had in my mind for a long time" in a letter to his mother at the end of 1919. Actually, its origins can be traced to 1914, the year the young poet finally left Harvard and crossed to Europe, settling first in Oxford, as the First World War began.

Eliot's "Oxford year" (1914-15) was decisive. It was then that he encountered Ezra Pound. Soon after, perhaps betrayed by his "genius for dancing", he met and married his first wife, Vivien(ne) Haigh-Wood. This self-inflicted wound, by many accounts, holds the key to *The Waste Land*, which became a mirror to all his most acute marital difficulties. "All I wanted of Vivien," he later wrote, cruelly, of this relationship, "was a flirtation." He had persuaded himself he was in love, "because I wanted to burn my boats" and stay in England with Pound. This instinct was correct. Eventually, Pound would play a decisive editorial role in the making of the poem.

Eliot's 1920 New Year resolution, to "get started" on his "long poem", came after some very difficult months. His marriage to Vivien (who was also sleeping with Bertrand Russell) was going from bad to worse, and he was struggling to make ends meet professionally. In extremis, Eliot began to compose the lines that would morph into a new poem, much longer than anything he had written before, with the working title "He Do the Police in Different Voices".

In The Love Song of J Alfred Prufrock, Eliot had perfected a radical modernist kind of dramatic monologue, given in a single voice. Now, he was experimenting with a cubist narrative and "different voices": a famous clairvoyant (Madame Sosostris), a neurotic wife ("My nerves are bad tonight"), two cockneys yakking in a pub ("if you don't give it him, there's others will, I said"), another distracted woman "the hyacinth girl", a wandering poet ("I had not thought death had undone so many") and a ragtime singer ("O O O O that Shakespeherian Rag …") to identify some of the most famous.

Intercut quasi-cinematically with these vernacular scraps are Eliot's other "fragments … shored against my ruins". These include half-stated Christian and Buddhist themes, mixed with Arthurian legend and classical mythology. In the final section "the Thunder" delivers some sonorous commands, until the crisis of the poem is brilliantly resolved with "Shantih shantih shantih".

In Eliot's own life, there were no commensurate reconciliations, just the daily torment of his marriage to Vivien, who suffered equally from her life with "Tom". At the end of 1919, she wrote: "Glad this awful year is over ... Next probably worse." Eliot, almost as fragile as his wife, took himself off to Lausanne to consult a therapist. It was here that he wrote the haunting last verses of his work-in-progress as if "in a trance".

By January 1922, *The Waste Land* was ready for submission to the *Dial* and, more importantly, Ezra Pound's maieutic brilliance. Pound had no doubt of its genius. "About enough, Eliot's poem," he wrote, "to make the rest of us shut up shop."

For Eliot, meanwhile, 1922 was almost as troubled as 1919. While he wrestled with the final draft of *The Waste Land*, his distracted wife Vivien was undergoing a new treatment, Ovarian Opocaps, distilled from "the glands of animals", plus a starvation diet. The result was colitis, high temperatures, insomnia and migraine. Rarely had life and art been so inextricably braided together.

The Waste Land is a poem of its time, and for all time. It is about ghosts and heroes, civilians and veterans, and recently mobilised wartime women exposed to predatory young men; it is about loss and despair, sex and madness, seduction and grief, and the poet's own anguished quest for meaning in a shattered and desolate world.

Ezra Pound would play the role of the midwife in delivering this disturbing and extraordinary new voice to the poetry-reading public and ultimately the canon, but crucial though his intervention undoubtedly was in focusing the text, his editor's scissors hardly touched the basic structure of Eliot's vision. The five parts of *The Waste Land* are: The Burial of the Dead; A Game of Chess; The Fire Sermon; Death by Water; What the Thunder Said.

The sections that Eliot (and Pound) agreed to drop include: Song. For the Opherion, The Death of the Duchess, Elegy and Dirge. Published in 1971, the facsimile and original transcript edition, edited by Valerie Eliot, the poet's widow, gives a remarkable insight into the process by which *The Waste Land* achieved its final form. For the critic Cyril Connolly, who came of age during the years of *The Waste Land*, this is the essential version: it was, he wrote, "indispensable for all lovers of poetry, students of the early 20th century, and survivors like myself".

In 1922, the original edition, a text of 434 lines, was followed by several pages of notes, which were requested by the New York publisher Horace Liveright, to justify publishing the work as a book.

Eliot himself affected a certain unease at the claims made for *The Waste Land*. He told one American literary friend that "various critics have done me the honour to interpret the poem in terms of criticism of the contemporary world, have considered it, indeed, as an important bit of social criticism. To me it was only the relief of a personal and wholly insignificant grouse against life; it is just a piece of rhythmical grumbling."

Three to compare:
JG Frazer: *The Golden Bough* (1890)
Jessie Weston: *From Ritual to Romance* (1920)
Robert Graves: *The White Goddess* (1948)

56. A Room of One's Own
by Virginia Woolf (1929)

A Room of One's Own is both a landmark in feminist thought and a rhetorical masterpiece, which started life as lectures to the literary societies of Newnham and Girton Colleges, Cambridge, in October 1928. It was then published by the Hogarth Press in 1929 in a revised and expanded edition that has never been out of print.

Barely 40,000 words long, addressed to audiences of female students in the hothouse atmosphere of interwar creativity, this became an unforgettable and passionate assertion of women's creative originality by one of the great writers of the 20th century. Ironically, she herself never favoured the term "feminist".

Virginia Woolf, no question, transformed the English literary landscape. But how, exactly? Was it through modernist innovation (*Mrs Dalloway; To the Lighthouse*)? Or flirting outrageously with historical fiction (*Orlando*)? Or in the provocative argument – in part a response to EM Forster's *Aspects of the Novel* – of a book like *A Room of One's Own*?

Well, all of the above. As many critics have noted, Woolf's writings – from letters and diaries to novels, essays and lectures – are of a piece. Open any one of her books and it's as though you have just stepped inside, and possibly interrupted, a fierce internal monologue about the world of literature.

Woolf herself assists this response. "But, you may say, we asked you to speak…" is the opening line to *A Room of One's Own* that backs its author into the limelight of an initially rambling, but finally urgent, polemic. "England is under the rule of a patriarchy," she declares on about page 30, and then proceeds to lay bare the structure of male privilege and female exclusion – from independence, income and education.

At first, she masks the narrator of her argument in the guise of several fictional Marys: Mary Beton, Mary Seton or Mary Carmichael, an allusion to a 16th century ballad about a woman hanged for rejecting marriage and motherhood. This "Mary" narrator identifies female writers such as herself as outsiders committed to jeopardy.

Quite soon, however, Woolf seems to abandon this contrivance. Now she is on fire, writing in her own voice:

"One might go even further and say that women have burnt like beacons in all the works of all the poets from the beginning of time – Clytemnestra, Antigone, Cleopatra, Lady Macbeth, Phèdre, Cressida, Rosalind, Desdemona, the Duchess of Malfi, among the dramatists; then among the prose writers: Millamant, Clarissa, Becky Sharp, Anna Karenina, Emma Bovary, Madame de Guermantes – the names flock to mind, nor do they recall women 'lacking in personality and character'. Indeed, if woman had no existence save in the fiction written by men, one would imagine her a person of the utmost importance; very various; heroic and mean; splendid and sordid; infinitely beautiful and hideous in the extreme; as great as a man, some think even greater. But this is woman in fiction. In fact … she was locked up, beaten and flung about the room.

A very queer, composite being thus emerges. Imaginatively she is of the highest importance; practically she is completely insignificant. She pervades poetry from cover to cover; she is all but absent from history. She dominates the lives of kings and conquerors in fiction; in fact she was the slave of any boy whose parents forced a ring upon her finger. Some of the most inspired words, some of the most profound thoughts in literature fall from her lips; in real life she could hardly read, could scarcely spell, and was the property of her husband."

Typically, Woolf takes herself to task as well, for her complacency:

"What I find deplorable ... is that nothing is known about women before the 18th century. I have no model in my mind to turn about this way and that. Here am I asking why women did not write poetry in the Elizabethan age, and I am not sure how they were educated ..."

Some of *A Room of One's Own*, while written in a white heat, is also very funny: "I thought of that old gentleman ... who declared that it was impossible for any woman, past, present, or to come, to have the genius of Shakespeare. He wrote to the papers about it ... Women cannot write the plays of William Shakespeare."

From this point forward, "Judith Shakespeare" becomes another polemical fiction who, like Woolf, had to stay at home, watch her brother go off to school, and become imprisoned in domesticity: "She was as adventurous, as imaginative, as agog to see the world as he was. But she was not sent to school." Eventually, Judith is shamed into a marriage of convenience by her family. Her brother makes his way in the world, while Judith is trapped at home, her genius unfulfilled.

Once Woolf has invented Judith Shakespeare, the poet's sister who eventually kills herself, she can embark on a review of the creative lives of her great predecessors – Jane Austen, George Eliot, and the Brontë sisters, of whom she wrote, that Charlotte Brontë, burnt by rage, died "at war with her lot ... young, cramped and thwarted". *En passant,* Woolf reviews the lives and careers of female writers such as Aphra Behn: "All women together ought to let flowers fall upon the tomb of Aphra Behn ... for it was she who earned them the right to speak their minds. It is she – shady and amorous as she was – who makes it not quite fantastic to say to you tonight: Earn five hundred a year by your wits."

It's at this juncture in her argument that Woolf proposes her now celebrated idea about the key to a woman's creative liberation: a room, plus some independent means. To a resident of Bloomsbury this, no doubt, seemed a feasible goal, the guarantee of two essential gifts – privacy and freedom, or time and solitude. In retrospect, a private room plus "five hundred a year" seems impossibly middle-class. And yet, at current prices, it's a sum that roughly translates into the figure that the Bailey's prize (formerly the Orange prize) for women's fiction (£30,000) awards to its annual winner. So perhaps Woolf's dream has been at least partly fulfilled.

So much of *A Room of One's Own* is so light and glancing that it's easy to overlook the urgency of Woolf's analysis. But she could be transgressive, and even mischievous, too. In another passage, describing the work of a fictional woman, Mary Carmichael, Woolf alludes to lesbian love in the novel, a passage almost certainly inspired by her relationship during the 1920s with Vita Sackville-West: "Then I may tell you that the very next words I read were these – 'Chloe liked Olivia...' Do not start. Do not blush. Let us admit in the privacy of our own society that these things sometimes happen. Sometimes women do like women."

Finally, Woolf breaks free from the feminist arguments of her essay, morphs towards her preferred androgyny, and makes a larger claim for the true literary imagination (as she sees it): "It is fatal for anyone who writes to think of their sex ... one must be woman-manly or man-womanly ... Some collaboration has to take place in the mind between the woman and the man before the art of creation can be accomplished. Some marriage of opposites has to be consummated. The whole of the mind must lie wide open ... There must be freedom and there must be peace. Not a wheel must grate, not a light glimmer. The curtain must be close drawn."

And then, in a few valedictory pages – replete with more powerful arguments about the importance of university education for women – she is done, closing with an appeal to the essential spirit of risk and originality, " the habit of freedom and the courage to write exactly what we think".

Three to compare:
Beatrice Webb: *My Apprenticeship* (1926)
EM Forster: *Aspects of the Novel* (1927)
Germaine Greer: *The Madwoman's Underclothes* (1986)

57. GOODBYE TO ALL THAT
BY ROBERT GRAVES (1929)

The First World War is renowned for poetry (Owen, Sassoon, Rosen

berg) more than prose, but there is one volume, this "autobiography", partly set in the trenches, that continues to enthral readers with its irreverent, comic, and often bawdy first-hand account of front-line action in France. Graves opens *Goodbye to All That* with a saucy, candid and even outrageous, statement of intent that will set the tone for all that follows: "The objects of this autobiography, written at the age of 33, are simple enough: an opportunity

for a goodbye to you and to you and to you and to me and to all that; forgetfulness, because once all this has been settled in my mind and written down and published it need never be thought about again; money."

Graves certainly made money from *Goodbye to All That*, and perhaps he did "say goodbye" as he intended, but he was never free from what he had just "written down and published". It was simply too good, and too entertaining, to be "never thought about again". And it also caught the war-weariness of the interwar years, in which the greatest sin (for the writer of memoir) was to be boring. Graves is never boring: "There was no patriotism in the trenches. That was too remote a sentiment, and rejected as fit only for civilians. A new arrival who talked 'patriotism' would soon be told to cut it out."

As the critic Paul Fussell writes in *The Great War and Modern Memory*, the indispensable guide to the literature of the First World War, Graves is, first and foremost, "a tongue-in-cheek neurasthenic *farceur* whose material is 'facts'".

The original 1929 edition, which varies significantly from the revised version of 1957 was completed, fast, in less than four months, inspired by Graves's lover and muse, the American poet Laura Riding, and composed in a spirit of burning-his-boats excitement: Graves wanted to raise enough money to retire to Majorca. This first version has a raw and ragged energy that's missing from the later edition, which eliminates Riding, from whom he had become estranged. As Andrew Motion has written, the 1929 printing contained "a version of events that told the poetic truth about his experiences, the emotional truth, rather than being primarily fact-driven". For instance, Graves also reports the killing of captured Germans by British troops, although Graves himself had not witnessed any massacres. He seems determined to shock his readers, cheerfully working bestseller ingredients into his story: "Nearly every instructor in the mess could quote specific instances of prisoners having been murdered on the way back. The commonest motives were, it seems, revenge for the death of friends or relatives, and jealousy of the prisoner's trip to a comfortable prison camp in England."

His account of trench life is the thing that still grips the reader 100 years on. In keeping with the account of modern warfare reported by his friend Siegfried Sassoon, Graves describes a campaign that's a succession of "bloody balls-ups", in which farcical incompetence and stupidity are responsible for a casual and gruesome slaughter. He, in turn, adds his wild protest by ruthlessly celebrating the horrors of trench life – rotting corpses, scattered brain-matter, and visceral, almost animal, suffering. It would be wrong to focus exclusively on his irreverence. Among several set pieces, Graves's account of the heroism of "Samson", who died in no man's land, is especially poignant: "The first dead body I came upon was Samson's. I found that he had forced his knuckles into his mouth to stop himself crying out and attracting any more men to their death. He had been hit in 17 places."

Subsequently, Graves's comic account of his own misreported death in action is another famous high point. He had been wounded by a German shell while leading his men through a cemetery on 20 July 1916. The wound had at first seemed so severe that his regiment erroneously reported his decease ("died of wounds" etc). In a richly entertaining coda to his passing, while also mourning his death, Graves's family received word from him that he was alive, and put an announcement to that effect in the newspapers. To add hilarity to pathos, he describes how his colonel wrote to him with: "I cannot tell you how pleased I am you are alive." Soon he was back in the trenches, but then invalided home where he got classified B-1, "fit for garrison service abroad". The armistice followed soon after: "The news sent me out walking along the dyke above the marshes of Rhuddlan ... cursing and sobbing and thinking of the dead."

After this, he catches Spanish flu, almost dies, and is tormented by a lot of bad dreams. *Goodbye to All That* ends with Graves sailing for Egypt to become professor of English at Cairo University. He would shortly write *I, Claudius*, the book for which he would become world-famous. *Goodbye to All That* remains his masterpiece, a classic of English autobiography, and a subversive tour de force that would inspire, among others, Evelyn Waugh's *Sword of Honour* trilogy.

Three to compare:
Siegfried Sassoon: *Memoirs of a Fox-Hunting Man* (1928)
Winston Churchill: *My Early Life* (1930)
Vera Brittain: *Testament of Youth* (1933)

58. MY EARLY LIFE: A ROVING COMMISSION
BY WINSTON CHURCHILL (1930)

Winston Churchill is renowned as an archetypal Great Briton (statesman, war leader, speechmaker and political maverick), with all the good and bad associations of such a description. He was also a prolific, occasionally inspired, writer who was awarded the Nobel prize for literature in 1953. That honour was principally to do with his fight against Hitler and the Nazis, and the citation saluted both his mastery of historical and biographical description, and his brilliant defence of "exalted human values". But the award was not misplaced. Churchill was one of the finest prose stylists of the last century, steeped in the works of Shakespeare, Gibbon and Macaulay. *My Early Life,* a precocious autobiography, is his masterpiece.

As usual with Churchill, it's a zesty cocktail of mixed ingredients, including rehashed newspaper articles, scraps of speechmaking, and many hours of dictated material. The bulk of the book was compiled during the parliamentary holidays in the summer of 1928. The happy author told Stanley Baldwin, "I have had a delightful month – building a cottage and dictating a book: 200 bricks and 2,000 words per day."

Churchill's delight in his own vivid experience is part of the book's enduring appeal. His first 25 years, indeed, were like pages torn from a *Boy's Own* adventure: colonial military service, skirmishes on the North-West Frontier, gruelling night marches, a great cavalry charge, and a daring escape from a Boer war prison. In his coming of age, Churchill's love of action and excitement were fully satisfied by two contrasting British institutions, Sandhurst and Fleet Street. Nothing gave him more satisfaction than the jeopardy of warfare or journalism, and he excelled at both.

My Early Life, however, is more than just a ripping yarn. It is also a surprisingly direct and reflective, even intimate, self-portrait of an extraordinary character during his formative years, full of ironic wit and self-deprecating good humour. Churchill is also candid about his peculiar upbringing as the child of an Anglo-American marriage, his adored but distant mother (Jeanette Jerome), his doomed father (Lord Randolph Churchill), and his own miserable schooling at Harrow. In a famous passage, he confesses his enduring love for Mrs Everest, his nanny. On her death, he wrote: "She had been my dearest and most intimate friend during the whole of the 20 years I had lived."

Elsewhere, he regrets his privileges as a junior member of the Marlborough family, and mourns the failure of his relationship with his father, Lord Randolph: "I would far rather have been apprenticed to a bricklayer's mate, or run errands as a messenger boy, or helped my father to dress the front windows of a grocer's shop. It would have been real … Also I should have got to know my father, which would have been a joy to me."

As well as elegiac and filial, Churchill is also funny. His account of learning the Latin noun 'mensa' is a classic:

> "But why 'O table?'" I persisted in genuine curiosity.
> "You would use it in speaking to a table."
> "But I never do," I blurted out in honest amazement.
> "If you are impertinent, you will be punished very severely."

Such was my introduction to the classics, from which, I have been told, many of our cleverest men have derived so much solace and profit.

In addition to his own life story, he is concerned to paint "a picture of a vanished age", the *fin-de-siècle* world that would morph into Edwardian England. Additionally, as a man of action, Churchill knows how to tell a story, and make it live. *My Early Life* has countless minor pleasures, and two great set-piece narratives, the Battle of Omdurman (1898) and, in another theatre of imperial conflict, Churchill's capture by the Boers (The Armoured Train) in 1899.

But the adventure that propelled Churchill on to the front pages of the jingoistic British press was his capture by, and daring escape from, the Boers in the episode of The Armoured Train in November 1899. Churchill at this point was not in uniform, but working as a journalist associated with the *Morning Post*.

None of that inhibited him from acts of considerable bravery when the armoured train on which he was travelling was ambushed by the Boers. Inevitably, he was seized as a prisoner of war ("the least unfortunate kind of prisoner to be"), and almost as inevitably, he managed to escape (having failed to argue for his release as a foreign correspondent). By Christmas Eve, he was back in Durban with a wonderful scoop (his own escape) and quickly found himself "a popular hero", though a few rival newspapers suggested that the Boers would have been entitled to execute him for muddling military and civilian roles.

A less secure writer and autobiographer might then have described his service in several cabinets, his career during the First World War, and his political life in the 1920s. But Churchill does not do that. He wanted to keep his book short, by his standards, and he wants to focus on his beginnings. He signs off with the cheerful and insouciant optimism of a man who also battled with depression ("the black dog"):

> "Events were soon to arise in the fiscal sphere which were to plunge me into new struggles and absorb my thoughts and energies at least until September 1908, when I married and lived happily ever afterwards."

Three to compare:
Siegfried Sassoon: *Memoirs of a Fox-Hunting Man* (1928)
George Orwell: *Down and Out in Paris and London* (1933)
Winston Churchill: *Their Finest Hour* (1949)

59. TESTAMENT OF YOUTH
BY VERA BRITTAIN (1933)

Testament of Youth was written by a woman approaching 40 who had spent some 17 years coming to terms with her singular experience of the First World War – as a girl, a fiancee, a feminist, a Voluntary Aid Detachment (VAD) nurse and, finally, as the sorrowing victim of intolerable grief. Brittain's is one of several memoirs inspired by the fighting in Flanders, but it made a lasting impact through the raw passion of its anti-war message and its rather modern confessional candour. After much redrafting in various genres, including fiction, it was the success of Sassoon's *Memoirs of a Fox-Hunting Man* (1928) and Graves's *Good-bye to All That* (1929) that showed Brittain the way forward, creatively. A modern classic, *Testament of Youth* is both an elegy and a memoir, a book for all seasons that would have a remarkable literary afterlife in the 1970s and 1980s.

Brittain's "autobiographical study" (she would never allow "autobiography") takes her readers on to the home front as much as into the trenches. A book that's based at first on her teenage diaries comes to France quite late in the narrative. Peripherally interested in the war, Brittain provides a fascinating picture of a young girl's tormented coming of age as the long summer of Edwardian England becomes overcast by the storms of total war.

Brittain is never less than disarmingly frank. "When the Great War broke out," she begins, "it came to me not as a superlative tragedy but as an interruption of the most exasperating kind to my personal plans." She had grown up in Macclesfield and Buxton, in a solid middle-class family, had become a "provincial debutante" in 1912, and was en route to Somerville College, Oxford. Her writing, at this stage, was an "incongruous mixture of war and tennis". In another life, she might have embarked on a post-Victorian "ladyhood". But that was not to be: "The train started. As the noisy group moved away from the door, he sprang onto the footboard, clung to my hand and, drawing my face down to his, kissed my lips in a sudden vehemence of despair. And I kissed his and just managed to whisper 'Goodbye.'"

Falling in love with Roland Leighton, and watching him go off to the trenches, changed everything. The young lovers grew up very fast and when, inevitably, the news came that Vera's fiancé had "died of wounds" just before Christmas 1915, Brittain's fate was sealed. Now, all her ambitions as a writer were bent towards expressing the agony of her loss.

Brittain's experience in war becomes emblematic of the slaughter, as her immediate circle is annihilated. After Roland, her beloved brother, Edward, is killed and then two close soldier friends, Geoffrey and Victor (Tah).

Testament of Youth, which sold hundreds of thousands of copies on publication, had and continues to have its own afterlife. Rediscovered by Virago in the 1970s, it found a new audience and was adapted for television, with Cheryl Campbell playing Brittain. Part of its success, in hindsight, was that it both articulated a longing for women's liberation while simultaneously celebrating a nostalgic vision of British middle-class comfort in the twilight of the Edwardian age. That dichotomy had been intrinsic to the book long before it was completed.

Brittain's ambition, she said at the outset, was "to write something which would show what the whole war and postwar period has meant to the men and women of my generation". Testament of Youth achieves this, then it goes further. It describes one woman's struggle in the dominantly masculine world of military action and her determination to humanise the experience of being in extremis. It is courageous and honest, a work of literature that fulfilled all its author's ambitions.

Three to compare:
Beatrice Webb: *My Apprenticeship* (1926);
Siegfried Sassoon: *Memoirs of a Fox-Hunting Man* (1928);
Irene Rathbone: *We That Were Young* (1932)

60. HOW TO WIN FRIENDS AND INFLUENCE PEOPLE
BY DALE CARNEGIE (1936)

The selling of the American self, and its dream of a better future, began with the Declaration of Independence and founding father Benjamin Franklin, who once observed that "God helps them that help themselves". Selling and salesmanship pervade American life and literature: *Sister Carrie* (Theodore Dreiser), *Babbitt* (Sinclair Lewis), *The Iceman Cometh* (Eugene O'Neill), *Death of a Salesman* (Arthur Miller), and *Glengarry Glen Ross* (David Mamet).

Exactly 80 years after *How to Win Friends* first appeared, it comes as no surprise to find a distorted, and sickeningly corrupt, version of Dale Carnegie's homespun and inspirational self-help manual flourishing in the presidential campaign of Donald Trump, bestselling author of *The Art of the Deal*. Trump, indeed, continues actively to extol a later Carnegie fan (Norman Vincent Peale, author of *The Power of Positive Thinking*) for his contribution to the American way of life.

Trump's diehard supporters are an apt reminder that, for many Americans, the pursuit of happiness is unsatisfying, success painfully elusive, and failure shameful and/or infuriating. The hunger for a better future remains a constant feature of the American sociopolitical landscape. In the depths of the Great Depression, it was this desperate need that Carnegie addressed *in How to Win Friends and Influence People*. Carnegie's message was to inspire go-getting Americans to look on the bright side, and sell themselves better. By the time of Carnegie's death in 1955, more than 5m copies had been sold, the book had been translated into more than 30 languages, and its title had passed into the language.

Carnegie himself, born in 1888, the same year as TS Eliot, embodied the American idea of self- or re-invention. He grew up the son of a failed Missouri farmer named Carnagey. Ambitious young Dale changed the spelling of his name more closely to associate himself with the great steel baron, Andrew Carnegie, a late 19th century household name, and embarked on a career as a salesman while also attempting to make a future in the theatre as an actor, auditioning successfully for the American Academy of Dramatic Arts. Theatre life

was hard. It was at this stage, he wrote, that "the dreams I had nour-
ished back in my college days turned into nightmares".

But he didn't give up, and it was from this pit of despair and disappointment that he conceived the idea of giving courses in public
speaking. Paraphrasing RW Emerson, he would say, "Do the thing
that you fear to do, and the death of fear is absolutely certain." By
1916, he was in a position to rent Carnegie Hall and lecture to full
houses about his self-help techniques. His first book, *Public Speaking: A
Practical Course for Business Men*, followed in 1926, and led inexorably
through his growing stateswide audience to *How to Win Friends*.

The key to this new iteration of his optimistic message was its 12
principles (which ranged from No 1, "The only way to get the best
of an argument is to avoid it", to No 12, "Throw down a challenge",
via No 6, "Let the other person do a great deal of the talking"). Each
principle was deftly illustrated by Carnegie's well-chosen examples of
influential and successful Americans in action.

Early on in his pitch for a mass audience, Carnegie mixed a simple
American credo with radical European thought. He writes: "Sigmund
Freud said that everything you and I do springs from two motives: the
sex urge and the desire to be great."

Carnegie also traded in folksy wisdom, in the manner of his idol,
Abraham Lincoln. His first chapter, If You Want to Gather Honey,
Don't Kick Over the Beehive, encourages a positive, warm and optimistic attitude in dealings with others. He argues against attacking or
criticising people. That will only make them aggressive towards you.
After that, successive chapters deal with: how to get people to act as
you want them to; how to make people like you; how to convince
people of your arguments; and finally, how to be a Leader ("Making
People Glad to Do What You Want"). All this was packaged into Carnegie's systematic method, an important key to his popular success.

The measure of Carnegie's extraordinary achievement can be seen
in his many imitators. The most immediate was Norman Vincent
Peale whose keynote sentence could have been written by Carnegie:
"If you feel that you are defeated and have lost confidence in your
ability to win, sit down, take a piece of paper and make a list, not of
the factors that are against you, but of those that are for you."

Unlike Carnegie, Peale was that now familiar American figure: a
charismatic preacher trading in a crude, faith-based optimism. The
officiating priest at the Marble Collegiate Church in Manhattan

for more than half a century, Peale first began to promote "positive thinking" on the radio with a programme entitled The Art of Living. The latest edition of *The Power of Positive Thinking* declares: "This Book Could Change Your Life", and specifically offers to enable "everyone to enjoy confidence, success and joy". Here, in about 300 pages, is a succinct expression of the American Dream in its purest form. From the outset, like Carnegie, Peale identifies squarely with the Common Man. His book, he declares, "was written for the plain people of this world, of whom certainly I am one". With a sly allusion to Abraham Lincoln's origins – a straight lift from Carnegie – he then makes a classic assertion of white American solidarity: "I was born and reared in humble midwestern circumstances in a dedicated Christian home. The everyday people of this land are my own kind whom I know and love and believe in with great faith." Then follows Peale's kicker: "When any one of them lets God have charge of his life the power and glory are amazingly demonstrated."

What Peale offered was not merely spiritual counselling (over the years, plenty of other preachers had already done that), but "a system of simple procedures" that would generate untold "peace of mind, improved health and a never-ceasing flow of energy". Extolling the common sense of his system, he goes on: "[This book] makes no pretence to literary excellence, nor does it seek to demonstrate any unusual scholarship on my part. This is simply a practical, direct-action, personal improvement manual."

After Peale, the other American titles that owe a huge debt to Carnegie include: *The One Minute Manager* by Ken Blanchard and Spencer Johnson (1982); *The 7 Habits of Highly Effective People* by Stephen R. Covey (1989); and *Become a Better You: 7 Keys to Improving Your Life Every Day* by Joel Osteen (2007). From these popular best-sellers, bought by people who probably possess almost no other books, it is only a short step to Trump's "*Make America Great Again*".

Dale Carnegie has something to answer for.

Three to compare:
Norman Vincent Peale: *The Power of Positive Thinking* (1952)
Donald Trump: *The Art of the Deal* (1987)
Malcolm Gladwell: Blink: *The Power of Thinking Without
     Thinking* (2005)

61. THE ROAD TO OXIANA
BY ROBERT BYRON (1937)

According to Robert Byron's Oxford contemporary Evelyn Waugh – never the most reliable witness – the future author of *The Road to Oxiana* used to delight in shouting "Down with abroad". Typical in striking a pose, Byron was an aggressive Oxford aesthete of the "Brideshead generation", a homosexual wanderer whose precocious career as a travel writer and art historian can be traced through a succession of prewar gems. (*Robert Byron* by James Knox, published by John Murray in 2003, remains the principal biographical source.)

Byron wrote *The Station*, aged 22, after a visit to Mount Athos on a mule, Fortnum & Mason saddlebags bursting with a soda siphon and chicken in aspic. This was followed by *The Byzantine Achievement* (1929) and *The Birth of Western Painting* (1930). In 1933, the publication *of First Russia, Then Tibet* confirmed Byron's reputation as a traveller and connoisseur. In the same year, accompanied by his friend Christopher Sykes, but tormented by his unrequited love for Desmond Parsons, Byron set out on a journey to Persia and Afghanistan, by way of Jerusalem, Damascus and Baghdad, in search of the origins of Islamic architecture. After many vicissitudes, *The Road to Oxiana* (the remote northern borderland of Afghanistan) became the record of his 11-month journey, a fabulous and intoxicating weave of surreal vignettes, journal entries and odd playlets. In these gorgeous pages, poetry, gossip and scholarship become braided into an exotic tapestry that dazzles as much today as it did on publication. As many critics have noted, unlike his contemporaries, such as Peter Fleming and Norman Douglas, Byron has not dated.

An enthusiastic literary critical response ranged from Graham Greene, who admired Byron's demotic, conversational brilliance, to the rivalrous Evelyn Waugh, who had to concede the book's high spirits, via the *Sunday Times*, which linked Byron to his namesake (no relation) and declared him "the last and finest fruit of the insolent humanism of the 18th century". Today, widely considered to be Byron's masterpiece, *The Road to Oxiana* stands as perhaps the greatest travel book of the 20th century.

It is a title that continues to inspire hyberbole. The American critic Paul Fussell, writing in *Abroad,* his important 1982 study of interwar literary travelling, has judged that "what *Ulysses* is to the novel between the wars, and what *The Waste Land* is to poetry, *The Road to Oxiana* is to the travel book".

This extravagant claim is supported by writers as varied as Bruce Chatwin, Colin Thubron and William Dalrymple. In their different ways, each shares a veneration for *The Road to Oxiana.* Chatwin, whose debt to Byron was profound, declared it to be "a sacred text", and campaigned to get the book back into print with Picador in 1981, after almost 50 years of obscurity.

Byron starts his quest, in medias res, with himself as a "joy-hog" in Venice, immersed in the sea at Lido. The bathing, on a calm day, must be the worst in Europe: water like hot saliva, cigar ends floating into one's mouth, and shoals of jellyfish. Once he is joined by Christopher Sykes, Byron begins to hit his stride as as an aphorist: "The King David hotel is the only good hotel in Asia this side of Shanghai." Lines such as these will remind Byron's readers that when, on a visit to Soviet Russia, he had encountered an Intourist guide, a Shakespeare-denier who insisted that the plays could never have been written by a grocer from Stratford, Byron had cheerfully replied: "They are exactly the sort of plays I would expect a grocer to write."

In the same spirit, Byron was untroubled by the perils of his trip. Crossing into Persia, his companion Sykes nervously rebukes him for disrespecting the shah out loud. He suggests: "Call him Mr Smith."

"I always call Mussolini Mr Smith in Italy."

"Well, Mr Brown."

"No, that's Stalin's name in Russia."

Further debate establishes that "Jones" is no good either. That's what Byron calls Hitler in Germany. (In 1938, together with Unity Mitford, Byron would attend the last Nuremberg rally.) Eventually, the two travellers settle on "Marjoribanks" for the shah ("Marjorib-anks" will recur throughout the subsequent pages of Byron's journey).

Byron was often as daring as he was witty. To enter the forbidden mosque of Goharshad, he disguised himself by blackening his face with charcoal. From Herat to Mazar-i-Sharif, he and Sykes were the first Englishmen to undertake what was, and remains, a highly dangerous route.

Byron was insouciant towards the risks he took. Many of his best passages are strikingly joyous and carefree, in prose that's lambent, simple and brilliantly observed, as in this conclusion to a sunset at the shrine of Niamatullah:

"While the cadent sun throws lurid copper streaks across the sand-blown sky, all the birds in Persia have gathered for a last chorus. Slowly, the darkness brings silence, and they settle themselves to sleep with diminishing flutterings, as of a child arranging its bedclothes."

Byron's grand journey plans were frustrated. He would never get further east than Afghanistan. The dividend, for his readers, is that he plunges himself into his Afghan adventures with infectious brio: in April, he's arrested for an "incident"; in May, we find him as a guest at the consul's ball; various kinds of transport break down or fail. Somehow, and very entertainingly, Byron ends up in Kabul.

"A winding hill road brought us down from the Charikar plateau to a smaller plain inside a ring of mountains; running water and corrugated iron glinted among its trees. At the entrance to the capital the police deprived the vicar and the curate of their rifles, to their great distress; but being in turbans, no one would believe they were government servants."

After the thrills of Kabul and the Khyber Pass, England looked – as it always looks upon that inevitable return home – "drab and ugly from the train". Suddenly deflated, Byron confesses to feeling "dazed at the prospect of coming to a stop, at the impending collision between 11 months' momentum and the immobility of a beloved home". Laconic, he writes: "The collision happened. Our dogs ran up. And then my mother – to whom, now it is finished, I deliver the whole record."

Byron was lost at sea on 24 February 1941, aged 35, when the Egypt-bound ship on which he was sailing was torpedoed by a German U-boat off Cape Wrath.

Three to compare:
Eric Newby: *A Short Walk in the Hindu Kush* (1958)
Bruce Chatwin: *In Patagonia* (1977)
Rory Stewart: *The Places in Between* (2004)

62. The Road to Wigan Pier
by George Orwell (1937)

"The first sound in the mornings was the clumping of the mill-girls'

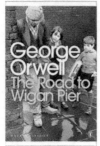

clogs down the cobbled street." This opening line is the sound of a great writer establishing his authentic voice. With absolute confidence, after several false starts, the mature George Orwell takes charge of this idiosyncratic account of working-class life from his first page.

Formerly Eric Blair, he was now writing with the urgency of a freelance with a much-needed commission, and also as a man just back from a journey through the industrial wastes of Yorkshire and Lancashire in the depths of the Great Depression.

Orwell had been signed up in the spring of 1936 for perhaps as little as £50 (plus expenses) by Victor Gollancz, the leftwing publisher who had championed *Down and Out in Paris and London*. Gollancz wanted a "condition of England" title to include in his Left Book Club, a bookselling experiment he had started to develop at the beginning of 1936. In fact, when Orwell delivered his manuscript at the end of the year, Gollancz was confronted with rather more than he'd bargained for, an infuriating but always compelling, personal quest by one of the strangest and most complicated figures in English literature.

The Road to Wigan Pier falls into two parts, a travelogue describing Orwell's journey through three northern towns, and a matching, but much more contentious, quest of heart and mind. It was, declared its author, a "political book", a mix of reportage and political commentary with a dash of autobiography. Orwell's contemporaries such as Cyril Connolly noted that, henceforth, he would be a socialist, but a socialist with an aura of secular saintliness that some found affected, even comical. And yet, with all its weaknesses, it would prove to be a milestone in his creative development.

Orwell's long-term publisher, Fred Warburg, described it as "one of the most contradictory books ever written", which is another way of saying that, as well as writing outstanding reportage from "Wigan Pier", Orwell was willing to be honest about himself as a refugee from the middle class, via Eton, Burma and the dosshouses of Paris and London. In these pages, finally, he began to carve out his peculiar place as a

British literary socialist, and to reconcile himself to himself.

The first half opens with a brilliant, stand-alone chapter about the Brookers' tripe shop-cum-lodging house, No 22 Darlington Street. From the squalor of working-class Wigan, Orwell plunges into meetings with the unemployed, with slum-dwellers, with coalminers, and dockers.

Anxious to return to his future wife, Eileen O'Shaughnessy, Orwell spent just two months in the north, and finally took the train home, closing his travels with a scene glimpsed from his railway carriage, the unforgettable image of a working-class woman trying to unblock a drain:

> "At the back of one of the houses a young woman was kneeling on the stones, poking a stick up the leaden waste pipe which ran from the sink inside and which I suppose was blocked … She looked up as the train passed, and I was almost near enough to catch her eye … it wore the most desolate, hopeless expression I have ever seen … She knew well enough what was happening to her – understood as well as I did how dreadful a destiny it was to be there in the bitter cold, on the slimy stones of a slum backyard, poking a stick up a foul drainpipe."

The second half of *Wigan Pier* is much more uneven, and famously provocative. Even now, Orwell's private encounter with English socialism can seem shocking. His determination "to see what mass unemployment is like at its worst" was principally to do with his own quest, a journey that was, he writes, "necessary to me as part of my approach to socialism".

For, he said, before you can be sure whether you are genuinely in favour of socialism, you must decide whether things at present are tolerable or not tolerable, and you must take up a definite attitude on the terribly difficult question of class.

Orwell is never less than self-lacerating. On the class question, he eviscerates himself: "The real reason why a European of bourgeois upbringing cannot without a hard effort think of a working man as his equal is summed up in four frightful words: the lower classes smell."

From here, an admission that continues to shock, and having described his adolescent self as "an odious little snob", he confesses his deep sense of inadequacy: "I had not much grasp of what socialism meant, and no notion that the working class were human beings … I could agonise over their sufferings, but I hated them and despised them whenever I came anywhere near them."

In conclusion, having fretted neurotically over the condition of domestic socialism, and his obligations towards it, he arrives at a kind of armistice in the war with himself: "To sum up – there is no chance of righting the conditions I described in the earlier chapters of this book, or of saving England from fascism, unless we can bring an effective socialist party into existence."

Rarely, in English literature, has a writer flayed himself so mercilessly in print, or published so many hostages to fortune. But the upshot of this uniquely strange book was a kind of creative liberation: Eric Blair, who was now unequivocally George Orwell, had found his voice and his identity. For the rest of his active life – barely 10 years – he would write as a British literary socialist. From this declaration of intent come his masterpieces: *Homage to Catalonia*, *Animal Farm* and, finally, *Nineteen Eighty-Four*. It's arguable that without *The Road to Wigan Pier* none of these would have been possible.

Three to compare:
JB Priestley: *English Journey* (1934)
Robert Byron: *The Road to Oxiana* (1937)
Richard Hoggart: *The Uses of Literacy* (1957)

63. ENEMIES OF PROMISE
BY CYRIL CONNOLLY (1938)

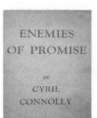

"A didactic inquiry into the problem of how to write a book which lasts 10 years", this interwar masterpiece of cultural criticism transformed the English literary conversation almost overnight, establishing phrases such as "the pram in the hall" at the heart of contemporary creative consciousness.

In the age of book blogs and digital publishing, Connolly's elevated dissection of the republic of letters might seem more redolent of another world, and different criteria. And yet, rarely in the beaten ways of Grub Street, has one writer so comprehensively nailed his subject. Connolly's observations about the habit and practice of literature remain excruciatingly accurate. At the point at which he sat down at a table under a plane tree in the south of France (with "a gramophone playing in the next room"), in the summer of 1937, he had spent all his professional life in various literary milieux, and knew in his marrow what made books and writers tick. From the outset, Connolly nurtured a deep fear for the influence of the press, an anxiety which remains as real today as it was in 1938: "Nothing dates like a sense of actuality than which there is nothing in journalism more valuable. A writer who takes up journalism abandons the slow tempo of literature for a faster one and the change will do him harm."

Connolly's anatomy of his trade is never less than inspired, and memorable: "In this verbal exchange Fleet Street is a kind of Bucket Shop which unloads words on the public for less than they are worth and in consequence the more honest literary bankers, who try to use their words to mean what they say, who are always "good for" the expressions they employ, find their currency constantly depreciating."

Almost as damaging, Connolly observes, are the hazards of success: "Success is a kind of moving staircase, from which the artist, once on, has great difficulty in getting off, for whether he goes on writing well or not, he is carried upwards, encouraged by publicity, by fan mail, by the tributes of critics and publishers and by the friendly clubmanship of his new companions ... Popular success is like a palace built for a writer by publishers, journalists, admirers, and professional reputation makers, in which a silent army of termites, rats, dry rot, and death watch beetles are tunnelling away till, at the very moment of completion, it is ready to fall down."

But *Enemies of Promise* was more than just a highly quotable essay on the threats to literary accomplishment of drink, conversation, politics, domesticity, journalism and worldly success. Connolly's purpose was to make a lasting and decisive evaluation of his gifted contemporaries, writers such as Auden, Joyce, Proust, Firbank, Woolf, Huxley, Hemingway, Faulkner and Waugh. Our contemporary understanding of Anglo-American literary modernism, from *The Waste Land* forwards, is shaped by Connolly's quotable and brilliant sentences about the books and writers of his time. His verdicts, moreover, remain freshly minted and remarkably perceptive, however much he crams them into the Procrustean bed of his analytical framework.

And then, just at the point when Connolly-as-critic is on the point of becoming insufferably show-off and omniscient, he undercuts his own lapidary self-confidence with the closing section of the book, eight chapters of *A Georgian Boyhood* in which he strips away the veil. "I have always disliked myself at any given moment," he writes, "the total of such moments is my life."

In this powerful climax, Connolly's mandarin criticism morphs into a kind of scintillating but abstract reportage that gives the book its timeless staying power. He and a boy named Eric Blair had attended the same south coast prep school, St Cyprian's. It's the measure of their inequality that Connolly's account of "St Wulfric's" is not half as lacerating as George Orwell's famous essay Such, Such Were the Joys, in which the young Eric Blair suffered a "world of force and fraud and secrecy", where a shy, sickly and unattractive boy surrounded by pupils from families much richer than his own, became "like a gold-fish" thrown "into a tank full of pike". For Connolly, by contrast, St Cyprian's was "a well run and vigorous example [of an English prep school] which did me a world of good".

Finally, by connecting his analytical brilliance to his painfully candid account of his schooling at Eton college, Connolly ensured that his ebullient celebration of some remarkable writers was edged with a poignant sense of personal failure. As a young man, he had known some golden moments of acclaim, and knew all about "power and popularity, success and failure, beauty and time". In fact, he was "as promising as the Emperor Tiberius retiring to Capri". The sweets of his gilded youth were not bestowed on Connolly's mature career, and in the end he would be eclipsed by his school friend and rival, Blair/Orwell, who established himself, in 1937, with another book that combines ideas and autobiography in an equally intoxicating combination, *The Road to Wigan Pier*.

Three to compare:
EM Forster: *Aspects of the Novel* (1927)
TS Eliot: *Selected Essays 1917-32* (1932)
FR Leavis: *The Common Pursuit* (1952)

64. How to Cook a Wolf
by MFK Fisher (1942)

To WH Auden, in 1963, she was America's "greatest writer". The poet

declared, "I do not know of anyone in the United States who writes better prose", a verdict that mixed provocation and tease in a way that would have delighted Mary Frances Kennedy Fisher.

The author of more than 25 inimitable books on food (each a highly original *macedoine* of cooking, travel, and autobiography) MFK Fisher was nothing if not singular, and had been so since childhood, growing up in California, the daughter of Rex Kennedy, the editor-proprietor of a string of small-town newspapers.

Food and writing became her obsession early on. While her father commissioned her to write for him, her mother indulged the young Mary "in a voluptuous riot of things like marshmallows in hot chocolate, thin pastry under the Tuesday hash, rare roast beef on Sunday instead of boiled hen". Not to be outdone, her father would serve "a local wine, red-ink he called it, with the steak; we ate grilled sweetbreads and skewered kidneys with a daring dash of sherry."

At the age of 21, Mary married her college sweetheart, Al Fisher, and, like many young Americans between the wars, moved to France, a life she would mythologise in retrospect: "We ate terrines of pate 10 years old under their tight crusts of mildewed fat. We tied napkins under our chins and splashed in great odorous bowls of écrevisses à la nage. We addled our palates with snipes hung so long they fell from their hooks, to be roasted then on cushions of toast softened with the paste of their rotted innards."

Her marriage failed; she had affairs, and was photographed by Man Ray, but always recognised her limits. "I wasn't so pretty that I didn't have to do something else," she said. As a single woman, she "spent hours in my kitchen cooking for people, trying to blast their safe, tidy little lives with a tureen of hot borscht and some garlic-toast and salad, instead of the fruit cocktail, fish, meat, vegetable, salad, dessert and coffee they tuck daintily away seven times a week." Now she discovered her vocation, which quickly became a passion indistinguishable from the others in her life.

Fisher's prose was remarkable in quality and quantity. She wrote hundreds of stories for the *New Yorker*, as well as 15 books of essays and memoir. She produced the best English translation of Brillat-Savarin's 1825 classic *The Physiology of Taste*, as well as a novel, a screenplay, a book for children and many travelogues. Other food writers would confine their writing to the recipes or the mundane details of a particular cuisine, but MFK Fisher used food as a metaphor. Inevitably, as she complained in a 1990 interview, her subject matter "caused serious writers and critics to dismiss me for many, many years. It was woman's stuff, a trifle." But she remained true to her self, described, in her 1943 volume, as *The Gastronomical Me*. Her critics eventually caught up. "In a properly run culture," wrote the *New York Times* Book Review, "Mary Frances Kennedy Fisher would be recognised as one of the great writers this country has produced in this century."

Her first book, *Serve It Forth* (1937), made this declaration: "if you have to eat to live, you may as well enjoy it." This theme was repeated in *Consider the Oyster* (1941): "An oyster leads a dreadful but exciting life. Indeed, his chance to live at all is slim, and if he should survive the arrows of his own outrageous fortune and in the two weeks of his carefree youth find a clean smooth place to fix on, the years afterwards are full of stress, passion and danger …"

Fisher's embrace of the slow, sensual pleasures of the table was matched by her cool acceptance of sudden jeopardy and violence. One critic of *How to Cook a Wolf* noted "the faintly Gothic perversity that makes Mrs Fisher's literature unique". For Fisher, *How to Cook a Wolf* was "about living as decently as possible with the ration cards and blackouts of World War II". It was also a poignant farewell to the author's youthful exuberance:

> "There are very few men and women, I suspect, who cooked and marketed their way though the past war without losing for ever some of the nonchalant extravagance of the 1920s. They will feel, until their final days on earth, a kind of culinary caution: butter, no matter how unlimited, is a precious substance; meats, too, and eggs, and all the far brought spices of the world, take on a new significance, having once been so rare."

It's in such passages that you can detect the strong affinities between Fisher and her British counterpart and contemporary, Elizabeth David. Even when the wolf was at the door, she was always a fierce advocate of a libertarian approach to cooking and eating. "Now, of all times in our history," she declares, "we should be using our minds to live gracefully if we live at all." Fisher hated the tyranny of the American diet.

The reviews of *How to Cook a Wolf* described it as "irresistibly seductive", "a book you can hardly wait to get your teeth into" and "a licence to dream". It's hard not to imagine that her critics were really describing MFK Fisher herself who, on the final page of *How to Cook a Wolf,* celebrated "the pleasures of the flesh".

Fisher's credo was to live a full life. She had no time for prudence, especially at the table. In *An Alphabet for Gourmets* (1949) she wrote:

> "A complete lack of caution is perhaps one of the true signs of a real gourmet: he has no need for it, being filled as he is with a God-given and intelligently self-cultivated sense of gastronomical freedom. He not only knows from everything admirable he has read that he will not like Irish whiskey with pineapple chilled in honey and vermouth, or a vintage Chambertin with poached lake perch; but every taste bud on both his actual and his spiritual palate wilts in revulsion at such thoughts. He does not serve these combinations, not because he has been told, but because he knows."

Three to compare:
Julia Child: *Mastering the Art of French Cooking* (1961)
Marcella Hazan: *The Classic Italian Cookbook* (1973)
Anthony Bourdain: *Kitchen Confidential: Adventures in the Culinary Underbelly* (2000)

65. BLACK BOY: A RECORD OF CHILDHOOD AND YOUTH BY RICHARD WRIGHT (1945)

Great coming-of-age memoirs have a potency rare in literature, and can be just as influential as great novels. Richard Wright, outstanding in both genres, was an important 20th century African American writer, renowned for his 1940 novel, *Native Son*. Together with Langston Hughes and Ralph Ellison, Wright was crucial in forging an authentic literary consciousness for the black community as it struggled to escape decades of oppression after the civil war.

The bestselling *Black Boy*, published in 1945 (its original title had been *Black Confession*), explored the background to *Native Son*, but was also a visceral and unforgettable account of a young black man's coming of age in the American south in the bitter decades before the civil rights movement.

Full of vivid scenes and arresting vignettes, it begins with four-year-old Richard ("angry, fretful and impatient") setting fire to the family home, a brilliant opening that establishes young Wright as a fiery protagonist. Indeed, he presents himself throughout *Black Boy* as a rebel, at odds with both his ailing mother, his faithless, improvident father and tyrannical "Granny". After the fire, the Wright family headed to Memphis, Tennessee where they lived in "a brick tenement".

Young Richard goes to school; his father deserts the family and his sons are put into care. Eventually, they move to Arkansas, where Wright broods on "the cultural barrenness of black life". For him, however, there is not even the consolation of religion. He's an atheist. In church, when his fellows sing: "Amazing grace, how sweet it sounds", he is humming under his breath: "A bulldog ran my grandma down."

Slowly, Wright's mature character formed itself: "At the age of 12 I had an attitude toward life that was to endure, that was to make me sceptical of everything while seeking everything, tolerant of all and yet critical."

This lifelong spirit, he writes, "made me love burrowing into psychology, into realistic and naturalistic fiction and art, into those whirlpools of politics that had the power to claim the whole of men's souls."

Thus driven, and to escape the shocking racism of the south, it becomes his ambition to head north to Chicago as soon as he can afford the trip. But first, he must start out in life as a young black man in Memphis.

The first half of Wright's "confession" is set exclusively in the south; the second part, describing his Chicago experiences, entitled The Horror and the Glory, was originally part of a longer book with the working title "American Hunger". For various commercial consider-ations, Wright's publishers requested that he focus on his Mississippi childhood and drop the final (Chicago) chapters. American Hunger became *Black Boy*, and would not be published with all parts fully restored until 1991, when the Library of America issued *Black Boy* (American Hunger).

The British, Vintage edition, though incomplete, is faithful to the 1945 version. It subtly mythologises Wright's African American upbringing and fearlessly confronts southern racism. For Wright, coming of age was all to do with claiming and celebrating his identity as a black man. The south, he declared, in a fierce passage, had only allowed him "to be natural, to be real, to be myself" through a negative form of self-expression, "in rejection, rebellion, and aggression". He continues:

> The white south said that it knew 'niggers', and I was what the white south called a 'nigger'. Well, the white south had never known me – never known what I thought, what I felt. The white south said I had a 'place' in life. Well, I had never felt my 'place'; or, rather, my deepest instincts had always made me reject the 'place' to which the white south had assigned me. It had never occurred to me that I was in any way an inferior being.

As a youngster in small-town Jackson, Wright knew only too well what it meant to be a "nigger", a second-class citizen. He worked as a porter in a clothing store; next he worked for an optician; then he moved to a drugstore, sweeping the sidewalk. But he had a fundamental problem. He "could not make subservience an automatic part of my behaviour".

Wright's closing words evoke the rhetoric of the civil rights movement, making a surprising and unexpected link between himself and Martin Luther King. He has, he writes, "a hazy notion that life could be lived with dignity, that men should be able to confront other men without fear or shame, and that if men were lucky in their living on earth they might win some redeeming meaning for their having struggled here beneath the stars."

Three to compare:
Ralph Ellison: *Invisible Man* (1952)
James Baldwin: *Notes of a Native Son* (1955)
Malcolm X (with Alex Haley): *The Autobiography of Malcolm X* (1965)

66. THE OPEN SOCIETY AND ITS ENEMIES
BY KARL POPPER (1945)

"If our civilisation is to survive," Karl Popper writes at the beginning

of this passionate defence of freedom and reason, "we must break with the habit of deference to great men."

The Open Society and Its Enemies, conceived in the 1930s, and completed in the 1940s, would become a key text of the 1960s, and its author a profound, sometimes thrilling, influence on a new genera-tion of college students. Thus, a book inspired by the Nazi invasion of Austria in 1938, but actually written in the secluded tranquillity of New Zealand's South Island, became a rallying cry, on behalf of western liberal democracy, for the postwar renewal of the European tradition.

Before the inevitable backlash, Popper, an émigré intellectual deter-mined to address "the difficulties faced by our civilisation", became a touchstone for progressive opinion. His fierce critique of Plato, Hegel and Marx was understood as an assault on totalitarian thought, and became widely fashionable, even when denounced by dissenting scholars and rivals. At the same time, *The Open Society and Its Enemies* (published in two volumes: *The Spell of Plato* and *The High Tide of Prophecy: Hegel, Marx, and the Aftermath*) was the product of the philoso-pher's own intellectual journey.

As a young man, Popper had adopted Marxism, a decision that would seriously influence many of his later ideas. For a few months in 1919 he had even considered himself a communist, becoming quite at home with the orthodoxies of class conflict, and the central tenets of Marxist economics and history. Although he quickly became disillusioned, this youthful flirtation with Marxist ideology would lead him to distance himself from those who believed in violent revolution. Eventually, during the long disillusionment of the 1920s, he came to realise that the sacrifice of human life must be a last resort, and that radical thought and conduct must be exercised with exemplary caution and prudence.

Popper was not only dismayed by the failure of democratic parties to prevent fascism from taking over Austrian politics in the 1920s and 1930s, he suffered directly from the consequences of this historic failure. The Nazis' annexation of Austria, with the Anschluss of 1938, forced the young philosopher into permanent exile. Henceforth, he would devote himself to a lifelong assault on totalitarian thought in general, and Marxism in particular.

His philosophical interests also concerned science and the uncertainty of knowledge. Some of his teaching, indeed, would eventually play an important part in the intellectual development of Thomas Kuhn. Popper questioned the idea that there were inexorable laws of human history, believing history to be influenced by the growth of knowledge, which is always unpredictable.

Popper had first expressed his arguments about science in *The Logic of Scientific Discovery* (1934), arguing that science proceeds through bold, competing conjectures subjected to rigorous testing. He once said that "next to music and art, science is the greatest, most beautiful and most enlightening achievement of the human spirit".

But it was as the sponsor of the idea of "the open society", and defender of democratic systems, that he became most widely known. *The Open Society and Its Enemies,* finally published in 1945, has been described as one of the most influential books of the 20th century. As well as popularising the open society, it argued that communism and fascism were philosophically linked, and demonstrated the subtle interconnections of politics and culture: "The contention that Plato's political programme is purely totalitarian, and the objections to this contention," writes Popper, "have led us to examine the part played, within this programme, by such moral ideas as Justice, Wisdom, Truth and Beauty." In response, Bertrand Russell, an important champion, declared Popper's work to be "a vigorous and profound defence of democracy, timely, interesting and very well written".

In the spirit of the cold war, and the political climate in which *The Open Society and Its Enemies* was first being read, Popper did not hesitate to declare Marxism "a major problem" and just "one of the many mistakes we have made in the perennial and dangerous struggle for building a better and freer world". Accordingly, Popper did not hesitate to identify "the darkness of the present world situation", claiming this to be his justification for his "severe treatment of Marx".

From the perspective of 2016, much of Popper's polemic seems almost as remote as medieval theology. Contingency and the *zeitgeist* will always have an important role to play in the making of such nonfiction classics. Popper's conclusion remains at once radical, and deeply conservative:

"Our greatest troubles spring from something that is as admirable and sound as it is dangerous – from our impatience to better the lot of our fellows. These troubles are the by-products of what is perhaps the greatest of all moral and spiritual revolutions of history, a movement which began three centuries ago. It is the longing of uncounted unknown men to free themselves and their minds from the tutelage of authority and prejudice. It is their attempt to build up an open society ... It is their unwillingness to sit back and leave the entire responsibility for ruling the world to human or superhuman authority ... This revolution had created powers of appalling destructiveness; but they may yet be conquered."

Three to compare:
Gilbert Ryle: *The Concept of Mind* (1949)
Willard Van Orman Quine: *From a Logical Point of View* (1953)
Thomas Kuhn: *The Structure of Scientific Revolutions* (1962)

67. HIROSHIMA
BY JOHN HERSEY (1946)

American print journalism, possibly thanks to its special place in the

US constitution, occasionally delivers exemplary knockout blows, world-class reporting on great subjects. John Hersey's *Hiroshima* stands at the head of this tradition. These 31,000 words of searing testimony were written and published just a year after the dropping of the first A-bomb on Japan in August 1945, a terrible act of war that killed 100,000 men, women and children and marked the beginning of a dark new chapter in human history.

Hiroshima was the result of an inspired commission about an event of global significance from a renowned war correspondent by a magazine editor of genius. It was in the spring of 1946 that William Shawn, the celebrated managing editor of the *New Yorker*, and *protégé* of its founder Harold Ross, invited his star reporter, John Hersey, to visit postwar Japan for an article about a country recovering from the shattering experience of the atomic bomb. The piece was intended to be a standard four-parter about Japan's ruined cities and devastated lives nine months on from the country's humiliating unconditional surrender.

On the Pacific sea voyage to Japan, however, Hersey chanced on a copy of Thornton Wilder's novel *The Bridge of San Luis Rey*, the tale of five people who are crossing an Inca rope bridge in Peru when it collapses, for which Wilder had won a Pulitzer prize. Accordingly, Hersey decided to focus his narrative on the lives of a few chosen Hiroshima witnesses. As soon as he reached the ravaged city, he found six survivors of the bombing whose personal narratives captured the horror of the tragedy from the awful moment of the explosion. This gave Hersey his opening sentence, a unique point of view, and a narrative thread through a chaotic and overwhelming mass of material. In a style later developed and popularised by the "new journalism" of the 1960s, the opening of *Hiroshima* pitches the reader into the heart of the story, from the viewpoint of one of its victims:

"At exactly 15 minutes past eight in the morning on 6 August, 1945, Japanese time, at the moment when the atomic bomb flashed above Hiroshima, Miss Toshiko Sasaki, a clerk in the personnel department of the East Asia Tin Works, had just sat down at her place in the plant office and was turning her head to speak to the girl at the next desk."

From here, Hersey embarks on an exploration of the lives of five other interlocutors: the Rev Mr Kiyoshi Tanimoto, of the Hiroshima Methodist church, who suffers radiation sickness; Mrs Hatsuyo Naka-mura, a widow with three children; one European, Father Wilhelm Kleinsorge, a German Jesuit priest who had endured exposure to radi-ation; and finally, two doctors – Masakazu Fujii and Terufumi Sasaki (not related to Miss Sasaki). Some of these interviewees had been less than 1,500 yards (1,370m) from the site of the explosion, and their harrowing accounts of vaporised, burnt and mutilated bodies, of blasted survivors, of hot winds and a devastated city tormented by raging fires, a scene from hell, gave a voice to a people with whom the US and its allies had been brutally at war only a year earlier. Hersey's brilliant reportage gave his story an existential dimension:

They still wonder why they lived when so many others died. Each of them counts many small items of chance or volition – a step taken in time, a decision to go indoors, catching one streetcar instead of the next – that spared him. And now each knows that in the act of survival he lived a dozen lives and saw more death than he ever thought he would see. At the time, none of them knew anything.

Hersey also used all his skill as a novelist and as a war reporter to bring home the horror of what he, one of the first correspondents into Hiroshima, had learned:

Dr Sasaki had not looked outside the hospital all day; the scene inside was so terrible and so compelling that it had not occurred to him to ask any questions about what had happened beyond the windows and doors. Ceilings and partitions had fallen; plaster, dust, blood, and vomit were everywhere. Patients were dying by the hundreds, but there was nobody to carry away the corpses. Some of the hospital staff distributed biscuits and rice balls, but the charnel-house smell was so strong that few were hungry. By three o'clock the next morning, after nineteen hours of his gruesome work, Dr Sasaki was incapable of dressing another wound.

Hersey's decision to use the testaments of Dr Sasaki, Mrs Namakura and the others, was both an inspired creative and also a tactically brilliant decision. The US army of occupation had prevented many US journalists from taking material out of the country, censoring photographs and tape-recordings alike. Hersey avoided such restrictions. He would stay only a few weeks in Hiroshima, but he returned to New York with a suitcase full of extraordinary first-hand material, and now set about fashioning a four-part piece for the *New Yorker.*

Part I, A Noiseless Flash, introduced Hersey's six witnesses. Part II, The Fire, reported the immediate, horrific aftermath of the explosion. Part III, Details are Being Investigated, described the wider, Japanese response to this unimaginable act of war. Part IV, Panic Grass and Feverfew, followed Father Kleinsorge and the sufferings of Hersey's other witnesses in the weeks after the bombing, describing the Japanese people's hatred for the Americans who had perpetrated this "war crime". So soon after the end of the Second World War, with feelings still running high, to achieve any kind of objectivity was a remarkable challenge.

In hindsight, Hersey frankly acknowledged the first technical difficulty he encountered with this story: there was no way he could bring his usual style to bear on his material, he said. "A show of passion would have brought me into the story as a mediator. I wanted to avoid such mediation, so the reader's experience would be as direct as possible." Instead, he went for cool and low key. As the *New Yorker* writer Hendrik

Herzberg has written: "Hersey's reporting was so meticulous, his sentences and paragraphs were so clear, calm and restrained, that the horror of the story he had to tell came through all the more chillingly." Hersey's flat, plain, deliberately unemotional style immediately caught the imagination of his editors, Ross and Shawn. In conditions of great secrecy, they decided to do something unprecedented: devote an entire edition of their magazine to the story of Hiroshima.

The ironic cover of the 31 August 1946 edition of the *New Yorker* gives nothing away: a summer-in-the-park illustration of a carefree picnic. It was not until the reader turned past Goings on About Town and the usual metropolitan advertisements for motor cars and diamonds that the editors' intentions were revealed in a simple statement: "TO OUR READERS. The *New Yorker* this week devotes its entire editorial space to an article on the almost complete obliteration of a city by one atomic bomb, and what happened to the people of that city. It does so in the conviction that few of us have yet comprehended the all but incredible destructive power of this weapon, and that everyone might well take time to consider the terrible implications of its use."

The impact of this *New Yorker* was extraordinary. The edition sold out 300,000 copies within hours of publication, inspiring a storm of commentary across the US, and abroad, especially on radio. Harold Ross said he had never got "as much satisfaction out of anything else" in his life. Hersey's piece was reprinted worldwide. Albert Einstein, an outspoken opponent of the bomb, who tried to buy a thousand copies of the *New Yorker* to send to fellow scientists, had to settle for a facsimile version. Copies of the original edition changed hands at many times the cover price.

Within a year, Knopf had published *Hiroshima* as a book. It has never since been out of print, and has now sold upwards of 3m copies.

John Hersey died in 1993.

Three to compare:
John Hersey: *A Bell for Adano* (1945)
John Hersey: *The Algiers Motel Incident* (1968)
Jonathan Schell: *The Fate of the Earth* (1982)

68. THE COMMON SENSE BOOK OF BABY AND CHILD
CARE BY DR BENJAMIN SPOOK (1946)

Practically speaking, Dr Spock's compendious *Baby and Child*

Care manual probably had a greater impact on the lives of postwar Americans (and some Britons) than any other title in this list. Spock came to shape the baby-boom generation like no other bestseller, mainly because his book was a bestseller like no other. It has sold more than 50 million copies in print and in 49 languages.

Spock's chapter titles convey both his approach and his pre-feminist perspective: "Watching him grow"; "He's apt to change his eating habits"; "The father as companion"; "Trouble with lessons". Nothing was too trivial to escape Spock's radar. In his pages, the worried parent could find help for virtually every problem.

Spock's secret, which comes as a shock on an initial reading, 70 years after first publication, was to offer fundamentally conventional, even banal, advice in a revolutionary way. For instance, in the most reassuring tones, as smooth as silk, he told postwar mothers that they knew more than they realised and should simply trust their maternal instincts. As an American, he also made the project of childhood a recapitulation of man's ascent from primeval swamps: "There's nothing in the world more fascinating than watching a child grow ... Each child as he develops is retracing the whole history of mankind, physically and spiritually, step by step."

Where previous American parenting guides were stern and repressive, Spock was humane, benign and borderline permissive, based on – this was really radical – his devout reading of Freud. After several years as a young paediatrician in New York during the 1930s, Spock's line to parents was "trust yourself". He established this earth-shattering credo from the very first sentence of Baby and Child Care: "You know more than you think you do." This would set the tone for the childcare of the postwar era and would sponsor the development of a generation of children raised in an atmosphere of self-conscious warmth and flexibility – at least on the surface.

Spock also projects a seductive, aw-shucks pragmatism on every page of *Baby and Child Care*. He insists his is not the last word, that mothers and fathers always know best and that "natural loving care" is the only way to go. Spock is also profoundly American in outlook. "Your baby is born to be a reasonable, friendly human being," he writes, in words that could have been written by Thomas Jefferson or Benjamin Franklin. Later, reflecting Enlightenment thought, he would argue quite passionately that the growing child is fundamentally and naturally good, sensible, joyful and healthy. At heart, Spock is anxious to swaddle the contentious and troubling business of parenthood in an aura of tolerance, restraint, common sense and tranquillity. He was against all forms of coercion and it was his conviction that children were likely to respond most positively to love and affection. He believed that adolescents should be taught that sex was "wholesome and natural and beautiful". Who, you ask, could possibly take issue with that?

Well, the social historian Christopher Lasch was one. In 1979, in *The Culture of Narcissism*, a brilliant study of the postwar American mind, this passionate critic of US liberalism conducted a revisionist assault on the unexamined influence of *Baby and Child Care*. He made the good, and overlooked, point that Spock, for all his alleged permissiveness, had actually encouraged parental authority. "Often blamed for the excesses of permissive child-rearing," wrote Lasch, "Spock should be seen instead as one of its critics, seeking to restore the rights of the parent in the face of an exaggerated concern for the rights of the child."

One difficulty with getting a clear reading on Spock comes from his midlife career as a radical peacenik during the many waves of protest against the Vietnam war. He had already been a fierce advocate of nuclear disarmament. Now, as he put it, he was "hooked for the peace movement". Having signed a declaration entitled A Call to Resist Illegitimate Authority and supported the burning of draft cards as an expression of free speech, he was charged and convicted of conspiracy to counsel, aid and abet resistance to the draft.

Thrust into the limelight for siding with the young generation, Spock found himself and his ideas under renewed scrutiny. Twenty years after he had first overturned conventional child-rearing wisdom, Spock was once again coming under fire, this time for helping to create a generation of self-centred narcissists, young people who lived only for themselves. Was it possible to trace mass anti-war protests to the pages of *Baby and Child Care*? Some people thought so and

Spock thereafter struggled to shake off the accusation that he was the father of America's psycho-social "decline". Whatever the long-term outcome of this debate, one thing is certain: *Baby and Child Care* is woven into the landscape of the American imagination.

Three to compare:
Mary Sheedy Kurcinka: *Raising Your Spirited Child* (2003)
Penelope Leach: *Your Baby and Child* (1977)
Alice Miller: *The Drama of the Gifted Child* (1981)

69. THE LAST DAYS OF HITLER
BY HUGH TREVOR-ROPER (1947)

"Now that the new order is past, and the thousand-year Reich has crumbled in a decade, we are able at last, picking among the still smoking rubble, to discover the truth about that fantastic and tragical episode." Some books simply exude excitement and self-confidence, as if the writer is on fire with ideas, or intoxicated with information. This is one such title.

From his commanding opening sentence, the author of this engrossing forensic masterpiece, a work of brilliant reportage, knows that the story he is about to unfold will be unputdownable, a scoop of epic proportions: history in the making. That, as we shall see, would come to haunt him at the end of a long and distinguished career.

In 1945, Hugh Trevor-Roper was a 31-year-old British intelligence officer, an academic historian who had been recruited to Bletchley Park to fight the secret war against the Nazis. When hostilities ended, Trevor-Roper found himself in occupied Germany. He was appointed by Dick White, then head of counterintelligence in the British zone, to find out what had happened to Hitler. The Nazi leader had, by then, been missing for more than four months since Germany's unconditional surrender on 7 May, becoming the subject of many bizarre and outlandish rumours inimical to a secure postwar settlement.

Trevor-Roper, working under the pseudonym of "Major Oughton", completed his report in record time. "The British Intelligence Report on the Death of Hitler" was delivered to the four-power intelligence committee in Berlin on 1 November 1945. To his credit, Dick White saw that there might be a book in it, and persuaded his *protegé* to undertake a revision of his material once his official duties were over. The outcome of one spy's intuition about a gifted subordinate, *The Last Days of Hitler* was published in March 1947 and became an immediate bestseller.

Trevor-Roper's contemporary and rival, the historian AJP Taylor, later wrote in the *Observer*: "Trevor-Roper's brilliant book demonstrated how a great historian can arrive at the truth even when much of the evidence is lacking or, as in this case, deliberately kept from him … This was all the doing of one incomparable scholar."

The remarkable luxury Trevor-Roper enjoyed as an investigative historian was that most of his informants were still available for interview. The stage was set for an enthralling quest into the heart of darkness, the smouldering ruins of the postwar Reich, a plot worthy of any thriller.

Trevor-Roper's narrative starts with a long scene-setter, describing Hitler, his court and the "vast system of bestial Nordic nonsense" with which the Nazi high command was obsessed. Goering, Speer, Himmler and Goebbels are memorably depicted with a rhetorical zest inspired by Trevor-Roper's admiration for great British historians such as Gibbon and Macaulay. Himmler, for instance, becomes "an inexorable monster whose cold, malignant rage no prayers, no human sacrifices can ever for one moment appease".

After this compelling introduction, the narrative moves swiftly to the impending defeat of April 1945, and the shocking physical deterioration of the Führer's final days, especially the drugs administered to him by a sinister cabal of Nazi doctors, to the point at which he became, in Trevor-Roper's words, "a physical wreck". Inside this murky hell-hole, there was, however, a figure of innocence, an Aryan maiden who would sacrifice herself for her hero.

At the moment when the young historian first investigated the bizarre and fascinating psychodrama of life in Hitler's bunker, Eva Braun, who would marry her lover in the last days of April, was still an unknown. His portrait of Hitler's devoted companion is one of the many mini-scoops scattered through these pages:

> "Braun had none of the colourful qualities of the conventional tyrant's mistress, writes Trevor-Roper. But then neither

was Hitler a typical tyrant. Behind his impassioned rages, his
enormous ambition, his gigantic self-confidence, there lay not the
indulgent ease of a voluptuary, but the trivial tastes, the conventional domesticity, of the petty-bourgeois. One cannot forget the
cream buns."

Hitler's 56th birthday fell on 20 April. Fifty feet underground, beneath
the garden of the Reich chancellery, the Fuhrer struggled to direct an
ever more desperate rearguard action as the allies, led by the Red Army,
closed in on Nazi Berlin. On 22 April there was a three-hour conference of war at which, famously, Hitler's rage exceeded all previous
eruptions. He shrieked; he railed; he denounced; finally, in exhaustion,
he declared that the end had come. By 27 April the heart of the city
was cut off from the rest of Germany. Now the Russians were shelling
it without mercy. As hope faded, Hitler's court bade farewell. Incredibly,
some were still reluctant to leave their master. However, at this juncture, there was a bitter distraction: the feuding at the top of the party
between Bormann, Goering and Himmler added to the air of crisis
surrounding life in the bunker.

After 27 April, Hitler's days were numbered. Life in the bunker
became progressively madder and more apocalyptic. Trevor-Roper
extracts maximum theatricality from his narrative, describing the inferno
of those last days. How, he asks, can the ordinary reader envisage the life
that was led in those doomed, subterranean bunkers, amid perpetual
shelling and bombing, often in total darkness, in which all count of
the hours was lost; when meals took place at wayward hours, and the
boundaries of night and day had been forgotten?

During the night of 27–28 April, with Red Army shelling cacopho-
nously overhead, Hitler rehearsed with his court their plans for suicide
and the various methods by which their corpses might be destroyed.
Two days later, word came that Himmler had set himself up as a new
Reichsführer, and was negotiating with the Swedes. In the delirium of
treachery surrounding Hitler, this was the end.

And now the Wagnerian climax was complete, with a doomed
protagonist to lend some weird poignancy to the drama. On Trevor-
Roper's account, Adolf Hitler presented a pathetic spectacle.

"His look was abstracted, his eyes glazed over with a film of
moisture. Some of those who saw him even suggested that he
had been drugged ... He walked in silence down the passage

and shook hands with all the women in turn … The suicide of the Führer was about to take place. Thereupon an unexpected thing happened. The terrible sorcerer, the tyrant who had charged their days with melodramatic tension, would soon be gone, and for a brief twilight moment they could play. In the canteen of the chancellery, where the orderlies took their meals, there was a dance."

Soon after, a single shot was heard. After Eva Braun had taken poison, Hitler shot himself in the mouth. It was 3.30pm on 30 April 1945.

When it was first published, *The Last Days of Hitler* had a quasi-propaganda purpose: to prove, definitively, by brilliant detective work, that the Hitler was not only dead, but had killed himself.

This, triumphantly, Trevor-Roper achieved. His account has never seriously been challenged. More than that, he also contrived to interweave into his narrative a critique of the Nazi state and its origins that would help shape the prodigious historiography of the Hitler regime that blossomed like a pernicious weed throughout the second half of the 20th century.

So magisterial was Trevor-Roper, now Lord Dacre, in relation to Hitler studies that when in 1983 Britain's *Sunday Times*, by then owned by Rupert Murdoch, acquired the rights to a set of notebooks purporting to be Hitler's personal diaries, the now ageing but immensely distinguished historian was cynically deployed to authenticate the "Hitler Diaries". In the media frenzy that surrounded the publication of "the scoop of the century", Murdoch threw Trevor-Roper to the wolves, dismissing the elderly historian's subsequent doubts with the memorably brutal: "Fuck Dacre. Publish."

In the uproar that preceded the exposure of these documents as shameless forgeries, Trevor-Roper was first humiliated, then pilloried. (Initially, he had expressed doubts, then changed his mind under duress, and declared that they could be genuine, before finally agreeing that they were a fake.) His reputation never recovered.

He died in 2003, but his influence lingers. He wrote the first best-seller about Adolf Hitler, and has unquestionably inspired many subsequent generations of popular historians, journalists and novelists to follow the same mesmerising path into the Nazi state's labyrinth of evil.

Three to compare:
Hugh Trevor-Roper: *Hitler's Table Talk* (1951)
Robert Harris: *Selling Hitler* (1986)
Joachim Fest: *Inside Hitler's Bunker* (2002)

70. THE GREAT TRADITION
BY FR LEAVIS (1948)

For about half of the 20th century, the English literary tradition was arbitrated by one critic whose ideas transformed the intellectual landscape of his time, and whose influence lingers still. I write this from personal experience: as a student, I was lucky enough to see FR Leavis in action. It's hard now to convey the peculiar fervour and excitement – the frisson – that surrounded this Cambridge don with his open white shirt and intense, bird-like demeanour, in front of his acolytes and disciples. And it's perhaps even harder to recognise how completely Leavis, and the literary critical consensus associated with his name, has been swept aside since his death in 1978.

To understand the hold Leavis had over the minds of students who came of age in the 60s and 70s, I want to quote from an interview given to *The Paris Review* by the writer and psychoanalyst, Adam Phillips, in which he describes the impact of Leavisite teaching on his adolescence:

"It was contagious and inspiring. My teacher had been taught by FR Leavis at Cambridge. Leavis was a literary critic who treated English literature as a secular religion, a kind of answer to what he thought was a post-Christian society. He had a fanatical assurance about literature ... And my teacher at school felt something comparably zealous ... It was conveyed to us that certain books really did matter and that you were involved in some rearguard action for the profound human values in these books. This was conveyed very powerfully – that the way to learn how to live and to live properly was to read English literature – and it worked for me. I was taught close, attentive reading, and to ironize the ambitions of grand theory."

As zealot-in-chief, FR (Frank Raymond) Leavis, born in Cambridge in 1895, was shaped by the non-conformism of an East Anglian upbringing. In his prime, his criticism was distinctive for its uncompromising association of literature and good values. Having served in the ambulance corps during the First World War, he went on to pioneer a new literary critical aesthetic from the early 1930s when, as a young don, he founded the quarterly review, *Scrutiny*. Leavis would edit this extraordinarily influential journal from 1932 to 1953. At the same time, he published the works that established his reputation, *New Bearings in English Poetry* (1932), *Revaluation* (1936), the immensely important essays from *The Common Pursuit* (1952) and, before that, perhaps his best-known critical statement, *The Great Tradition*.

In this polemical *tour de force*, Leavis expounded his belief in an inalienable connection between literature and morality, with special reference to the work of just five great novelists, his chosen representatives of "the great tradition" – Jane Austen, George Eliot, Henry James, Joseph Conrad and DH Lawrence.

Not everyone accepted the moral ferocity of Leavis's judgement. To some in the academic critical establishment, Leavis was anathema. He, however, never wavered in his opposition to what he saw as the frivolous and dilettante ways of Bloomsbury, always insisting that "form" was the novelist's first responsibility, and that novels that expressed an indifference to "form" would always be less important.

In the broader evaluation of the English literary tradition, Leavis never took prisoners. He pronounced Milton as "negligible", dismissed "the Romantics", and believed that, after John Donne, there is "no poet we need bother about except Hopkins and Eliot".

And when it came to English fiction, Leavis believed that "some challenging discriminations are very much called for". Nevertheless, he claimed it would be a misrepresentation of his views to suggest that, apart from Austen, Eliot, James and Conrad, "there are no novelists in English worth reading".

The knockabout opening chapter of *The Great Tradition* is still an entertaining, sometimes shocking, read:

> "Fielding hasn't the kind of classical distinction we are invited to credit him with. He is important not because he leads to Mr JB Priestley but because he leads to Jane Austen, to appreciate whose distinction is to feel that life isn't long enough to permit of one's giving much time to Fielding or any to Mr Priestley."

Having, so to speak, cleared his throat, Leavis goes on to swat Laurence Sterne as "irresponsible, nasty and trifling", exclude Dickens (finally reprieved in a later chapter about *Hard Times*), declare *Wuthering Heights* to be "a kind of sport", belatedly admit DH Lawrence ("the great genius of our time") to his pantheon, and set the scene for the majestic essays (on Eliot, James and Conrad) that follow. These giants, says Leavis, "are distinguished by a vital capacity for experience, a kind of reverent openness before life, and a marked moral intensity".

The impact of Leavis on the literary imaginations of some late 20th century writers is possibly exemplified by the response of his former student, the Man Booker prizewinning novelist Howard Jacobson, who confesses, in a self-lacerating account of his tutorials with Leavis, the agony he suffered at the feet of the master critic.

"The work that strained my capacity for reverence most," writes Jacobson, "was *The Great Tradition*, especially the opening essay with its footnote dismissive of Laurence Sterne. Not because I admire *Tristram Shandy*; although I am what is sometimes called a comic novelist, I never did find *Tristram Shandy* anything but as 'trifling' as Leavis found it, ditto the tradition of laborious jocosity it continues to spawn. But the other adjectives employed in Leavis's dismissal – 'irresponsible' and 'nasty' – made me uncomfortable. 'Irresponsible' can point to virtues (think of Henry James's praise for 'irresponsible plasticity') no less than vices. And 'nasty' is not a convincing critical term, just as 'pornographer' was never a convincing description of Kingsley Amis."

There are, in conclusion, many things to be said against Leavis: he exercised a kind of cultural tyranny; half his nominations for his "great tradition" weren't English; he was a better critic of poetry than fiction, and so on. That's all true, no doubt. But in the end, we must concede that he offered, to the serious reader of fiction, a moment of exemplary clarity – something that's missing today. As Jacobson puts it, so well, at the end of his appreciation, "Leavis told a particular story about English literature. It's not the only one. But we owe it to him to show that, so far, nobody has told a better one, or told it with a braver conviction of why it matters to tell it at all."

Three to compare:
QD Leavis: *Fiction and the Reading Public* (1932)
Raymond Williams: *Culture & Society* (1958)
Lionel Trilling: *Sincerity and Authenticity* (1972)

71. A BOOK OF MEDITERRANEAN FOOD
BY ELIZABETH DAVID (1950)

A Book of Mediterranean Food, written and published in an age of postwar rationing, when food coupons were still in force and the national diet was dominated by bread and gristle rissoles, dehydrated onions and carrots, and toad in the hole made with corned beef, was a *cri de coeur* by a sensual British woman on behalf of those places where wild garlic is intrinsic to every recipe and where, in the words of Marcel Boulestin, "peace and happiness reign".

Mediterranean Food is one woman's response to the new challenges of peacetime, a *macedoine* of elegy, *joie de vivre*, requiem and manifesto. Elizabeth David, returning to Britain after the war, became a food writer on *Harper's Bazaar* initially to make money, to remind herself of the sunnier world she had left behind – she had spent much of the war in the Mediterranean – and finally to mount a one-woman challenge to the bleakness of austerity Britain.

From the first pages of *Mediterranean Food*, however, it was not merely the exotic cuisine of those alluring southern climes that Elizabeth David was celebrating, but the English language itself. Mrs David (as she was known) never over-egged her prose, but her recipes were rich with loving evocations of rare and spicy ingredients. "There are," she writes, "endless varieties of currants and raisins, figs from Smyrna on long strings, dates, almonds, pistachios and pine kernel nuts, dried melon seeds and sheets of apricot paste which is dissolved in water to make a cooling drink."

Mediterranean Food, which was swiftly followed, in the same style, by *French Country Cooking* (1951), *Italian Food* (1954) and *Summer Cooking* (1955), was a surreptitiously literary experience, replete with anecdotes about Gertrude Stein's cook, and long quotations from the likes of Osbert Sitwell, DH Lawrence, Henry James, and her friends Norman Douglas and Lawrence Durrell. As well as indulging the reader in some discrete treasures of English prose, David wanted her readers to escape from "the frustration of buying the weekly rations" and "to read about real food cooked with wine and oil, eggs and butter and cream, and dishes richly flavoured with onions, garlic, herbs and brightly coloured southern vegetables". This, she conceded, might be "over-picturesque for every day; but then who wants to eat the same food every day?"

In 1950, this was a call to arms, fuelled by her indignation at the horrors of the national diet. With mouthwatering recipes for *moules marinières* and *kokkoretsi, bocconcini, bouillabaisse* and *bourride, lièvre à la royale, paella Valenciana* and *boeuf en daube*, she challenged her readers to break out of the Home Front straitjacket and sally forth into Soho. In words that seem as quaint as Beatrix Potter's, she wrote, "Those who make an occasional marketing expedition to the region of Tottenham Court Road can buy Greek cheese and Calamata olives, Tahina paste from the Middle East, little birds preserved in oil from Cyprus, stuffed vine leaves from Turkey, Spanish sausages, Egyptian brown beans, even occasionally Neapolitan Mozzarella cheese, and honey from Mount Hymettus."

Mrs David was never an ordinary cookery writer. Overnight, it seems, she became a household name, a liberator, a kitchen goddess, and a provocation. "I remember when *A Book of Mediterranean Food* came out," writes Jane Grigson, another fine cookery writer, looking back. "Basil then was no more than the name of bachelor uncles, *courgette* was printed in italics as an alien word, and few of us knew how to eat spaghetti or pick a globe artichoke to pieces." In a world where tiny bottles of olive oil could only be bought in Boots the Chemist (for aural hygiene), where BBC television could famously conduct an April Fool's day report on the "spaghetti harvest", and where food meant "marge, evaporated milk and Woolton Pie", Mrs David burst in "like sunshine".

From the outset, the quality of David's writing, and the radicalism of her attitude, attracted good reviews. The *TLS* wrote, of *Mediterranean Food*: "More than a collection of recipes, this book is in effect a readable and discerning dissertation on Italian food and regional dishes, and their preparation in the English kitchen." The *Observer*, rhapsodising, declared that "Mrs David ... may be counted among the benefactors of humanity." Her fans included John Arlott and Evelyn Waugh.

Elizabeth David's later work, once published in paperback, became an essential feature in millions of British kitchens. *French Provincial Cooking* (1960), her most enduringly popular title, was eventually joined by a collection of her journalism, *An Omelette and a Glass of Wine* (1984), which became a bestseller.

Mediterranean Food earns its place on this list for three reasons. First, it has profoundly influenced generations of food writers, from Julia Child to Nigella Lawson. Second, it inspired a revolution whose happy aftermath can be seen in the food aisles of Waitrose, Sainsbury and Tesco, and perhaps even in the popularity of MasterChef and The Great British Bake Off. Finally, all her work expresses a credo about cooking that, with equal justice, might apply to English prose at its finest and most natural: "Good cooking is honest, sincere and simple, and by this I do not mean to imply that you will find in this, or indeed in any other book, the secret of turning out first-class food in a few minutes with no trouble. Good food is always a trouble and its preparation should be regarded as a labour of love, and this book is intended for those who actually and positively enjoy the labour involved in entertaining their friends."

Three to compare:
Elizabeth David: *French Country Cooking* (1951)
Julia Child: *Mastering the Art of French Cooking* (1961)
Nigella Lawson: *How to Be a Domestic Goddess: Baking and the Art of Comfort Cooking* (2000)

72. WAITING FOR GODOT
BY SAMUEL BECKETT (1952/53)

Waiting for Godot was not just a two-act play in which, as one wit

put it, "nothing happens, twice", it was a theatrical revolution, the beginning of the theatre of the absurd. Together with some essential volumes of poetry, this extraordinary drama would not only exert a profound influence on the postwar imagination, it would provide a metaphor for existence. Arguably, the great plays and poetry identified by this series transcend their genres to contribute tangibly to our sense of "who we are", the guiding principle of this list.

Thus, from the moment Vladimir and Estragon step on to an empty stage furnished with nothing more than a bare tree and utter the famous opening line: "Nothing to be done", the audience is pitched into a world in which the idea of boredom becomes a prolonged metaphor about the nature of existence, a strangely entertaining and finally moving "tragicomedy" (Beckett's description) sustained by two tramps in vaudeville costume and the ever-absent "Mr Godot."

The author of *En Attendant Godot* was certainly a member of the European *avant garde*, but an unlikely theatrical innovator. Beckett had never written a staged play before. Born in Dublin on Good Friday, 1906, Beckett had moved to Paris as a young man to sit at the feet of James Joyce, whose secretary and amanuensis he briefly became.

Between the wars, Beckett developed his genius as a writer in the shadow of modernism and, closer to home, *Ulysses* and *Finnegans Wake*. His first novel, *Murphy*, rejected many times, was finally published in 1938, coincidentally the same year as *Scoop* (Evelyn Waugh) and *The Code of the Woosters* (PG Wodehouse). It opened with a brilliantly alienated first line – "The sun shone, having no alternative, on the nothing new" – puzzled a lot of reviewers, was praised by Dylan Thomas and sold very badly.

Then the war came, and the Nazi panzers rolled into Paris. Beckett fled south and lived for part of the war as a near vagrant and possible resistance fighter, in and around Roussillon. Returning to Paris after the liberation in 1944, he published a brilliant trilogy *(Molloy, Malone Dies, The Unnamable)* and established a modest reputation as a writer's writer, an avant gardist with a quirky wit.

He wrote *En Attendant Godot* in French and it received its première in Paris at the Théâtre de Babylone on 5 January 1953 [see chronological note, below]. The common view that it flopped is disputed by the record. James Knowlson's and Deidre Bair's biographies (*Damned to Fame* (1996) and *Samuel Beckett: A Biography* (1978)) confirm that, actually, the play, which was produced on a shoestring with a scratch cast, did quite well, with some favourable reviews.

The text of the play, now in Beckett's translation, crossed the Channel and landed on the desk of a young director Peter Hall who, admitting that he hadn't "the foggiest idea" what it meant, produced it at the Arts Theatre, London in August 1955. Almost immediately, the two most influential London critics, Kenneth Tynan (the *Observer*) and Harold Hobson (the *Sunday Times*) hailed it as a masterpiece.

Within the decade, Beckett was established as the most innovative, radical and important English-language playwright of the century, one of the founding fathers of the theatre of the absurd. Eventually, his work would profoundly influence the work of Harold Pinter, Tom

Stoppard, David Mamet and Sam Shepard, among many others.

The circumstances of *Waiting for Godot* are bleak and existential, but the main characters, "Didi" and "Gogo", exhibit a manic energy and utter dialogue of such entrancing polyphony, laced with moments of profound and resonant silence, that the experience for the audience can be a mood of optimism and often hilarity. Beckett's vision might be dark, but his touch is supremely light. Some snatches of the dialogue are more Laurel and Hardy than Kafka:

> VLADIMIR: I don't understand.
> ESTRAGON: Use your intelligence, can't you?

Vladimir uses his intelligence.

> VLADIMIR: (finally) I remain in the dark.

Tellingly, his characters acknowledge their part in the illusion of action that's unfolding in front of us:

> ESTRAGON: We always find something, eh Didi, to give us the impression we exist?
> VLADIMIR: Yes, yes, we're magicians.

The tramps also delight in teasing each other, and the audience, with their predicament:

> ESTRAGON: I can't go on like this.
> VLADIMIR: That's what you think.

The meaning of *Waiting for Godot has* been debated about for more than 60 years now. The elusive Godot himself, most notably, has been the object of intense, and occasionally deranged, speculation. Beckett was offhand about his "meaning". In Deidre Bair's controversial biography, he is quoted, saying that it would be "fatuous of me to pretend that I am not aware of the meanings attached to the word 'Godot', and the opinion of many that it means 'God'." He was, however, insistent that "I wrote the play in French, and if I did have that meaning in my mind, it was somewhere in my unconscious and I was not overtly aware of it."

For such speculation, Beckett has an answer, in one of Vladimir's great speeches:

VLADIMIR: Let us not waste time in idle discourse! (Pause. Vehemently.) Let us do something, while we have the chance! It is not every day that we are needed. Not indeed that we personally are needed. Others would meet the case equally well, if not better. To all mankind they were addressed, those cries for help still ringing in our ears! But at this place, at this moment of time, all mankind is us, whether we like it or not. Let us make the most of it, before it is too late! Let us represent worthily for once the foul brood to which a cruel fate consigned us! What do you say? (Estragon says nothing.) It is true that when with folded arms we weigh the pros and cons we are no less a credit to our species. The tiger bounds to the help of his congeners without the least reflection, or else he slinks away into the depths of the thickets. But that is not the question. What are we doing here, that is the question. And we are blessed in this, that we happen to know the answer. Yes, in the immense confusion one thing alone is clear. We are waiting for Godot to come –

And of course, at the end of act two, with no sign of Godot, none of this has come to anything.

VLADIMIR: Well? Shall we go?
ESTRAGON: Yes, let's go.

They do not move.

Chronological note:
Beckett's original French text was composed between October 1948 and January 1949. On 17 February 1952, an abridged version of the play was performed in a Paris recording studio and broadcast on French radio. Beckett sent an introductory note in which he confessed: "I don't know who Godot is", but did not himself turn up. The French (Editions Minuit) text appeared in print on 17 October 1952 in advance of the play's first unabridged theatrical performance. This premiere of Beckett's French version took place on 5 January 1953 in the Théâtre de Babylone, Paris. Beckett's English translation of his play was published during 1954 by the Grove Press, in the US. The first English language version of *Waiting for Godot* was premiered in London in 1955 at the Arts Theatre, and was subsequently published in the UK by Faber & Faber in 1956.

Three to compare:
Samuel Beckett: *Endgame* (1957)
Harold Pinter: *The Caretaker* (1960)
Tom Stoppard: *Rosencrantz and Guildenstern Are Dead* (1966)

73. THE HEDGEHOG AND THE FOX
BY ISAIAH BERLIN (1953)

"The fox knows many things, but the hedgehog knows one big thing." When Isaiah Berlin, as a young Oxford don in the late 1930s, first encountered this tantalising fragment of verse by the 7th century BC Greek poet Archilochus, it became an entertaining way by which Berlin and his circle could categorise their friends: as hedgehogs or foxes. However, this mysterious shard of wisdom stuck in Berlin's mind and eventually became the animating principle for an extraordinary essay on Tolstoy, dictated in the course of two days, and originally entitled Lev Tolstoy's Historical Scepticism. (It was the publisher George Weidenfeld who suggested the substitution.) As well as interrogating the text of *War and Peace*, Berlin explored the fundamental distinction that exists between those who are fascinated by the infinite variety of things (foxes) and those who relate everything to a central, all-embracing system (hedgehogs).

By then, and in subsequent critical discourse, the division of humanity into hedgehogs and foxes had become not only a witty means of classification, but also an existential way of confronting reality. Foxes, for instance, will come to understand that they know many things, that a coherent worldview is probably beyond them and that they must be reconciled to the limits of what they know. In his life of Isaiah Berlin, the biographer Michael Ignatieff quotes Berlin thus: "We are part of a larger scheme of things than we can understand; we ourselves live in this whole and by it, and are wise only in the measure to which we make our peace with it."

Berlin's hedgehog, by contrast, never makes peace with the world and remains unreconciled. His or her purpose is to know one big thing and, in Ignatieff's words, "strive without ceasing to give reality a unifying shape. Foxes settle for what they know and may live happy lives. Hedgehogs will not settle and their lives may not be happy."

Berlin's famous essay, however, is not about wildlife. Addressing the supreme creative artist's intellectual personality, he begins with an act of division, describing Dante, Pascal, Ibsen and Proust (inter alia) as hedgehogs and Shakespeare, Herodotus, Aristotle, Montaigne, Balzac, Goethe and Joyce as foxes.

From here, passing through a catalogue of great Russian writers – Pushkin, Dostoevsky, Turgenev, Chekhov and Gogol – Berlin arrives at the curious case of Count Lev Nikolayevich Tolstoy and confesses himself to be baffled. Ask whether Tolstoy's "vision is of one or of many, whether he is of a single substance or compounded of heterogenous elements" and, he admits, "there is no clear or immediate answer".

Here, *The Hedgehog and the Fox* becomes an essay about Tolstoy's philosophy of art and history (as expressed in *War and Peace*), a dazzling *tour de force* of fewer than a hundred pages. It was acclaimed from the first. "This little book," wrote the *Observer*, "is so entertaining as well as acute that the reader hardly notices that it is learned too." Across the Atlantic, the *New York Times* declared: "Not only does Mr Berlin command all the materials of erudition, literary and philosophical, for his task, but he has a deep and subtle feeling for the puzzle of Tolstoy's personality, and he writes throughout with a wonderful eloquence."

In correspondence with the great American critic Edmund Wilson, Berlin summarised his essay quite simply thus: "Tolstoy I maintain was by nature and gifts a fox who terribly believed in hedgehogs and wished to vivisect himself into one. Hence the crack inside him which everyone knows." This "crack" is universal: humanity will always be reconciled to life as it is, while, at the same time, longing for a simple, unitary truth, underlying existence, that provides a deep and consoling explanation.

The heroism of the hedgehog is that he or she rejects limitations and will probably never be reconciled to quotidian restriction. As Ignatieff has written, Tolstoy was contemptuous of all kinds of doctrine, both religious and secular, yet could never quite give up on the possibility of an ultimate explanation. "Tolstoy's sense of reality," writes Berlin, "was until the end too devastating to be compatible with any moral ideal which he was able to construct out of the fragments into which his intellect shivered the world, and he dedicated all of his vast strength of mind and will to the lifelong denial of this fact."

The distinction between the pluralistic fox and the single-minded hedgehog has become a staple of modern cultural analysis. The ultimate accolade: Berlin's brilliant exploitation of the concept has also inspired parody. In *Punch* (24 February 1954), John Bowle, with apologies to Edward Lear, divided the world into "owls" and "pussycats", the former "wise, ghostly and detached", the latter "round, fluffy and predacious".

Berlin's great essay endures because it is a rhetorical masterpiece, an intellectual firework display by a modern master, a brilliant investigation of a great writer and his work and perhaps because almost everyone is divided between living like foxes or hedgehogs. Berlin, who later said: "I am very sorry to have called my own book *The Hedgehog and the Fox*. I wish I hadn't now", ultimately accepted that he was "probably a fox".

Three to compare:
George Steiner: *Tolstoy or Dostoevsky, An Essay in Contrast* (1960)
Isaiah Berlin: *Against The Current, Essays in the History of Ideas* (1979)
Edmund Wilson: *The Fifties: From Notebooks and Diaries*
    of the Period, ed Leon Edel (1986)

74. THE NUDE: A STUDY OF IDEAL ART
BY KENNETH CLARK (1956)

To *Private Eye*, he was, immortally, "Lord Clark of Civilisation", an accolade that probably made this patrician art historian better known to the British public than any other contemporary critic in any genre, a household name to stand alongside Fry, Gombrich and Pevsner. The epitome of the Great and the Good, equally at home with princes, patrons, and prime ministers, Clark was also a scholar with a showman's instincts, who kept a beady eye on his audience. He relished provocative observations, and began this controversial study by opposing the naked ("huddled and defenceless") with the nude ("balanced, prosperous and confident ... the body re-formed"). Appropriately, this pioneering history of the depiction of the human body, which began with the 1953 Mellon Lectures, was largely written in the home of Bernard Berenson, the art historical master to whom it is dedicated.

In the context of its time, the mid-1950s, Clark's account of the nude in the history of art, from the Greeks and the Romans to Picasso and the postimpressionists, is a wide-ranging, secular celebration of an important classical tradition. In ancient times, the nude had been used to express fundamental human needs, for instance, the need for harmony and order (Apollo) versus the need to sublimate sexual desire (Venus). Writing in postwar Europe, Clark's ambition was to restore the human body in the public mind as an object of myth and wonder, not (as it had become in the 30s) the tool of fascist brutalism.

Clark, the most refined and sophisticated of critics, was also surreptitiously advancing a very British kind of popular paganism through his acknowledgment of the power of Eros. In hindsight, *The Nude* can be identified as a turning point for the incipient sexual revolution of the 60s.

Probably no one would be more surprised at this suggestion than Clark. His own indifference to what would later be identified by his many critics as "the politics of vision" makes him an unlikely radical. In his writing, the former academic historian aims to celebrate and admire the sensuality of the naked human form, expressing himself elegantly and without over-complication. As it happens, he is only partly successful.

In *The Nude*, the transition from the male nudes of Michelangelo, via the great Venuses of Giorgione and Titian, to the female nudes of Rubens and Ingres, sponsors an irruption of excitement into Clark's narrative. He starts using a kind of language no art historian had explored before:

> "The Venus of Giorgione is sleeping, without a thought of her nakedness. Compared with Titian's Venus of Urbino, she is like a bud, wrapped in its sheath, each petal folded so firmly as to give us the feeling of inflexible purpose. With Titian, the bud has opened ... replaced by renaissance satisfaction in the here and now."

Having broken the taboo, Clark's prose becomes decorously, but never deliriously, liberated. Describing François Boucher's portrait of Miss O'Murphy he writes:

> "Freshness of desire has seldom been more delicately expressed than by [her] round young limbs, as they sprawl with undisguised satisfaction on the silken cushions of her sofa. By art

Boucher has enabled us to enjoy her with as little shame as she is enjoying herself. One false note and we should be embarrassingly back in the world of sin."

Throughout the composition of this remarkable monograph, Clark was not merely battling his own inhibitions, he was having to find new ways to sustain his narrative line. As he admits in his preface to *The Nude:* "I soon discovered, that the subject is extremely difficult to handle. There is difficulty of form; a chronological survey would be long and repetitive, but almost every other pattern is unworkable. And there is a difficulty of scope; no responsible art historian would have attempted to cover both antique and post-medieval art."

Clark's solution was to devote three long chapters at the heart of *The Nude* to the themes of energy, pathos and ecstasy, corresponding to classical (athletes and heroes), Christian (crucifixions and pietas) and finally some bacchanalian and gothic nudes. Throughout his narrative, Clark is fully alive to the ironies of his analysis, especially as he probes the depiction of the medieval nude:

"During the long banishment of the body there arose one symbol of pathos more poignant and more compelling than all the others: Our Lord on the Cross. Nothing in our subject shows more decisively the ideal character of the antique nude than that, in spite of the Christian horror of nakedness, it was the undraped figure of Christ which was finally accepted as canonical in representations of the Crucifixion."

An instinctive quest for our civilisation and its towering humanistic values was never far from the core of Clark's writing. The success of *The Nude* in the 1950s and 60s, before the sensational success of *Civilisation*, and before the critics, led by John Berger, turned on him, possibly indicates the deep and unconscious imperatives behind the Anglo-American passion for culture.

Three to compare:
Bernard Berenson: *The Drawings of the Florentine Painters* (1903)
Kenneth Clark: *Civilisation, a Personal View* (1969)
John Berger: *Ways of Seeing* (1972)

75. NOTES OF A NATIVE SON
BY JAMES BALDWIN (1955)

In the spring of 1820, Thomas Jefferson, who, in an early draft of

the Declaration of Independence, had launched a withering assault on slavery, confessed to an associate that the plight of the American negro was a momentous question, which, "like a fire bell in the night, awakened and filled me with terror".

Race, still the greatest of the unresolved issues within America, has inspired one entry on this list – *Dreams From My Father* by Barack Obama. With James Baldwin, African-American literature reaches one

of its 20th century masters in fiction (*Go Tell It on the Mountain* and *Giovanni's Room*), a name to stand alongside Langston Hughes, Richard Wright and, most recently, Nobel laureate Toni Morrison.

Baldwin is also the author of some important nonfiction, several landmark essays of great power and beauty about the place of the black writer in white America. In this genre, *Notes of a Native Son* is a recent classic. For Henry Louis Gates Jr, it was Baldwin who "named for me the things you feel but couldn't utter … articulated for the first time to white America what it meant to be American and a black American at the same time". The 10 essays collected in *Notes of a Native Son* – on subjects ranging from *Uncle Tom's Cabin* to 1940s Harlem – distil Baldwin's thinking. It is a source book for a subject that Langston Hughes described in a review of Notes as "the troubled problems of this troubled Earth".

Baldwin frames his work as a crucial journey of self-discovery. He had, for instance, first to confront his complex relationship with his father, a preacher: "He [Baldwin's father] could be chilling in the pulpit and indescribably cruel in his personal life and he was certainly the most bitter man I have ever met; yet it must be said that there was something else in him, buried in him, which lent him his tremendous power and, even, a rather crushing charm."

At the same time, almost as taxing, he had to investigate himself: "I was trying to discover myself – on the whole, when examined, a somewhat dubious notion, since I was also trying to avoid myself."

In *Notes*, Baldwin is much franker about the "condundrum of colour" than the complexity of his life as a gay man, perhaps because race could be rhetorically linked to a historical crime: "It is a fearful inheritance, for which untold multitudes, long ago, sold their birthright. Multitudes are doing so, until today. This horror has so welded past and present that it is virtually impossible and certainly meaningless to speak of it as occurring in time.

Describing himself as "a survivor", Baldwin senses the stirrings of liberation in postwar America and notes the changes that have begun to occur in his lifetime:

> "When I was young, I was being told it will take time before a black person can be treated as a human being, but it will happen. We will help to make it happen."

Throughout his writing, Baldwin never shies away from a frank and disquieting acknowledgement of feelings: "There is no negro living in America who has not felt, briefly or for long periods … naked and unanswerable hatred; who has not wanted to smash any white face he may encounter; to violate, out of motives of cruellest vengeance, their women, to break the bodies of all white people..."

Despite this admission of rage, Baldwin can also be entertainingly satirical, as in his essay on Carmen Jones: "Hollywood's peculiar ability to milk, so to speak, the cow and the goat at the same time – and then to peddle the results as ginger ale – has seldom produced anything more arresting than the 1955 production of Carmen Jones."

All of the foregoing culminates in the title essay, Baldwin's declaration of independence. Speaking of his struggle to vindicate himself as an artist, he writes: "This fight begins, however, in the heart and it has now been laid to my charge to keep my own heart free of hatred and despair."

This becomes a statement of intent which Baldwin would fulfill many times over in the career that followed.

Three to compare:
Richard Wright: *Black Boy* (1945)
Ralph Ellison: *Shadow and Act* (1964)
Alex Haley: *The Autobiography of Malcolm X* (1965)

76. The Uses of Literacy: Aspects of Working-Class Life (1957) by Richard Hoggart.

Lists such as this occasionally face difficult, perhaps even imposs-

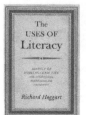

ible, choices. In 1957, a 100-page monograph by a brilliant young American linguist, a book regularly nominated for an automatic place in contemporary "most influential" and "modern classic" selections, was published by a small Dutch publishing house (Mouton & Co) in the Hague.

The text in question is *Syntactic Structures*, "part of an attempt to construct a formalised general theory of linguistic structure". Its author, Noam Chomsky, celebrated as the founder of modern linguistics, is one of the foremost public intellectuals of the age, and the fierce conscience of progressive America, acclaimed as much for his polemics against US foreign policy as for his theories about language and mind.

And yet, despite an immersion in his "masterpiece", a summary of a much longer 1,000-page work entitled *The Logical Structure of Linguistic Theory,* I have to confess, after two baffled readings, that I cannot inflict Chomsky on the subscribers to this list. If his prose was otherwise lovely, I would forgive *Syntactic Structures* its forbidding and impenetrable mask of technical language (aka jargon). If his ideas were profoundly obscure, but ultimately recoverable as deep and thrilling, I would take a chance.

To this reader, sadly, apart from one arresting piece of brilliant nonsense ("Colourless green ideas sleep furiously"), Chomsky's masterpiece is unreadable. I'm sorry: no doubt, as some have suggested, *Syntactic Structures* is comparable to the work of Keynes or Freud. On my reading, on behalf of the common reader, the presumed audience for a list such as this, it is also unintelligible.

What, for instance, are we to make of Chomsky's declared "fundamental concern"? This, he writes, is "the problem of justification of grammars". Seeking clarity, but still mystifying this reader, he goes on to define "a grammar of the language L" as "essentially a theory of L". This is also, he declares, in a further clarification, "a device that generates all of the grammatical sequences of L and none of the ungrammatical ones".

There are, maybe, lists on which this short and singular book should be at home. For *Observer* readers, I believe that *Syntactic Structures* would be a hideous imposition. Instead, from the same year, 1957, I am choosing Richard Hoggart's beautifully written and profoundly influential, classic of British postwar cultural analysis,

This attempt to understand the changes in British culture after the Second World War in which the mobilisation of the home front had ushered in "massification" – mass society and mass culture – will resonate with any reader struggling to make sense of the Brexit referendum vote.

In this deeply autobiographical study, written from within the experience of growing up in industrial Leeds, Hoggart argued that Britain was squandering the hard-won skills of education and literacy by moving towards a new kind of society dominated by new and troubling values. The upshot of this, he said, would be that an urban, working-class culture "of the people" would be destroyed.

Originally, Hoggart's passionate alarm-call was to have been called The Abuses of Literacy, and some of his most memorable passages attack the "mass publicists" who, as he saw it, were destroying the delicate web of close-knit neighbourhood communities based on local libraries, corner shops and working-mens' clubs. Hoggart is aware of the dangers inherent in his analysis, finding himself, he writes "constantly having to resist a strong inner pressure to make the old much more admirable than the new".

His book falls into two parts ("An 'Older' Order" and "Yielding Place to New"): first an impassioned narrative of former working-class values, followed by an extended portrait of the changes that had occurred in Britain between, roughly, the election of the Attlee government and the coming of the Beatles.

Hoggart, who was plainly influenced by the George Orwell of *The Road To Wigan Pier*, interrogates the popular songs, newspapers, magazines, and mass market paperbacks of the 1950s for clues to the transformation of the popular imagination.

Some of this strayed into the realm of fiction. To evade British libel laws, Hoggart was forced to invent titles for the sex and crime pulp fiction he was excoriating. (One of these, *Death Cab for Cutie,* had an extraordinary afterlife becoming a comedy rock song for the Bonzo Dog Doo-Dah Band, and subsequently performed by the Beatles in their 1967 television film Magical Mystery Tour.)

Whatever the multiplicity of its sources, the deep authenticity of

Hoggart's writing is unmistakable. As with the greatest books in this series, *The Uses of Literacy* focuses on a case study – the particular plight of the poor and underprivileged, in relation to the available mass media (tabloid newspapers, pulp magazines, local radio).

From this microcosm, Hoggart derives a work resonant with universal truths about the interaction between the many and the few; the ordinary person and the dominant elites. Ultimately, Hoggart provides an anatomy of an archetypal conflict: the street versus the ivory tower.

In his preface, Hoggart, implicitly rebuking academics who preach only to the choir, observes that he thought of himself "as addressing first of all the serious 'common reader' or 'intelligent layman' from any class. I have written as clearly as my understanding of the subject allowed".

He concludes: "One of the most striking and ominous features of our present cultural situation is the division between the technical language of the experts and the extraordinarily low level of the organs of mass communication."

We shall probably never know if he was familiar with *Syntactic Structures.*

Three to compare:
George Orwell: *The Road to Wigan Pier* (1937)
Raymond Williams: *Culture and Society* (1958)
EP Thompson: *The Making of the English Working Class* (1963)

77. THE AFFLUENT SOCIETY
BY JOHN KENNETH GALBRAITH (1958)

From its urbane opening line – "Wealth is not without its advantages..." – John Kenneth Galbraith's bestselling assault on some of America's most treasured economic myths survives as the apotheosis of an impressive public intellectual's restatement of classic liberalism: provocative, humane and entertaining, a book that shaped the American mind from the 50s and 60s to the fall of the Berlin Wall.

As well as tackling economic shibboleths, Galbraith also coined some striking and influential concepts of his own. "The conventional wisdom", the title of his opening chapter, for instance, has now passed into the language. At first, this book was intended to be a study of poverty entitled 'Why the Poor Are Poor', until Galbraith's wife suggested the more upbeat *The Affluent Society*. Certainly, some of its entertaining iconoclasm derives from that first draft. In the end, however, it expressed a marriage of British theory, especially Keynesianism, with American industrial experience, making a mid-Atlantic bestseller for the postwar world.

Before reaching its central message, the first half of *The Affluent Society* is devoted to demonstrating how classical economic theory, from Adam Smith to Malthus to David Ricardo, projects a grim view of human prospects, casting an air of pessimism over the socioeconomic study of the human condition. This Galbraith is at pains to dispel. He is a witty and engaging optimist for whom GDP is "the accepted measure not only of economic but of larger social achievement".

The idea that the production of goods and services should be the measure of civilised success plainly bears the influence of its time, but he also disputed the idea that increased material production is the only indicator of economic wellbeing. Through his book, Galbraith, a Canadian who became an important figure in American life, especially as a favoured confidant of President John F Kennedy, first began to emerge as an unofficial spokesman for a more progressive American materialism during the 60s, an era in which capitalism and the cold war became inextricably interwoven. As a disciple of Keynes, he argued that the US should invest dynamically in roads, schools and hospitals.

Galbraith, the inveterate populariser, is never less than quotable: "The study of money, above all other fields in economics," he once wrote, "is one in which complexity is used to disguise truth or to evade truth, not to reveal it. The process by which banks create money is so simple the mind is repelled. With something so important, a deeper mystery seems only decent."

In this spirit, the second half of *The Affluent Society* assaults some deeply held economic myths. What is the meaning of productivity if many of the goods we produce are simply artificial needs promoted by the advertising media of mass society? "As a society becomes increasingly affluent," writes Galbraith, "wants are increasingly created by the process by which they are satisfied." In addition to this Dependence Effect, why ignore waste and extravagance in the private sector while simultaneously speaking of government expenditure "squandered" on public works?

Galbraith is not just an articulate and contrarian cheerleader for a superior kind of American consumerism. He is also, quite presciently, keen to strike a note of warning about inflation. But in the end, he is contemptuous of a society in which "the bland lead the bland". His main project is to break "the thralldom of a myth – that the production of goods is the central problem of our lives".

With the perspective of hindsight, much of Galbraith reads like a long footnote to the great American claim that the true goal of a free society should be "life, liberty and the pursuit of happiness". In 1979, almost a generation after he first completed this essay in economic optimism, Galbraith ventilated a few second thoughts: "Let us put elimination of poverty on the social and political agenda. And let us protect our affluence from those who, in the name of defending it, would leave the planet only with its ashes. The affluent society is not without its flaws. But it is well worth saving from its own adverse or destructive tendencies."

At the end of his life, speaking on US television, he articulated a fundamental liberal pragmatism: "Where the market works, I'm for that. Where the government is necessary, I'm for that. I'm deeply suspicious of somebody who says, 'I'm in favour of privatisation', or, 'I'm deeply in favour of public ownership.' I'm in favour of whatever works in the particular case."

Three to compare:
JK Galbraith: *The Great Crash 1929* (1955)
JK Galbraith: *The New Industrial State* (1967)
Vance Packard: *The Hidden Persuaders* (1957)

78. THE ELEMENTS OF STYLE
BY WILLIAM STRUNK AND EB WHITE (1959)

Dorothy Parker once wrote: "If you have any young friends who aspire to become writers, the second greatest favour you can do them is to present them with copies of *The Elements of Style*. The first greatest, of course, is to shoot them now, while they're happy."

Many Americans, who believe that writing can be taught, will turn to *The Elements of Style* as the indispensable road map through a trackless desert of whirling words. From the Great War to the Cold War, this little book of scarcely 90 pages, was just one college professor's attempt to cut "the vast tangle of English rhetoric down to size and write its rules and principles on the head of a pin".

Those are the words of EB White, who, having been taught English at Cornell University by Prof William Strunk Jr, was commissioned in 1957 by the publishers Macmillan to revise Strunk's privately printed course book on style for the general reader as well as the college market. In Britain, whose relationship to the English language has been more mandarin, the equivalent title is HW Fowler's *A Dictionary of Modern English Usage* (1926).

In its original, privately printed guise, *The Elements of Style* was a 43-page summary of, in White's words, "the case for cleanliness, accuracy and brevity in the use of English". After half a century, he conceded, it was still "a barely tarnished gem", so little broken that it barely required fixing. "Seven rules of usage, 11 principles of composition, a few matters of form, and a list of words and expressions commonly misused – that was the sum and substance of Professor Strunk's work."

White added his own chapter "on writing" – about English prose composition, and that was that. "Strunk & White", a title routinely chosen as one of the most influential books ever written in English, was ready to take its place in the front line of the ongoing battle to save the language from corruption, marching to war against the horrors of jargon, prolixity and grammatical solecism beneath a banner inscribed with one simple slogan: "Omit needless words".

In the *New Yorker* of 1957, addressing the task he had undertaken, EB White recalled that when, in college, "I was sitting in [Strunk's] class, he omitted so many needless words, and omitted them so forcibly and with such eagerness and obvious relish, that he often seemed in the position of having short-changed himself – a man left with nothing more to say yet with time to fill, a radio prophet who had outdistanced the clock. Will Strunk got out of this predicament by a simple trick: he uttered every sentence three times."

As Lewis Carroll once observed, "What I tell you three times is true." *The Elements of Style* is replete with many timeless truths about modern English usage, truths that have trickled down into the literary consciousness of many generations of journalists and writers. Some of Strunk's wisdom is still chiefly revered in the US, but his explication of the nature and beauty of brevity is almost poetic: "vigorous writing is concise. A sentence should contain no unnecessary words, a paragraph no unnecessary sentences, for the same reason that a drawing should have no unnecessary lines and a machine no unnecessary parts. This requires not that the writer make all his sentences short, or that he avoid all detail and treat his subjects only in outline, but that every word tell."

Everyone immersed in the joys of the English language – school teachers, journalists, poets, diarists and doodlers – knows that many rules of style are a matter of personal choice (Strunk happened to loathe "forceful" and "the fact that") and even that some established rules of grammar are open to challenge. Shakespeare, it's often pointed out, broke almost every rule in the book.

"The best writers," admitted Strunk, "sometimes disregard the rules of rhetoric." At the same time, his guidelines, based on generations of accumulated custom and practice, will help the ordinary beginner to find clarity, brevity and candour in self-expression. It won't teach you to write, but it will make what you do write a lot more readable, vigorous, and persuasive.

EB White published two revisions of his 1959 edition (in 1972 and 1979). By then, the world in which Strunk had first addressed split infinitives; the importance of the comma "before a conjunction introducing a dependent clause"; and the difference between "anticipate" and "expect", had been almost completely swept away by the cultural avalanche of mass communications, multiculturalism, and the so-called "permissive society".

In a time of acute change, *The Elements of Style* could seem fuddy-duddy and redundant. In 2005, the *Boston Globe*, breaking ranks with the *New York Times* and *the Washington Post*, many of whose journalists continue to revere Strunk and White, declared it to have become an "ageing zombie of a book ... a hodgepodge, its now-antiquated pet peeves jostling for space with 1970s taboos and 1990s computer advice".

And yet, despite the passage of time, changes in fashion, and the ravages of the IT revolution, there were some, like the writer Stephen King, who refused to back down in the face of change. In his excellent style manual, *On Writing* (2000), King observed, "There is little or no detectable bullshit in that book. (Of course, it's short; at 85 pages it's much shorter than this one.) I'll tell you right now that every aspiring writer should read *The Elements of Style*."

In Britain, where Strunk & White is still not widely known, but where a misplaced apostrophe can still look like the end of civilisation as we know it, the journalist Lynne Truss published a long and passionate footnote to *The Elements of Style* in 2003, with her bestselling "zero tolerance approach to punctuation", *Eats, Shoots and Leaves*. By now matters of taste and grammar had become hand-to-hand fighting against trolls and Visigoths on the barricades of the contemporary culture war.

Truss's guide was highly entertaining, but a long way from the sobriety and poise of Prof Strunk and his gifted disciple, the author of another American classic, *Charlotte's Web*. Let White, writing in 1979, have the last word: "... standing, in a drafty time, erect, resolute, and assured, I still find the Strunkian wisdom a comfort, the Strunkian humour a delight, and the Strunkian attitude towards right and wrong a blessing undisguised".

Three to compare:
HW Fowler: *A Dictionary of Modern English Usage* (1926)
Eric Partridge: *A Dictionary of Slang and Unconventional English* (1969)
Lynne Truss: *Eats, Shoots and Leaves* (2003)

79. A GRIEF OBSERVED
BY CS LEWIS (1961)

"No one ever told me that grief felt so much like fear." From its famous opening line, *A Grief Observed* propelled its readers into a no-man's-land of mourning and loss. It dramatises bereavement and ruthlessly confronts the desolate survivor with an insistent and overwhelming question: "Where is God?"

Lewis's answer to this existential conundrum resonates through the rest of the book with a kind of tangible fury: "Go to Him when your need is desperate, when all other help is vain, and what do you find? A door slammed in your face, and a sound of bolting and double-bolting on the inside. After that, silence. You may as well turn away. The longer you wait, the more emphatic the silence will become. There are no lights in the windows. It might be an empty house. Was it ever inhabited? It seemed so once. And that seeming was as strong as this. What can this mean? Why is He so present a commander in our time of prosperity and so very absent a help in time of trouble?"

Even a confused non-believer can appreciate the deep sense of betrayal here. In good times of happiness and security, you might have no sense of needing any consolation and might even assume that God will not be available when he is needed. For a believer, writes Lewis, bitterly, "the conclusion I dread is not 'so there's no God after all', but 'so this is what God's really like. Deceive yourself no longer.'"

Much of his text is quasi-theological; other parts have a self-help flavour that quickly morphs into lyricism: "Sorrow," instructs Lewis, "turns out to be not a state but a process. It needs not a map but a history, and if I don't stop writing that history at some arbitrary point, there's no reason why I should ever stop. There is something to be chronicled every day. Grief is like a long valley, a winding valley where any bend may reveal a totally new landscape."

A Grief Observed is an unsettling book for a secular age, plunging the reader, as it does, into allusions to St Augustine, considerations of heaven and eternity, coupled with some intense, self-analytical discussions about separation, solitude and Christian suffering. Some of Lewis's exclamations are raw and modern. "Cancer, and cancer, and cancer. My mother, my father, my wife. I wonder who is next in the queue."

Once the reader has tuned his or her sensibility to Lewis's wavelength, this unsentimental, even bracing, account of one man's dialogue with despair becomes both compelling and consoling in several intriguing ways not necessarily associated with death. As Rowan Williams has written: "If the anguish of loss can be honestly lived in (not 'through'), it must be with a clear recognition of the impossibility of possessing or absorbing anyone we love."

Indeed, some of Lewis's best passages recall the intensity of an earlier and very passionate essay, The Four Loves: "We have seen the faces of those we know best so variously, from so many angles, in so many lights, with so many expressions – waking, sleeping, laughing, crying, eating, talking, thinking – that all the impressions crowd into our memory together and cancel out in a mere blur."

This series of nonfiction greats does not typically narrate the backstory to the classics it selects, but the circumstances of A Grief Observed are worth repeating. Throughout his life, "Jack" Lewis was a man tortured by the tragedies of love. He was born in Northern Ireland in 1898, enjoyed a quasi-public school education in England, and then served as an officer in the First World War, where he was quite badly wounded in action. For him, the horror of the trenches was just another kind of association with death. He had lost his mother as a small boy, aged 10. In Surprised by Joy, he says that, when his mother died, "grief was overwhelmed by terror" at the sight of her dead body.

Thereafter, in honour of a pact made on the battlefield with a fallen fellow soldier, he formed a highly unconventional relationship with Jane Moore, a woman 26 years older than him, whom he referred to as "mother", and who eventually died of dementia in 1951.

When, in 1956, he abandoned his bachelor security for Joy Davidman, an American poet, he experienced a kind of conversion to the joys of feminine intimacy, and also acquired two stepsons through his marriage. This late flowering was cut short when Joy was diagnosed with cancer. Four years later, she was dead. Her death plunged Lewis into the crisis of faith he addresses in A Grief Observed. Perhaps he was more deeply wounded by his loss than he realised. Lewis died a week before his 65th birthday in November 1963.

The typescript of this fifty-something page text [Readers' Edition, Faber, 2015] was submitted to Faber as the work of a pseudonymous author, Dimidius, by a literary agent, Curtis Brown, who declared he was neither at liberty to reveal the author's name, nor much interested in further inquiries about it. The first person to read the text, TS Eliot, a Faber director, claimed to have "guessed the name of the author", typically kept his hunch to himself, recommended immediate publication and requested a less contrived pseudonym. (Dimidius, in Latin, implies "cut in half".) CS Lewis at once suggested an alternative, and *A Grief Observed* by NW Clerk was published in the autumn of 1961. Thanks to Eliot's connections and support, this little book attracted a disproportionate attention for the work of an unknown. When Lewis died a couple of years later, early in 1964, his estate gave permission for the book to be republished under his own name, adding to its growing status as a contemporary classic.

Three to compare:
CS Lewis: *Surprised by Joy: The Shape of My Early Life* (1955)
Joan Didion: *The Year of Magical Thinking* (2005)
Paul Kalanithi: *When Breath Becomes Air* (2015)

80. THE STRUCTURE OF SCIENTIFIC REVOLUTIONS BY THOMAS S KUHN (1962)

Thomas Kuhn (1922-1996) did not invent the concept of scientific revolution, but he gave it a special meaning and created a phrase – "paradigm shift" – so popular that it received the ultimate accolade: no fewer than four *New Yorker* spoofings (from 1974 to 2009). On its first appearance, we find a sexy young woman in bell-bottom trousers at a Manhattan cocktail party flattering a balding metropolitan with: "Dynamite, Mr Gerston. You're the first person I heard use the word 'paradigm' in real life."

The Structure of Scientific Revolutions (hereafter *The Structure*) commands the attention of a list such as this for its remarkable influence on our understanding of science and also its continued grip on our interpretative response to scientific history. *The Structure* is a work of ideas more than style (its prose can sometimes seem rather heavy going), but one might argue that Kuhn, an American physicist and philosopher of science, had triggered his own paradigm shift with the publication of this seminal monograph, a book demonstrating that however powerful science might be, it remains as flawed as the scientists who explore its many mysteries.

Kuhn's account of science and its development differed radically from traditional versions. Previously, the standard account saw steady, cumulative "progress". Kuhn, however, only saw discontinuities – "normal" and "revolutionary" phases in which scientific communities would be thrown into periods of crisis and uncertainty. Such revolutionary phases, Kuhn argues, correspond to those conceptual breakthroughs that lay the foundations for the periods of continuity that follow.

The Structure is very much a book of the late 20th century. It began forming in Kuhn's mind in the late 1940s, when he was just a graduate student in theoretical physics. As is often pointed out, a book that has reshaped the philosophy of science was actually conceived and written by a physicist who, having taught an undergraduate course on "physical science for the non-scientist", was exposed to scientific history, and (to his surprise) found his basic conceptions about the nature of the discipline radically undermined. So *The Structure* is, in a profound sense, a young man's book, rooted in its time. The science it addresses is dominated by the post-Einstein physics of the cold war. Indeed, 1962, the year in which Kuhn's ideas were first published, was also the year of the Cuban missile crisis. And while physics was undoubtedly the alpha male among the sciences when *The Structure* was being written, change was already afoot. With *The Double Helix* (1968), we shall see how, after the 1950s, the molecular biology of DNA was set to sweep the board. Since then, biotechnology and the marriage of computer science with genetics and even neurology have become the cutting edge of scientific research.

Yet, against the odds, Kuhn remains evergreen. His great insight, which owed something to Kant, but was based on his own study of the Copernican revolution, was provocatively at odds with Karl Popper. Kuhn's description of the dialectic of change in science (the making of a paradigm; the recognition of anomalies, with an ensuing crisis; finally, the resolution of the crisis by a new paradigm) still holds true today, albeit in a radically different intellectual environment dominated by information science and biotechnology. Kuhn's argument for an episodic model of scientific development in which periods of continuity are interrupted by passages of revolutionary science remains disputed by some, but is widely accepted within most circles.

He himself has written that, "because I insist that what scientists share is not sufficient to command uniform assent about such matters as the choice between competing theories or the distinction between an ordinary anomaly and a crisis-provoking one, I am occasionally accused of glorifying subjectivity and even irrationality."

Kuhn's challenge to long-standing linear notions of scientific progress and his argument that transformative ideas do not spring from a gradual process of experimentation, but from eureka moments that disrupt conventional wisdom and offer unanticipated breakthroughs, were themselves a revolution. If turning a world of thought upside down is the mark of a superior paradigm, then *The Structure* has been, for more than half a century now, a howling success. As the *Observer*'s John Naughton has written: "A Google search for [the phrase paradigm shift] returns more than 10m hits." More significantly, it scores a reference inside no fewer than 18,300 titles sold by Amazon. Kuhn's scholarly monograph, says Naughton, is also "one of the most cited academic books of all time. If ever a big idea went viral, this is it".

Kuhn's *Structure* continues to be hugely influential in the history of science and in many related areas (economics, sociology, philosophy and history). Since publication, it has sold more than 1.4m copies, been widely translated and is routinely listed as one of the books most frequently cited in the arts and humanities of the latter half of the 20th century. In highbrow commentary, lowbrow marketing and psephological analysis, "paradigm shift" has become a cliché of social and political change.

Three to compare:
Immanuel Kant: *The Critique of Pure Reason* (1781)
Karl Popper: *The Open Society and Its Enemies* (1945)
Thomas S Kuhn: *The Essential Tension* (1977)

81. SILENT SPRING
BY RACHEL CARSON (1962)

America is a society founded on the words of the Declaration of Independence, the arguments of writers like Tom Paine (the author of *Common Sense*), James Madison (co-author of *The Federalist Papers*) and ultimately on the US constitution and its 33 amendments. As a country largely made by lawyers and journalists through ink and paper, it continues to redefine itself through the English language. From generation to generation, its citizens, uniquely, turn to books and newspapers to argue for change.

Silent Spring is a classic of American advocacy, a book that sparked a nationwide outcry against the use of pesticides, inspired legislation that would endeavour to control pollution, and thereby launched the modern environmental movement in the US. The great nature writer Peter Matthiessen identified its "fearless and succinct" prose as "the cornerstone of the new environmentalism". In a few limpid chapters, and fewer than 300 pages, Rachel Carson described the death of rivers and seas, the scorching of the soil, the annihilation of plant life and forests, the silencing of the nation's birds, the perils of crop spraying, the poisoning of humanity ("beyond the dreams of the Borgias") and the genetic threats posed by all of the above, especially in its carcinogenic manifestations.

"We stand now," writes Carson, "where two roads diverge." There is, she goes on, the superhighway that leads to "disaster", and there is (echoing Robert Frost) "the road less travelled", on which US citizens can find their voice, and are heard.

The unrestricted use of pesticides in North America had boomed after the Second World War. Carson, whose early work for the US Bureau of Fisheries had given her a special understanding of marine pollution, was one of the first to realise that DDT, a radical new pesticide, had severe ecological consequences. As the great ethnobiologist Edward O Wilson has written: "The effects of pesticides on the environment and public health had been well-documented before *Silent Spring*, but in bits and pieces scattered through the technical literature. Environmental scientists were aware of the problem but they focused only on the narrow sector of their personal expertise."

Carson's achievement was to synthesise this information into a single message (her unforgettable image of a "silent spring") that scientists and the general public could relate to and understand.

When Carson, who had written extensively on conservation issues throughout the 1950s, began to research *Silent Spring*, the word "ecology" was still barely understood. Conservation biology did not exist. "At the time," Wilson later recalled, "the scientific culture was fixated on the spectacular success of the molecular revolution, which had placed physics and chemistry at the foundation of biology." Later would come *The Double Helix* (Number 86 in this list) and the excitement generated by discoveries like DNA, but at the time, Carson's work was beyond the scope of scientific concerns.

Carson was also battling the postwar renewal of the US economy. By the late 1950s, exuberant economic growth and a dynamic national quest for limitless progress meant that science and technology attracted uncritical national support. Environmental warnings were viewed as an irritating distraction from the American project. *Silent Spring* would be published in the same year as the Cuban missile crisis: the cold war was at its height.

To the chemical industry, which had championed DDT as central to the nation's domestic agriculture, an unofficial part of the war effort, Carson was seen as triply dangerous. First, she was an outsider; second, she was a humble biologist with no academic background; and third, she was a woman who addressed herself to the general public (writing radio scripts and bestselling books like *The Sea Around Us*, 1951). In a word, she was unqualified and unpatriotic.

In a hostile intellectual climate, Carson had to find support wherever she could. As she immersed herself in a contentious subject, she approached sympathetic writers and journalists to back her cause, notably the *New Yorker* writer, and author of *Charlotte's Web,* EB White. It was White's response to Carson's passionate advocacy that led to a commission from the *New Yorker* for a major article, a piece that would become *Silent Spring*. She was additionally helped in her efforts by the outbreak of the "Great Cranberry Scare" of 1959, in which the US cranberry harvest was found to contain high levels of a carcinogenic herbicide. The FDA's prohibition of cranberry sales and subsequent congressional hearings gave the anti-pesticide lobby renewed publicity and encouraged Carson to focus on the dark side of some pesticide programmes, and to do this with a quiet indignation that was both rhetorically effective and neatly expressed:

> "If Darwin were alive today, the insect world would delight
> and astound him with its impressive verification of his theories
> of the survival of the fittest. Under the stress of intensive
> chemical spraying, the weaker members of the insect population
> are being weeded out."

In her conclusion to *Silent Spring*, Carson allowed her rage on behalf
of nature to become almost majestic:

> "The 'control of nature' is a phrase conceived in arrogance,
> born of the Neanderthal age of biology and philosophy, when
> it was supposed that nature exists for the convenience of man
> … It is our alarming misfortune that so primitive a science has
> armed itself with the most modern and terrible weapons, and
> that turning them against the insects it has also turned them
> against the earth."

As Carson's biographer, Linda Lear, has written, she deliberately "challenged the wisdom of a government that allowed toxic chemicals to
be put into the environment before knowing the long-term consequences of their use. Writing in language that everyone could understand and cleverly using the public's knowledge of atomic fallout as
a reference point, Carson described how chlorinated hydrocarbons
and organic phosphorus insecticides altered the cellular processes of
plants, animals and humans … Carson challenged the moral right
of government to leave its citizens unprotected from substances they
could neither physically avoid nor publicly question."

Once *Silent Spring* was complete, the *New Yorker* stepped in again,
this time with a pre-publication serialisation that helped propel
Carson's work to the top of the bestseller lists. In part, she was helped
by the fury of the public debate, which reached as far as President
Kennedy and the White House, and also the outrage felt by the chemical industry. Carson's opponents vilified her, in Linda Lear's words,
as "a hysterical woman whose alarming view of the future could be
ignored or, if necessary, suppressed. She was a 'bird and bunny lover',
a woman who kept cats and was therefore clearly suspect. She was a
romantic 'spinster' who was simply overwrought about genetics. In
short, Carson was a woman out of control. She had overstepped the

bounds of her gender and her science".

Tragically, however, she was unable to rebut these slurs or even participate in the publicity campaign for her book; Rachel Carson was now mortally ill with breast cancer, and died 18 months after publication, on 14 April 1964. In its own way, however, *Silent Spring* marked a profoundly important historical moment, which some have compared in social importance to Harriet Beecher Stowe's anti-slavery classic *Uncle Tom's Cabin*.

Wilson's verdict is unequivocal. *Silent Spring* became, he writes, "a national political force, largely responsible for the establishment of the Environmental Protection Agency". It also "resulted in the passage in 1973 of the Endangered Species Act ... easily the most important piece of conservation legislation in the nation's history". This was the act that also sponsored the saving of the American alligator, the grey whale, the bald eagle and the peregrine falcon, as well as the east coast population of the brown pelican.

Three to compare:
Henry Thoreau: *Walden* (1854)
Edward O Wilson: *The Ants* (1991)
Elizabeth Kolbert: *Field Notes from a Catastrophe* (2006).

82. THE MAKING OF THE ENGLISH WORKING CLASS BY EP THOMPSON (1963)

"I am seeking to rescue the poor stockinger, the luddite cropper, the 'obsolete' hand-loom weaver, the 'utopian' artisan ... from the enormous condescension of posterity." With these stirring words, a virtually unknown provincial historian launched a revolution in social and cultural history that would influence the minds and attitudes of a college generation in a way almost unparalleled in late 20th century Britain. After Thompson, "popular culture" would become a settled touchstone of progressive intellectual concern.

Thompson was a northerner who had both served with a tank regiment in north Africa during the second world war, and also been active in the Communist party throughout the 1940s and 50s. Indeed, in 1946, he had joined the Communist Party Historians Group. Like many in the CP, he left the movement in the late 50s, disillusioned by the Soviet response to the Hungarian Uprising of 1956, and the direction of the USSR after Stalin. When he came to write *The Making of the English Working Class* (first commissioned as "Working Class Politics 1790-1921"), he wrote as a patriot and a political radical wanting to express a passionate engagement with the dissenting cultural traditions of his country whose proto-working-class protagonists he venerated.

As Thompson writes in one stirring passage: "Their crafts and traditions may have been dying. Their hostility to the new industrialism may have been backward-looking. Their communitarian ideals may have been fantasies. Their insurrectionary conspiracies may have been foolhardy. But they lived through these times of acute social disturbance, and we did not. Their aspirations were valid in terms of their own experience; and, if they were casualties of history, they remain, condemned in their own lives, as casualties."

Thompson's profound and addictive sympathy for his subject was almost novelistic. As a student of rural ritual, he owed a debt to the William Cobbett of *Rural Rides* (1822). As a historian, he was an outsider, a maverick and a lifelong idealist. Where previous historians of English labour had for decades focused on unemployment figures, wage differentials and urban population statistics, on Chartism and the rise of the Independent Labour Party, Thompson approached a democratic theme with an appropriate humility, researching and writing about his subject bottom-up not top-down. For Thompson, class was an expression of "community", not – as Marx had instructed – one component of a mechanistic structure. What mattered to Thompson were the numerous, semi-articulate expressions of English working men's fraternity – among the countless artisans, weavers, printers, blacksmiths, and domestic servants – that labour historians had ignored, patronised, or glossed over.

For Thompson, it was the mundane, half-forgotten details of everyday working life that told the all-important story of working-class aspirations. He was among the first to refer extensively to small-town customs, parish-pump traditions, squibs and broadsheets, semi-literate letters and diaries, and faded, repressed pamphlets, even to cite the evidence of popular ditties or quote from the ink-stained minutes of working men's clubs.

In hindsight, Thompson was painstakingly compiling an anatomy of pre-industrial Britain. He was also describing, in a very English way, the lost experience of the common man (his critics would complain that he had largely overlooked the story of working-class women), a theme traceable to Anglo-Saxon England. In part, too, as the white heat of technological change in the 1960s engulfed many ancient English communities, *The Making of the English Working Class* was an unconscious elegy for a way of life that – we can now see – has been lost for ever.

Edward Thompson was a trailblazer and a pioneer who deeply influenced a generation of English and American historiography. But he was, unwittingly, on the wrong side of history. Although he was writing in a golden age of Marxist history, around him more than a century of sociopolitical egalitarian struggle was drawing to close. Today, a generation after 1989, and the comprehensive dismantling of a once-proud intellectual tradition, it's easy to place Thompson in Trotsky's "dustbin of history", but that would be wrong. His book is, in its understated way, a revolutionary rhetorical document, showing how a dynamic culture and political consciousness of astonishing vitality were forged in the teeth of official opposition, and the dehumanising blight of mass industrialisation.

Summarising Thompson's achievement, the distinguished professor of political thought Michael Kenny has said that *The Making of the English Working Class* is one of the most influential and widely read works of English history published after 1945. To the *Observer*, it was, and remains, "a masterpiece".

Three to compare:
Christopher Hill: *The World Turned Upside Down – Radical Ideas During the English Revolution* (1972)
Eric Hobsbawm: *The Age of Revolution* (1962)
Angus Calder: *The People's War* (1969)

83. THE FEMININE MYSTIQUE
BY BETTY FRIEDAN (1963)

Betty Friedan, the godmother of the postwar US women's movement,

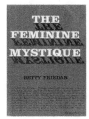

was an accidental feminist. "Until I started writing [*The Feminine Mystique*]" she confessed in 1973, "I wasn't even conscious of the woman problem." Friedan had begun her research into "the problem that has no name" – a catchy homage to "the love that dare not speak its name" of Oscar Wilde's *fin-de-siècle* disgrace – as part of her work for a question-naire of her former college classmates on their 15th reunion in 1957, thinking that she would "disprove the current notion that education had fitted us ill for our role as women".

When Friedan discovered that many of her former classmates were unhappy with their lives as women in society she pitched an article based on the questionnaire to *McCall's* magazine, which "turned the piece down in horror". By now, she was sure she was "on the track of something. But what?" Gradually, "from somewhere deep within me", a project that was now becoming a book began to take shape. "I have never experienced anything as powerful, truly mystical, as the forces that seemed to take me over when I was writing *The Feminine Mystique*", she wrote later, in an almost perfect summary of that pecu-liar literary phenomenon, the '*zeitgeist*' book.

As the critic Jay Parini has written, Friedan's work "almost single-handedly ignited a revolutionary phase that has deeply affected the lives of countless American women and men". Or, as Alvin Toffler put it, hers was a book "that pulled the trigger on history". Rarely has a title in this series flown off the shelves as this did, selling 300,000 within the first year. Thirteen foreign language translations followed. Within three years of the book's publication, Friedan had sold more than 3m copies.

Friedan herself professed puzzlement about what it was she had identified, right up to publication. After five years research and hard work in the New York Public Library, she continued to see herself as the prisoner of "that mystique, which kept us passive". Indeed, in common with many American women of the early 1960s, she "thought there was something wrong with me because I didn't have an orgasm waxing the kitchen floor. I was a freak, writing that book."

Today, *The Feminine Mystique* seems far from freaky, at times even staid verging on reactionary. Still, it retains a polemical undertow that's plainly designed to shift the minds of her readers. Compared to the other classic postwar statement of feminism, *The Second Sex* by Simone de Beauvoir, Friedan speaks quite practically to the concerns of middle-class American housewives, but mainly about the independent woman's life in house and home. "The problem," begins Friedan's narrative, "lay buried, unspoken, for many years in the minds of American women. Each suburban wife struggled with it alone. As she made the beds, shopped for groceries, chauffeured Cub Scouts and Brownies, lay beside her husband at night – she was afraid to ask even of herself the silent question – 'Is this all?'"

In a society famously dedicated to "the pursuit of happiness", Friedan reported that American women had lost their smiles. "I feel empty," declared this first generation of desperate housewives. Friedan intensified her argument by braiding it with one of many personal admissions: a slave to the feminine mystique, she had made her own sacrifices for "the dream of love", and become frustrated. (She, and her estranged husband, Carl, would fight about their marriage up to and beyond their eventual divorce.) Away from her failing home life, as a seasoned magazine journalist she conducted more reportage into the condition of female college students ("I don't want a career I'll have to give up", says one) following this up with a fairly simplistic assault on Freud ("the puritan old maid who sees sex everywhere") and then against social anthropology, and Margaret Mead, whom Friedan convicts for "the glorification of the female role".

Having anatomised this crisis of identity among American women, at least to her own satisfaction, Friedan wrenches her argument back to the present. She and her generation, she argues, are victims of the 20th century, specifically the depression, the Second World War, and the *anomie* of the atomic age. The baby boom, she says, was a reaction to more than a decade of dehumanising crisis, an instinctive quest for the traditional comforts of hearth and home. She is not really against this, rather determined to level the playing field for husbands and wives.

As Friedan's narrative works through sex, consumerism and dehumanisation, she builds to her stirring conclusion: "the feminine mystique has succeeded in burying millions of American women alive".

Finally, after a call to have contemporary women taking up roles "requiring initiative, leadership and responsibility", her book becomes a rallying cry, exhorting women to make change happen for themselves. Now was the time for a final breakthrough: "In the light of women's long battle for emancipation, the recent sexual counter-revolution [of the 1950s] has been perhaps a final crisis before the larva breaks out of the shell into maturity." Women, who had allowed the liberation of wartime to be taken away from them, would soon recognise their self-incarceration and break free, sexually and socially.

Friedan's sometimes awkward, occasionally inspired rhetoric would underpin women's lib, which in turn would morph into the ongoing feminist revolution in the writing of Susan Brownmiller, Germaine Greer, Gloria Steinem, Kate Millett, even Naomi Wolf's *The Beauty Myth* (1991), and many more. Few books in this series have enjoyed such a direct and immediate influence on their readership. Friedan, who died in 2006, was a magazine journalist more than a literary writer, but unquestionably a 20th century icon. To her admirers, she was the woman who changed the course of history for American women. In her obituary notice, Germaine Greer wrote a more careful verdict. Friedan had pioneered something important, even if subsequent feminists were uneasy in her company, and "though her behaviour was often tiresome, she had a point. Women don't get the respect they deserve unless they are wielding male-shaped power."

Three to compare:
AC Kinsey, *Sexual Behavior in the Human Male* (1948)
Kate Millett: *Sexual Politics* (1969)
Susan Brownmiller: *Against Our Will* (1975)

84. ARIEL
BY SYLVIA PLATH (1965)

Birthday Letters (Number 97) identifies the radioactivity buried within the work of Ted Hughes and Sylvia Plath, and recognises their place in the canon. With *Ariel*, Plath's second volume of poems, we approach the catalyst for 20th century poetry's thermonuclear explosion.

First, the terrible circumstances surrounding the first appearance of *Ariel* are essential to any reading of Plath's work. In the early years of her marriage to Ted Hughes, Plath had been the junior partner. She was known as the author of *The Colossus: and Other Poems* (1960), a well-received first collection, described by the *Guardian* as an "outstanding technical accomplishment", but not yet indicating the extraordinary power locked within Plath's literary psyche.

The key to Plath's final years, on top of the disintegration of her marriage to Hughes, lies in her lifelong fascination with her own death. As she expresses it in *Ariel,* her title poem, "I am the arrow... that flies. Suicidal, at one with the drive. Into the red eye..." Everything she wrote now was shadowed by this obsession.

Between 1961 and '62, working fast and urgently, she completed her autobiographical novel, *The Bell Jar*, writing to her mother that what she had done "is to throw together events from my own life, fictionalising to add colour – I think it will show how isolated a person feels when he is suffering a breakdown ... I've tried to picture my world and the people in it as seen through the distorting lens of a bell jar."

The Bell Jar was released by William Heinemann (publisher of *The Colossus*) in London on 14 January 1963 under the pseudonym Victoria Lucas. This was a decision inspired by Plath's desire to spare the feelings of her mother and a number of real-life characters in the novel. Plath's first novel appeared in the midst of the most bitter English winter of the century, and aroused virtually no comment.

Meanwhile, in early 1962, Plath had begun to put together the manuscript that became the framework for *Ariel*. Restlessly focusing her poetic intention, she had changed its title from *The Rival* to *A Birthday Present to Daddy* to *The Rabbit Catcher* and finally to *Ariel and*

Other Poems. She was now separated from Ted Hughes, whose affair with Assia Wevill had precipitated their break-up, and living alone with her two small children, Nick and Frieda, near Primrose Hill, London, in a house, 23 Fitzroy Road, once occupied by WB Yeats. By November 1962, she was done.

Then, in the early morning hours of her last few weeks, she wrote those poems that, as she herself predicted, would "make my name". All the poems written during the autumn of 1962, and into the new year, had been inspired by the intense solitude of her situation, and many of the final poems in *Ariel* are attributable to her predicament as a young single mother, but also to her clinical depression and the incipient breakdown that culminated in her suicide in the early morning of 11 February 1963. (Al Alvarez's account of this tragedy in his study of suicide, *The Savage God*, remains the indispensable portrait of this psychodrama.)

The poignant circumstances of Plath's death, as they became known, intensified the Anglo-American literary interest in the poet and her work. In 1965, *The Bell Jar* was republished under her own name and quickly recognised as a dark classic of contemporary feminism. But it was the publication of *Ariel* in the same year (1966 in the US) that set the seal on her posthumous fame and reputation. Here was a collection of strange, disturbing, and confessional poems whose wild and exhilarating ferocity exerted a remarkable grip on the imagination of a new generation.

Robert Lowell, in his preface to the first edition of *Ariel,* describes these as poems that are "playing Russian roulette with six cartridges in the cylinder". He was acknowledging what countless subsequent readers would discover for themselves: that *Ariel* is the volume on which Plath's reputation as one of the most original, daring and gifted poets of the last century rests.

The manuscript Plath had left behind on her death was titled *Ariel and Other Poems.* But that manuscript would not appear for more than 40 years. Instead, a rather different book called simply *Ariel* (published by Faber & Faber) reached bookshops in the UK in 1965 and sold a phenomenal 15,000 copies in 10 months. In the US edition (varying slightly from the UK edition), 12 of Plath's chosen poems were cut, 15 new ones added in their place; and several other poems moved from their original order.

Ted Hughes – of whom, towards the end of her life, she had

written "I hate and despise him so I can hardly speak" – had made the changes, inviting many searching and explosive questions about his apparent conflict of interest as Plath's executor and also the subject of her poetry. A generation would pass before an enraged feminist critique softened into a belated recognition that Hughes had fulfilled an almost impossible task with remarkable sensitivity and understanding. After all, the manuscript left behind at her death was still a work in progress.

Among these groundbreaking, and often difficult, poems are numbered several classics: Lady Lazarus, Ariel, The Moon and the Yew Tree, Daddy and Stings. Plath's fierce interrogation of herself and her feelings, and her unflinching honesty, came as a shocking revelation to poetry readers in the mid-1960s. Eventually, the *Ariel* of 1965, edited by Ted Hughes, was complemented in 2004 by a new edition, masterminded by Frieda Hughes, Plath's faithful daughter, which for the first time restored the selection and arrangement of the poems as her mother had left them.

In addition, finally, there is Ted Hughes's own response (in *Birthday Letters*) to his dead wife's phoenix-like resurgence. One of the most disturbing poems here is Suttee, his record of Plath's emergence as a poet, in which Hughes casts himself as a midwife delivering an "explosion / Of screams" and before being "engulfed / In a flood, a dam-burst thunder / Of a new myth", a birth that "sucked the oxygen out of both of us".

Many of the poems in *Birthday Letters* address the conundrum of Plath's other self. Hughes had already rehearsed this line of thought in his 1982 foreword to the first edition of Plath's journals, claiming that, although he had "spent every day with her for six years, and was rarely separated from her for more than two or three hours at a time", he had never seen "her show her real self to anybody – except, perhaps, in the last three months of her life".

Despite the unreconciled dialogue between husband and wife, in many conflicting registers, *Ariel* survives the obsessive extra-literary attention directed towards Plath and Hughes in the more than 50 years since Plath's suicide. For many readers, it is likely to remain one of the great volumes in the Anglo-American canon.

Three to compare:
A Alvarez: *The Savage God* (1974)
Sylvia Plath: *Letters Home: Correspondence 1950-63*
(ed Aurelia Plath) (1975)
Sylvia Plath: *The Unabridged Journals* (ed Karen V Kukil) (2000)

85. AGAINST INTERPRETATION
BY SUSAN SONTAG (1966)

Susan Sontag saw herself as a novelist. However, the years between 1962, when she completed her first novel, *The Bene-factor*, and 1965, when she began her second, *Death Kit*, were for Sontag "a sharply defined period" in which she wrote many of the literary critical and cultural pieces that came to define her even more strongly than her fiction.

In her *Paris Review* interview of 1994, Sontag confessed: "Writing essays has always been laborious. They go through many drafts, and the end result may bear little relation to the first draft; often I completely change my mind in the course of writing an essay. Fiction comes much easier, in the sense that the first draft contains the essentials – tone, lexicon, velocity, passions – of what I eventually end up with." Sontag's earliest essays, nonetheless, have a heady and self-confident originality. This collection for instance contains two modern classics, Against Interpretation and Notes on Camp, as well as discussions of Lévi-Strauss, Sartre, Camus, Beckett, Godard, a memorable demolition of Ionesco, together with psychoanalysis and science fiction cinema. Sontag, who came to influence generations of readers around the world and saw herself at war with philistinism, was nothing if not transgressive. And always intensely varied.

In the same *Paris Review* interview, she said of her writing that "it's supposed to be diverse, though of course there is a unity of temperament, of preoccupation – certain predicaments, certain emotions that recur – ardour and melancholy. And an obsessive concern with human cruelty, whether cruelty in personal relations or the cruelty of war."

Notes on Camp, which first appeared in 1964 in the *Partisan Review*, an early patron, fell to one side of that "unity", but caused a sensation that propelled Sontag to instant prominence in American intellectual circles. Summarising Sontag's reputation, *Time* magazine declared that "she has come to symbolise the writer and thinker in many variations: as analyst, rhapsodist, and roving eye, as public scold and portable conscience".

Sontag would have been gratified by such a description. "I had come to New York at the start of the 1960s," she wrote later, "eager to put to work the writer I had pledged myself to become." Her aesthetic was, and would remain, omnivorous. "My idea of a writer: someone interested in 'everything' … The only surprise was that there weren't more people like me."

But of course there weren't. Sontag was inimitable, in both life and work. Her writing quickly became the quintessential commentary to the 1960s, which was unfolding, raucously, and sometimes violently, around her in New York. Typically, she spurned any kind of easy pigeonhole. "It wasn't the 60s then. For me it was chiefly the time when I wrote my first and second novels, and began to discharge some of the cargo of ideas about art and culture and the proper business of consciousness which had distracted me from writing fiction. I was filled with evangelical zeal."

In its review of this volume, the *New York Times* latched on to Sontag's moralistic side, describing her as a "thoroughly American figure standing at the centre of Against Interpretation. The dress is new, true enough, and the images strange. The haunting image is that of a lady of intelligence and apparent beauty hastening along city streets at the violet hour, nervous, knowing, strained, excruciated (as she says) by self-consciousness, bound for the incomprehensible cinema, or for the concert hall where non-music is non-played, or for the loft where cherry bombs explode in her face and flour sacks are flapped close to her, where her ears are filled with mumbling, senseless sound and she is teased, abused, enveloped, deliberately frustrated until – until we, her audience, make out suddenly that this scene is, simply, hell, and that the figure in it (but naturally) is old-shoe-American: a pilgrim come again, a flagellant, one more self-lacerating Puritan."

This is super-fine, as far as it goes, but it misses Sontag's appetite for intellectual exhibitionism. There was, I think, always more than a touch of Oscar Wilde about "Miss Sontag". Like Wilde, she was a self-confessed "pugnacious aesthete"; like Wilde she revelled in aphorism; and, like Wilde, she absolutely refused to play safe. Despite the promise of her brilliant university career, she had other ideas. "I was not going to settle for being an academic: I would pitch my tent outside the seductive, stony safety of the university world."

Like her contemporary, Germaine Greer, Sontag was for "freedom", a throwing off of "old hierarchies", but she was also self-consciously placing herself squarely in a line of American thought: "The ardours I was advocating seemed to me – still seem to me – quite traditional. I saw myself as a newly minted warrior in a very old battle: against philistinism, against ethical and aesthetic shallowness and indifference."

As well as commenting on the 60s, Sontag came to embody the decade. "How one wishes," she wrote later, "that some of its boldness, its optimism, its disdain for commerce had survived. The two poles of distinctively modern sentiment are nostalgia and utopia. Perhaps the most interesting characteristic of the time now labelled 'the 60s' was that there was so little nostalgia. In that sense, it was indeed a utopian moment. The world in which these essays were written no longer exists."

Sontag's work, however, unequivocally outlives her. The title essay, which even carries an epigraph from Wilde ("It is only shallow people who do not judge by appearances. The mystery of the world is the visible, not the invisible") sounds a passionate appeal for "an erotics of art".

Sontag's Wildean provocations reached their apogee in her famous 1964 essay, Notes on Camp, also collected here. The debt to Wilde is manifest on almost every page. Remarkably, Sontag holds her own with verve. "The essence of camp," she begins, "is its love of the unnatural: of artifice and exaggeration. And Camp is esoteric – something of a private code, a badge of identity, even, among small urban cliques." Cleverly recognising that "it's embarrassing to be solemn and treatise-like about Camp" and run the risk of having perpetrated "a very inferior piece of Camp", Sontag proceeds to set out 58 witty and coruscating numbered "notes", culminating in the ultimate Camp statement: "It's good because it's awful."

What we need now, more than ever: this kind of originality and risk.

Three to compare:
Susan Sontag: *Illness As Metaphor* (1978)
Camille Paglia: *Vamps & Tramps* (1994)
Susan Sontag: *In America* (2000)

86. THE DOUBLE HELIX
BY JAMES D WATSON (1968)

Jim Watson was just 24 when, in collaboration with Francis Crick,

he decoded the structure of DNA, "the molecule of life". This was a 20th century watershed, the solution to one of the great enigmas of the life sciences that would revolutionise biochemistry. In human history, without exaggeration, nothing would ever be the same again.

Watson arrived at the Cavendish Laboratory, Cambridge University, during the autumn of 1951 looking for success, fame and the love of women.

He was brash, brilliant and American; a graduate zoologist from the mid-west who dreamed of winning the Nobel prize. Watson, as arrogant as he was obscure, found himself working with an equally self-possessed but somewhat overlooked older man at the Cavendish, Francis Crick, a 35-year-old would-be biophysicist who had seen service as a scientist in the Second World War. In his breezy, tactless way, Watson describes his new colleague as "totally unknown [and] often not appreciated. Most people thought he talked too much."

Soon, however, they became inseparable, habitually meeting in the Eagle, a popular Cambridge pub, a test tube's throw from their lab. It was here that they would chew over the science issues of the day. Crick and Watson both knew that the structure of deoxyribonucleic acid (DNA) and its role in human heredity was the unconquered Everest of contemporary biochemistry. Research teams in London, Europe and California had been struggling with this mystery for at least a decade. It was the postwar science story. Watson seems to have become the catalyst for Crick's frustrated creativity. With a surprisingly modest combined experience of advanced biochemistry, this maverick duo set out to solve the 20th century's greatest scientific conundrum: the secret of life itself.

Watson's personal account of their quest is both uncompromisingly honest and extraordinarily exciting, a searing portrait of two young men taking on the Anglo-American scientific establishment and winning against the odds. As some wounded participants in this story later observed, Watson's American brashness translates into the Pepys-like candour, even naivete, of "honest Jim", of whom the best one can say is that he is almost as hard on himself as anyone else. *The Double Helix* portrays a young scientist who will pick your intellectual pocket while chatting you up at your laboratory bench, before haring off to chase another Cambridge au pair girl, or "popsy", in his American slang. Crick himself never fell out with his colleague, but he did take issue with the reckless candour of Watson's account – a unique, compelling, and partisan picture of a scientific community riven with rivalries, hatreds, feuds and ambitions. Peter Medawar, the best science writer of the 60s, identified it immediately as "a classic".

From 1951 to 1953, Crick and Watson embarked on a race for immortality. They faced formidable but flawed competition. Linus Pauling in California and Maurice Wilkins in London had both been studying ways to crack DNA for years, and were close to a breakthrough. But Pauling, despite massive resources, was prone to catastrophic errors. Closer to home, Wilkins (a friend of Crick's) was at loggerheads with his brilliant x-ray crystallographer, the troubled figure of Dr Rosalind Franklin. Could Crick and Watson, two carpetbaggers from the Cavendish, acquire enough data to begin the advanced thought-experiment required to demonstrate and verify the structure of DNA?

Watson, the inevitable protagonist of *The Double Helix*, managed to get himself invited to a Franklin lecture in London and saw at once that her x-ray crystallography work held the key to the mystery of DNA. With hindsight, Franklin was too close to her research to grasp its significance. She was also mired in a toxic professional relationship with Wilkins, her boss. Nevertheless, Watson's account of Franklin, the tragic figure in this story, remains exceedingly distasteful: cruel, misogynist, and flippant.

Subsequently, a full-blown biography by Brenda Maddox, subtitled *The Dark Lady of DNA*, has described the degree to which Franklin, who died from ovarian cancer in 1958, had perhaps unwittingly established the context of the work that Crick and Watson would develop and conclude so triumphantly. In his tight-lipped epilogue, Watson acknowledges this, conceding that Franklin "definitely [established] the essential helical parameters [of the DNA molecule] and locating the ribonucleic chain halfway out from the central axis" – a crucial admission.

He also makes a belated kind of apology to her memory, conceding how he and Crick had come to appreciate "her personal honesty and generosity, realising years too late the struggles that the intelligent woman faces to be accepted by a scientific world which often regards women as mere diversions from serious thinking."

With a sombre expression of feeling distinctly absent from his portrait of the woman he had nicknamed "Rosy", Watson concludes that "Rosalind's exemplary courage and integrity were apparent to all when, knowing she was mortally ill, she did not complain but continued working on a high level until a few weeks before her death."

Slowly, the "helical theory" took shape. Proving this still-controversial working hypothesis was the problem. "Crick and the American", as they were known in Cambridge, were hardly helped by their bosses. "Francis and I," writes Watson, were told that they must "give up on DNA" because there was "nothing original" in their approach. Watson describes feeling "up the creek" after this decision. By the middle of 1951, he writes, the prospect "that anyone on the British side of the Atlantic would crack DNA looked dim". Meanwhile, far away in California, Pauling was known to be making steady progress.

But Watson had not abandoned his quest for glory. Covertly, he continued to work after hours at the Cavendish on the "helical" structure of DNA. By late 1952, Pauling had still made no new announcement. This was encouraging. "If Pauling had found a really exciting answer," writes Watson, "the secret could not be kept for long. One of his graduate students must certainly know what his model looked like, and the rumour would have quickly reached us." As it turned out, the news from California was far better than the Cambridge team could have expected. When, finally, Pauling did publish his latest theory, it contained a basic and fundamental flaw. Watson could not conceal his exhilaration: "Though the odds still appeared against us, Linus had not yet won his Nobel."

In retrospect, though progress seemed agonisingly protracted and uncertain, Crick and Watson's breakthrough occurred at warp speed, driven by "the American's" obsessive ambition. Watson, indeed, never stopped testing new hypotheses for the structure of DNA against Crick's wiser scepticism. Eventually, chance took a hand. It was a casual conversation Watson had with "an American crystallographer", who had fortuitously been assigned to his lab, that provided the germ of the idea that would survive Crick's scrutiny. On Watson's account, it was during the late winter of 1953 that "Francis winged into the Eagle to tell everyone that we had found the secret of life".

The "double helix", commissioned by Watson, was at once supremely beautiful, wonderfully elegant and fundamentally simple. In Watson's words: "Immediately [Crick] caught on to the complementary relation between the two chains and saw how an equivalence of adenine with thymine and guanine with cystosine was a logical consequence of the regular repeating shape of the sugar-phosphate backbone."

Towards the end of March 1953, Crick and Watson began to write the 900-word article for *Nature* that would change biochemistry for ever, and add their names to the roll call of great scientists: "We wish to suggest a structure for the salt of deoxyribonucleic acid (DNA). This structure has novel features which are of considerable biological interest." Rarely have two English sentences contained so much exhilarated understatement.

Watson's research career, described in *The Double Helix*, a wide-eyed, whirlwind account of unheated university lodgings, handwritten correspondence, chance encounters in pubs or on the Cambridge train and unexpected phone calls, is a world away from the science of today. It is more than slightly personal and unequivocally "heroic"; it celebrates contingency and chance and the unscientific qualities of pride, secrecy, chauvinism and low cunning. It is raw, rash and unputdownable. In taking an impossibly complex subject and rendering an account for the ordinary reader, it has inspired a generation of accessible science writing as well as, perhaps, the popularising work of writers such as Malcolm Gladwell (*Blink*; *Outliers*) and Michael Lewis (*The New New Thing*).

Three to compare:
Erwin Schrödinger: *What Is Life?* (1944)
Francis Crick: *Of Molecules and Men* (1966)
Brenda Maddox: Rosalind Franklin: *The Dark Lady of DNA* (2002)

87. Awopbopaloobop Alopbamboom
by Nik Cohn (1969)

Pop, the cultural revolution of the late 20th century, has touched art, poetry, fiction, and everything musical, with its hot white wand. In the beginning, in the 1960s, pop was sex and drugs and rock'n'roll: a way of life. A lot of young journalists covered it, but very few transcended the genre to create a narrative that would outlive the generation that hoped it would die before it got old. *Awopbop ...*, however, a luminously clear, aerial survey of an extraordinary phenomenon, set the gold standard that others would follow.

Nik Cohn's dispatch from the frontline of rock is about to turn 50 (its author is now in his 70s) and is still as evergreen and wild-eyed as it was when it burst on to the scene, with a snarl and a stamping foot, in 1969. Since then, many Scandinavian forests have been laid waste to describe the pop revolution, with names such as Greil Marcus, Philip Norman and Jon Savage jostling for attention at the front of a crowded field, but Nik Cohn was the first. No one had taken the subject quite as seriously as he did. There was nothing before him and there has been nothing quite as raw or as memorable since. Different, yes; sweeter, for sure; more searching, possibly; but never as fearless, flashy or straight-out thrilling. Written in a white heat, like some of the best journalism, *Awopbop ...* supplied the last word. Here, in 250 pages, was a new form: rock criticism.

This was a new kind of critical discourse, the strange fruit of a personal and passionate love affair, smoking with teenage intensity. "From the first blast of Tutti Frutti," writes Cohn, "rock'n'roll had possessed me, body and soul." From 1956 to 1968, the year Cohn signed off, he covered the "first mad rush" of a phenomenon that would eventually morph into disco, heavy metal, grunge, glam, techno, punk and many bizarre sub-genres.

At first, Cohn wrote as a freelance, prowling the streets of Soho, and later for the uber-cool *Queen* magazine. Eventually, he got a job "pontificating on yoof" for the *Observer*. The celebrated record producer (and manager of the Who) Kit Lambert recalls Cohn showing up "about 1963" as a "thin young man – he looked about 14 – wearing carefully dirtied-down sneakers". Cohn's approach was perfectly in tune with his subject. He writes: "Rock in the late 60s was still a spontaneous combustion. Nobody bothered with long-term strategies; hanging on once the thrill was gone was unthinkable. If anyone had told me then that the Stones or The Who would still be treading the boards in 30-plus years, I'd have thought they were out of their minds."

Cohn, the son of the historian Norman Cohn, author of a cult classic, *The Pursuit of the Millennium*, had grown up in Ireland, but escaped to London by 1963, "the year the Beatles broke through, and the climate seemed to change by the day". The metropolitan feeding frenzy he became part of was not confined to rock'n'roll. He writes that "newspaper editors, book publishers, fashion mags and film financiers were all caught up in the same fever. Almost overnight, being a teen degenerate was the hottest ticket around."

By the time he was 22, these heady days were done. "Even as I was pigging out on the moment," Cohn recalls, "rock and pop were already changing. The world I knew and savoured was basically an outlaw trade, peopled with adventurers, snake-oil salesmen, inspired lunatics. But their time was almost over. The scene was becoming more industrial. Accountants and corporate fat cats were fast driving out the wild men." Before long, rock had become "just another branch of commerce, no more or less exotic than autos or detergents".

Cohn's account of this "mad rush" is at once an elegy, a retrospective and a lingering goodbye. In 1968, he took a publisher's advance and holed up in Connemara for seven weeks to write the first draft of what would become a kind of farewell to arms. "My purpose was simple," he said later, "to catch the feel, the pulse of rock, as I had lived through it ... I simply wrote off the top of my head, whatever and however the spirit moved me. Accuracy didn't seem of prime importance. What I was after was guts, and flash, and energy, and speed. Those were the things I'd treasured in the rock I'd loved."

Awopbop ... was the result: subjective, unruly and unintentionally definitive. Questions about good and/or bad were afterthoughts and accidental. Cohn was riffing off memories and impressions. "Did Dion's Ruby Baby have any aesthetic value?" he asks. "Who cared? What it had was dirty magic – the slurred, sex-drunk vocal, those shambolic handclaps, the whole glorious unmade bed."

From Bill Haley to Jimi Hendrix, Cohn runs the gamut of rock'n'roll, with chapters on Elvis Presley, the twist, Phil Spector, the

Beatles, the Rolling Stones, the Who, Bob Dylan, even the Monkees. "What I've written about," he concludes, "has been the rise and fall of Superpop, the noise machine, and the image, hype and beautiful flash of rock'n'roll music. Elvis riding in his golden Cadillac, James Brown throwing off his robes in a fit, Pete Townshend slaughtering his audience with his machine-gun guitar, Mick Jagger hanging off his mike like Tarzan Weissmuller in the jungle, PJ Proby – all the heroic acts of pulp." Cohn was never American, but the wild chords of 60s' new journalism had left their mark on his style, shaping it into the perfect medium for a new kind of reportage, the journalism of correspondents in motley and denim, not mufti or combat fatigues. Finally, the last war was over, replaced by peace and love and the illusion of immortality.

Three to compare:
George Melly: *Revolt Into Style* (1970)
Greil Marcus: *Mystery Train* (1975)
Jon Savage: *England's Dreaming: The Sex Pistols and Punk Rock* (1991)

88. THE FEMALE EUNUCH
BY GERMAINE GREER (1970)

Some of the outstanding books in this series are polemical and

rhetorical as much as revolutionary. In the literature of gender identity, *The Female Eunuch* is already a classic, a bestselling masterpiece of passionate free expression by a writer steeped in the English literary tradition. Australia's Germaine Greer, the woman who has described herself as "an anarchist, basically", was captured in an *Observer* profile of 2003:

"She has been in the business of shaking up a complacent establishment for nearly 40 years now, and was employing the most elemental shock tactic of getting naked in public both long before and long after it ever crossed Madonna's mind. Indeed, she has never shied away from exposing herself; whether photographically, in counterculture periodicals such as *Oz* and the unambiguously titled *Suck*, or in memoirs such as her 1990 book *Daddy, We Hardly Knew You*. She has repeatedly written about her own experiences of lesbian sex, rape, abortion, infertility, failed marriage (in the 1960s she was married to a construction worker for three weeks) and the menopause, thereby leaving herself open to claims that she shamelessly extrapolates from her own condition to the rest of womankind and calls it a theory. She is the original mother of reinvention."

Greer is always her own best material. It's her voice that sets her work apart, and her inimitable tone – earthy erudition spliced with abrasive advocacy – that gives *The Female Eunuch* its unique narrative power. When he reviewed *The Female Eunuch* in the *Observer*, Kenneth Tynan recognised this. He wrote that Greer "has converted me to women's lib, as much by her bawdy sense of humour as by the bite of her polemic".

From first publication, this liberating, sometimes intimidating, book soon became mythologised. As a revolutionary manifesto, there are many things it's not: principally, it's not about sexual equality for women of the world, though that may have been a message her readers took away. Greer's explicit liberation struggle focuses on the self, not the collective. She wants a new society in which women write their own script, set their own agenda, and make their own deep personal choices. The "women" Greer addresses are not the majority of womankind – she concedes that she does not "know" poor people – but people like herself, university graduates, the comparatively privileged members of the western democracies. The books her work complements are Betty Friedan's *The Feminine Mystique* and Kate Millett's *Sexual Politics*, both of which are less accessible, and more earnestly part of the women's movement in its early days. From that springboard Greer, the self-confessed "anarchist" (elsewhere, a "privileged escapee"), was able to vault over a lot of tedious barricade-building before establishing her own risky and raucous front line in the sex wars of the late 20th century.

Greer herself was under no illusions about her place in the maelstrom of socio-cultural change that exploded around her in the late 1960s. Her work, she declared on the first page of *The Female Eunuch*, was just "part of the second feminist wave". This, for some, was about the forging of a classless society and the withering away of the state. Not Greer. Where once, in suffragette days, genteel middle-class ladies had clamoured for reform, the Greer of circa 1970 wanted one thing: freedom. "Freedom to be a person, with the dignity, integrity, nobility, passion, and pride that constitutes personhood. Freedom to run, shout, to talk loudly and sit with your knees apart."

In retrospect, perhaps disingenuously, she hoped her book would "quickly date and disappear" as the feminist revolution swept all before it. The movement, of course, did no such thing, and Greer's bright hopes for "a new breed of women" for whom her analysis of "sex oppression in the developed world in the second half of the 20th century would be utterly irrelevant" still remain unfulfilled. But the temptation now to read *The Female Eunuch* as outmoded, suffering the fate of all polemical literature, would be to overlook its staying power as an inspiring beacon amid a hurricane of social change.

The incandescent energy that promoted *The Female Eunuch's* ecstatic iconoclasm, especially to the new generation of the 1970s, came from a young woman who was just 31 on publication, craving freedom from the suffocations and cruelties of patriarchy, freedom from condescension, casual humiliation and abuse. Greer's was a manifesto for a showdown with the opposite sex. "Most of the women in the world," she writes, "are still afraid, still hungry, still mute and loaded by religion with all kinds of fetters, masked, muzzled, mutilated and beaten". However, the argument she makes about female submission in a patriarchal society is framed in terms of "liberation", not "equality". Despite occasional references to the new left, there is a striking absence of class war in *The Female Eunuch*.

She opens with a section on the body, because it is impossible, she declares, "to argue a case for female liberation if there is no certainty about the degree of inferiority or natural dependence which is unalterably female... We know what we are, but know not what we may be, or what we might have been."

Juxtaposed with the body is not the mind, as one might expect, but the soul, which is enslaved to the subtle tyranny of all-pervasive male fantasies, anatomised in a passionate sequence entitled "the stereotype". It's here that the narrative and many of its more fervent declarations ("I am sick of the Powder Room") now read like a first draft for its author's autobiography, and sometimes even like a fragment of literary criticism.

The Female Eunuch closes with a call to arms, a passionate but vague appeal for revolution, a rhetorical flourish which must, to any committed 21st century feminist, seem almost comically thin. "The surest guide to the correctness of the path that women must take," instructs Greer in her closing pages, "is joy in the struggle". What might that be? "Revolution," she declares, "is the festival of the oppressed. For a long time there may be no perceptible reward for women other than their new sense of purpose and integrity. Joy does not mean riotous glee, but it does mean the purposive employment of energy in a self-chosen enterprise." These words might almost be a definition of Germaine Greer's subsequent career path.

Social earthquakes of any consequence have their absurdities and confusions. Going over the top is part of every revolutionary's job description. The radical feminism of the 1970s has worn about as well as the radical socialism that preceded the Thatcher counter-revolution, which is to say: quite badly. Nevertheless women's lib, combined with the new left, did achieve lasting social and cultural change. *The Female Eunuch* was one of many catalysts in that ferment, with Germaine Greer its merry, and dazzling provocateur, a mischievous hybrid of lab assistant and sorcerer's apprentice. Nearly 50 years on, who could not find it in their hearts to salute the queen of such revels?

Three to compare:
Betty Friedan: *The Feminine Mystique* (1963)
Kate Millett: *Sexual Politics* (1970)
Germaine Greer: *The Whole Woman* (1999)

89. AWAKENINGS
BY OLIVER SACKS (1973)

Among the great books in this series that address the human condi-

tion, *Awakenings* stands out as a profoundly influential medical classic from the 1970s, whose extraordinary narrative continues to reverberate.

Awakenings has inspired short stories, poems, novels and plays, notably Harold Pinter's *A Kind of Alaska*. Its central themes – falling asleep, being turned to stone, being awakened, decades later, to a world no longer one's own – grip the imagination like the best drama, with this difference: the events described by the late Oliver Sacks actually happened.

The "sleepy sickness" pandemic of 1916-17, which persisted into the 1920s, ravaged the lives of nearly 5 million people before it disappeared, as mysteriously and suddenly as it had appeared, in 1927. A third of those afflicted by *encephalitis lethargica* died in its acute stages, in advanced states of coma or sleeplessness. Other patients who suffered an extremely severe somnolent/insomnia attack often failed ever to recover their original vitality and lived out their days, cut off from humanity, in a deeply strange, inaccessible, frozen state ("a kind of Alaska"), oblivious to the passage of time or what had befallen them. These survivors were described by the doctor who first identified *encephalitis lethargica* as "extinct volcanoes". They would sit motionless and speechless all day in their chairs, totally lacking energy, impetus, initiative, motive, appetite or desire.

In the majority of cases, these patients had their thoughts and feelings unchangingly fixed at the point at which their long "sleep" had closed in on them. For many survivors, this was the 1920s, a time that would remain more real to them than any subsequent decade. Their minds, however, remained clear and unclouded. And yet, unable to work or see to their needs, frequently abandoned by their friends and families, these patients were put away in hospitals, nursing homes and lunatic asylums and forgotten, like lepers of the 20th century. Yet some lived on, getting older and frailer, inmates of institutions, profoundly isolated, deprived of experience, half-forgetting, half-dreaming of the world they had once lived in.

In 1969, after more than 40 years of lives as insubstantial as ghosts and as passive as zombies, these "extinct volcanoes", scattered in hospitals for chronic neurological disability in Britain, Europe and the US, erupted into life through the intervention of a remarkable new "awakening" drug, L-Dopa *(laevodihydroxyphenylalanine)*. In one hospital in particular – the Beth Abraham in the Bronx – some 80 patients, long regarded as effectively moribund, returned explosively to life.

Oliver Sacks was the brilliant young neurologist who administered the wonder drug, keeping meticulous notes on his patients' recovery. *Awakenings* became his account of a unique experience, the return to humanity of men and women whose personalities had become immured in post-encephalitic torpor. This could be a rollercoaster ride. Some of L-Dopa's side-effects had a frightening intensity: in one patient's words: "I can no more control it than I could control a spring tide. I just ride it out and wait for the storm to clear ... That L-Dopa, that stuff should be given its proper name – Hell-Dopa!"

While such cerebral storms raged, Sacks took notes. "I cannot think back on this time without profound emotion," he wrote later. "It was the most significant and extraordinary moment in my life, no less than in the lives of our patients. All of us at Mount Carmel [Beth Abraham] were caught up with the emotion, the excitement, with something akin to enchantment, even awe."

Young Dr Sacks was not just a gifted neurologist blessed with a brilliant idea for a revolutionary treatment – he was also a passionate writer, committed to reporting an extraordinary story that was unfolding before him from day to day. In the spring of 1969, he writes: "I moved to an apartment a hundred yards from the hospital and would sometimes spend 12 or 15 hours a day with our patients – observing them, talking with them, getting them to keep notebooks, and keeping voluminous notes myself, thousands of words each day. And if I had a pen in one hand, I had a camera in the other: I was seeing such things as had never, perhaps, been seen before – and which, in all probability, would never be seen again." It was, said Sacks, his duty and his joy "to record and bear witness". The upshot was *Awakenings.*

The strangeness of life in Sacks's Mount Carmel is captured in the concluding moments of the life of Magda B, who had "a sudden premonition of death". In Sacks's account, "her tone was quite sober and factual, wholly unexcited ... In the evening Mrs B went round the ward, with a laughter-silencing dignity, shaking hands and saying 'Goodbye' to everyone there. She went to bed," Sacks continues, "and she died in the night." *Awakenings*, which pitches the reader into the drama of many such moments, is a voyage into the strange and often disturbing mystery of the human brain.

Sacks's stories become a kind of memoir, a neurological romance and a profoundly sympathetic essay on the human condition. Readers who watch Duncan Dallas's TV documentary *Awakenings,* in conjunction with the book, will have an unforgettable insight into a unique neurological experiment.

Three to compare:

Jean-Martin Charcot: *De la paralysie agitant: Leçons sur les maladies du système nerveux* (1880)

Harold Pinter: *A Kind of Alaska* (1982)

Oliver Sacks: *The Man Who Mistook His Wife for a Hat* (1985)

90. NORTH
BY SEAMUS HEANEY (1975)

Alongside his friend Ted Hughes, Seamus Heaney was among the finest late 20th century poets writing in the English language. Heaney's greatness was cultural as well as lyrical: he saw it as his inescapable duty to attempt a mood of reconciliation among his community. His work, rooted in his native Ireland, always had to navigate the murderous vicissitudes of the Troubles, the civil war that traumatised Northern Ireland for 30 terrible years, from the civil rights march of October 1968 to the Good Friday agreement of April 1998.

To be a writer, especially a famous poet, in this war zone was to confront a challenge that was political, artistic and tribal. Both Heaney's parents came from Roman Catholic families in Protestant Ulster. Throughout his life, his origins placed him at the lethal crossroads of sectarian conflict and Irish nationalism. That was an unenviable and dangerous location at the best of times, and he learned to become highly attuned to the history and heritage of oppression. He always contrived to move, as he put it, "like a double agent among the big concepts".

Heaney's *North,* published during one of the darkest times in a vicious war, reflects this instinctive ambivalence while being, at the same time, one of his most passionate collections, acknowledging both his roots and his loyalties. Crucially, whatever his deepest feelings, Heaney is never strident. Throughout this volume there's a steady undertow of irony. For the poet, that is fundamental to Ulster life. When I interviewed him in Dublin for the *Observer* in 2009, he spoke about the "articulate mockery" deployed by all the combatants in the Troubles. "The irony is so important," he said. "In the north, northern irony has allowed people to stand at the edge of the rift and shout across to each other."

Rereading *North*, more than 40 years on, in the 21st century, it's surprising to discover how raw and unguarded some of its emotions turn out to be. In *North*, an early collection, Heaney is not as diplomatic as he would later become, especially after winning the Nobel prize in 1995. In Whatever You Say, Say Nothing, he notes with dread the fearsome "eructation of Orange drums", and describes the "crater of fresh clay" left by a roadside bomb, and the "machine-gun posts" set up by the British army. This, he says, is "our little destiny".

Heaney's own destiny was to steer a middle path. "I am," he wrote in Exposure, the concluding poem in *North*, "neither internee nor informer." He would remain an "inner émigré" for the rest of his life, steadily articulating a vision of Ireland that, finally, coheres into a most resonant and seductive myth. He never denied the tragedies and violence that blighted the lives of an Irish generation, but he linked the darkness of his own times to memories of English and Scandinavian invasions from the past, as if to suggest that lives conducted in extremis, on the edge, have more to teach than visions of the pastoral.

Indeed, Heaney finds a kind of consolation in the savagery of the past, and locates this in the narrative of PV Glob's *The Bog People*, published by his Faber editor, Charles Monteith. This popular but scholarly account of the discovery of Tollund Man, and many related victims of prehistoric rituals and forgotten atrocities, was notable for its graphic black-and-white photographs of bodies that had become perfectly preserved in the peat bogs of Denmark. Glob's *Bog People* directly inspired four poems: Bog Queen, The Grauballe Man, Punishment, and Strange Fruit, as well as references to primitive violence in Funeral Rites and North, the title poem. These follow Tollund Man, which had appeared in *Wintering Out* (1972). In *North*, these horrific images have begun to acquire a much deeper meaning for the poet, supplying what he identified as "symbols adequate to our predicament".

Critics will doubtless continue to argue about the focus and subject of that "predicament". Was it addressed to "the north" as a whole, or just the Roman Catholics of Heaney's province? The poet himself never wanted to be drawn into that argument. Now that he is dead, too young at 74, the question is academic. Besides, shading into art, *North* transcends politics. Some readers will prefer his first collection, *Death of a Naturalist*, but for me it's the brilliant reconciliation of art with politics that sets *North* apart from the rest of Heaney's oeuvre and gives it a kind of dark majesty.

In *Death of a Naturalist*, he found his voice; in *North* he put that voice to the service of his people. He told me: "Your language has a lot to do with your confidence, your sense of place and authority" and added that speaking his own language, Irish English, was to acquire a trust in the pronunciation and in the quirks of vocabulary, and "to go through a kind of political reawakening".

Three to compare:
Paul Muldoon: *Why Brownlee Left* (1980)
Michael Longley: *The Weather in Japan* (2000)
Derek Mahon: *Harbour Lights* (2005)

91. THE SELFISH GENE
BY RICHARD DAWKINS (1976)

What is man, and what are we for? Remarkably, it was not until

Charles Darwin published *On the Origin of Species* in 1859 that anyone, in our history, had thought methodically to address the reason for our existence. Darwin's answer to this simple question was to show that every earthly species – chimps or humans, lizards or fungus – had evolved over about 3bn years by the process known as natural selection.

But then, after the furious controversy surrounding that publication, Darwin's celebrated theory fell into neglect and misuse. A hundred years later, in the heady, innovative atmosphere of the 1960s, a new generation of young and ambitious evolutionary biologists found themselves confronted with a rare opportunity: the rediscovery and renewal of evolutionary theory. Enter Richard Dawkins, a young Oxford zoologist who had been born, and partly raised, in Africa. Following some notable pioneers such as WD Hamilton and GC Williams, Dawkins pulled together many disparate strands of thought about the nature of natural selection, and organised them into a conceptual framework with far-reaching implications for our understanding of Darwin's ideas. He called it *The Selfish Gene*, a title he later considered to contain an unconscious echo of Oscar Wilde's *The Selfish Giant*. Dawkins was convinced that an amplified and developed version of neo-Darwinism "could make everything about life fall into place, in the heart as well as in the brain". His book would extol, he wrote, a "gene's-eye view of evolution".

It was Dawkins's simple, but profound, proposition that "the funda-mental unit of selection, and therefore of self-interest, is not the species, nor the group, nor even, strictly, the individual. It is the gene, the unit of heredity." He acknowledged that this might sound "at first like an extreme view" but proceeded to explore all the major themes of social theory in the light of this idea, conducting his survey in a highly readable and entertaining way. With chapters such as "Genesmanship", "Battle of the Sexes", and "Nice Guys Finish First", he tackled concepts of altruism and selfishness, the evolution of aggressive behaviour, kinship theory, sex ratio theory, reciprocal altruism, deceit, and the natural selection of sex differences. In hindsight, it seems appropriate that *The Selfish Gene* should have been published soon after *The Joy of Sex* and *The Female Eunuch*.

From his first page, Dawkins unfolds an exhilarating and combative narrative of the gene's-eye view of life with infectious brio. *The Selfish Gene*, he declares, should be read "almost as though it were science fiction. It is designed to appeal to the imagination." Part of the book's compulsion derives from Dawkins's appealing certainty that he is exploring a scientific world in which "we are survival machines – robot vehicles blindly programmed to preserve the selfish molecules known as genes". This insight, he reports, is "a truth which still fills me with astonishment".

Much of this book's appeal lies in its author's barely suppressed excitement, prose that bubbles over with the intoxication of a brilliant new approach. He buttonholes his readers; he dazzles with paradox and provocation. In an introduction to a later edition of *The Selfish Gene*, Dawkins describes its gestation: it was a book written in extremis (the power cuts and industrial strife of the early 1970s) and, as he says, "in a fever of excitement". For the young author, it was, in hindsight, "one of those mysterious periods in which new ideas are hovering in the air".

So much part of the *zeitgeist* was it that, from first publication, the reception of *The Selfish Gene* was highly favourable. Initially, it was not seen as a controversial book, Dawkins wrote later. "Its reputation for contentiousness took years to grow." Eventually it would become regarded as a work of extreme radicalism. But, he goes on, "over the very same years as the book's reputation for extremism has escalated, its actual content has seemed less and less extreme".

This is undeniable: while *The Selfish Gene* grew out of orthodox neo-Darwinian ideas, it actually expressed Darwinism in a way that Darwin himself might have welcomed. Rather than focus on the individual organism, it looked at nature from the perspective of the gene. It was, claimed Dawkins, "a different way of seeing, not a different theory".

It also addressed itself to "three imaginary readers": the generalist, the expert and the student. This was a high-low cohort that swiftly propelled it on to bestseller lists worldwide. Moreover, in keeping with the temper of the times, *The Selfish Gene* announced itself, from the first, as "a book about animal behaviour", arguing that "we, like all other animals, are (survival) machines created by our genes". For Dawkins, "we" did not mean just people. He wanted his description to embrace all animals, plants, bacteria and viruses. "The total number of survival machines on Earth," he wrote, "is very difficult to count." Even the total number of species is unknown, he conceded. "Taking just insects alone, the number of individual insects may be a million million million."

Dawkins – in a style that would recur in later polemical books such as *The God Delusion* – was never less than comprehensive in his ambitions. Here, he used "survival machine" rather than "animal" because he wanted to encompass all plants and humans, too. His argument should apply, he said, to any and all "evolved beings".

Orthodox neo-Darwinian he might be, but in chapter 11, he coined an idea about cultural transmission that quickly went viral within the global intellectual community: the meme, or replicator, a unit of imitation. Examples of memes include tunes, idea, catch-phrases, clothes fashions, ways of making pots or of building arches: "Just as genes propagate themselves in the gene pool by leaping from body to body via sperms or eggs, so memes propagate themselves in the meme pool by leaping from brain to brain via a process which, in the broad sense, can be called imitation." Shortly after this analysis, Dawkins characterised "God" as a meme. Thus, pages 192-193 of *The Selfish Gene* might be said to encapsulate most of Richard Dawkins's brilliant career, in which the theory of evolution came to offer such a satisfying and complete explanation for the complexity of life on Earth that there could no longer be a place for the possibility of God's design.

Three to compare:
GC Williams: *Adaptation and Natural Selection* (1961)
EO Wilson: *On Human Nature* (1978)
WD Hamilton: *Narrow Roads of Gene Land*, Vol I (1996)

92. Dispatches
by Michael Herr (1977)

Despite every other kind of progress, humanity still lives and dies in

conditions of either war or peace, a truth reflected in our literature. There is still a place for a great war book such as *Dispatches*. Like its precursors, from Homer to Hemingway, whose company it keeps, *Dispatches* seems to begin mid-sentence, plunging its readers into the war zone before they can take up defensive positions. As visitors to a place that could not be mapped ("for years now there had been no country here but the war"), Michael Herr's readers

must quickly acclimatise to the surreal experience of Vietnam in 1967, as though they have no choice: there's a war on.

Combined with the compelling urgency of Herr's narration – every line set down as if it's about to be interrupted by incoming shell-fire – there's Herr's mesmerising voice itself, perhaps the single greatest achievement of a book that, nearly 40 years on, offers the definitive account of war in our time, especially the Vietnam war – among the most terrible of the postwar wars. Inspired by the example of 1960s New Journalism, Herr's voice (after Tom Wolfe) is his own shit-scared, or doped-out, interior monologue spliced with scraps of rock'n'roll and the everyday jargon of the "grunts", the American GIs in the swamps, jungles and choppers of 'Nam in their search-and-destroy missions against "Charlie", the Viet Cong:

As well as the relentless jeopardy and the unforgettable voice in *Dispatches*, there's also Michael Herr's profound sympathy for, and grasp of, the psychology of men in combat. Thanks to his reckless immersion in the war at one of its craziest moments – working as a magazine journalist during the Tet offensive of 1967 and its aftermath – he catches the mix of humour, madness and drugs, setting it all down on the page with a rare combination of precision and compassion so that, as the reader, you think: I was there. Finally, as if all this were not enough, Herr in Vietnam (sadly, never since) is an excellent writer:

> "In Saigon I always went to sleep stoned so I always lost my dreams, probably just as well, sock in deep and dim under that information and get whatever rest you could, wake up tapped

of all images but the one remembered from the day before, with only the taste of a bad dream in your mouth like you'd been chewing on a roll of dirty old pennies in your sleep."

Some of Herr's best and most quotable passages read like hallucinations, and some simply are just that: descriptions of being stoned on the front line, like a character in *Apocalypse Now*, a film classic whose script Herr also contributed to:

"Just lying there tracking the rotations of the ceiling fan, reaching for the fat roach that sat on my Zippo in a yellow disc of grass tar. There were mornings when I'd do it before my feet even hit the floor. Dear Mom, stoned again. In the Highlands, where the Montagnards would trade you a pound of legendary grass for a carton of Salems, I got stoned with some infantry from the 4th ..."

Herr can be funny, too. Describing the US mission, he writes that "At the bottom was the shit-faced grunt, at the top of a Command trinity: a blue-eyed, hero-faced general, a geriatrics-emergency ambassador and a hale, heartless CIA performer". Namechecking an in-country spook, Robert "Blowtorch" Kromer, Herr drily adds that "if William Blake had 'reported' to him that he'd seen angels in the trees, Kromer would have tried to talk him out of it. Failing there, he'd have ordered defoliation".

Herr hooked up with an English war photographer, Tim Page, and Errol Flynn's son, Sean, who would later go missing on assignment, and went chopper-hopping round the war zone, taking huge risks, getting stranded in Khe Sanh in the winter of 1968 during its infamous siege (a brilliant set piece at the heart of *Dispatches*), surviving against the odds. Herr stuck it out till 1969, then came back to New York City with a heap of notes, a file of *Esquire* pieces, and a bat cave of toxic memories. Within 18 months of coming home, he was in the midst of a near-disabling depression, and perhaps the writing of *Dispatches* became part of his route out of hell.

The upshot was a book, published in 1977, which every journalist and writer who had ever been in a war zone – from John le Carré to Robert Stone – wished they'd written. Comparisons were made with books like *The Red Badge of Courage* and *All Quiet on the Western Front*, but this was different: it was by a writer not a soldier, and it was the writer's sensibility that made his book captivate a whole generation of readers. Another celebrated New Journalist, Hunter S Thompson, spoke for the profession when he said: "We have all spent 10 years trying to explain what happened to our heads and our lives in the decade we finally survived – but Michael Herr's *Dispatches* puts the rest of us in the shade."

Here in the UK, where Herr lived for a while during the 1980s, British war correspondents such as my *Observer* colleague Ed Vulliamy would make a point of getting an introduction: "Every writer who has tried his or her hand at war journalism," wrote Vulliamy, "would go to meet Michael Herr rather like a student of the cello would approach Mstislav Rostropovich. Apart from learning by listening, the gratifying thing is to find that one's own follies and fears are echoes of Herr's; one almost feels validated in one's quirks of judgment in the aftermath of war."

Now in a new century, and a new geopolitical landscape, it's as though everything, and nothing, has changed. As Herr writes, in another of his most haunting passages, the US army "took space back quickly, expensively, with total panic and close to maximum brutality. Our machine was devastating. And versatile. It could do everything but stop."

Three to compare:
Joseph Heller: *Catch-22* (1961)
David Halberstam: *The Best and the Brightest* (1972)
Neil Sheehan: *A Bright Shining Lie: John Paul Vann and America in Vietnam* (1988)

93. ORIENTALISM
BY EDWARD SAID (1978)

Next to the suicide bombings, the air strikes, and the beheadings, a

closely argued 300-page monograph devoted to a radical post-colonial thesis might seem to suggest a modest literary intervention. Yet in the ongoing, brutal clash of Islam and the west, Edward Said's analysis remains the book to which no combatant can be indifferent.

Orientalism is a profoundly influential and controversial study of the way in which, for at least 2,000 years, ever since the wars between the ancient Greeks and the Persians, the west has fought with, and largely dominated, the east through a persuasive colonial version of its culture and politics. Said's masterpiece has been topical ever since its publication shortly before the 1979 Iranian revolution. Today, in an even more unstable world, it must be ranked high on any list of key texts related to the contemporary sociopolitical crises of the 21st century.

Said, a highly sophisticated and brilliant public intellectual, drew on his experience as an Arab-Palestinian living in the west to examine the way in which, from culture to religion, the west imperialised the ancient and complex societies of north Africa, the Middle East, and Asia. He would argue that the Gulf wars, and the catastrophe of Iraq, are a direct consequence of a fateful and crude ideology rooted deeply in the western mind.

Any summary of Said's immensely subtle analysis of western attitudes and conduct towards the east risks becoming a travesty. However, in simplified terms, *Orientalism* examines the history of how the west, especially the empires of Britain and France, created a thought process to deal with the "otherness" of eastern society, customs and beliefs. As Said himself puts it, "I study orientalism as a dynamic exchange between individual authors and the large political concerns shaped by the three great empires (British, French, American), in whose intellectual and imaginative territory the writing was produced."

The authors in question include Homer and the Greek playwrights such as Aeschylus who first characterised the Persians of "the east" in their dramas as exotic and inscrutable, stereotypes that Said shows subsequently to permeate the works of writers such as Flaubert, the young Disraeli, and Kipling, whose accounts of "the east" fed the west's fascination with the orient. Said further sharpened the political edge of this narrative by showing how such ideas could be seen as a direct reflection of European racism and imperialism.

After the publication of *Orientalism* set off a firestorm of criticism from every angle of the east-west divide, Said declared, in a retrospective essay, that "the orient-versus-occident opposition was both misleading and highly undesirable; the less it was given credit for actually describing anything more than a fascinating history of interpretations and contesting interests, the better".

These were vain hopes. In the nearly 40 years since *Orientalism* first appeared, the Middle East, the Arabs and Islam have continued to fuel enormous change, struggle, controversy and, most recently, warfare. Said, a pugnacious advocate for an independent state of Palestine became drawn into some visceral arguments in a way that helped politicise a book whose scholarly first intent had been to use, in Said's words, a "humanistic critique to introduce a longer sequence of thought and analysis to replace the short bursts of thought-stopping fury that so imprison us".

Just before Said died in 2003, he noted with dismay the continuing impact of "orientalist" ideology on the west: "Bookstores in the US," he wrote, "are filled with shabby screeds bearing screaming headlines about Islam and terror, Islam exposed, the Arab threat and the Muslim menace, all of them written by political polemicists pretending to knowledge imparted by experts who have supposedly penetrated to the heart of these strange oriental people..."

As the US and the western powers continue to grapple with the crisis of Islam in Syria, Iraq, Egypt, and Libya, while desperately appeasing the oil-rich princes of Arabia, *Orientalism* will remain the text to which the Foreign Office and the State Department will have to return to replenish their search for mutual understanding in the conflict between east and west.

Said was always a vociferous enemy of theories about the "clash of civilisations". With great elegance and clarity, he argued for intellectual progress. "One of the great advances," he wrote as the *Orientalism* controversy raged around him, "is the realisation that cultures are hybrid and heterogeneous, and that cultures and civilisations are so interrelated and interdependent as to beggar any simply delineated description of their individuality." How, he went on, "can one speak of 'western civilisation' except as an ideological fiction that gave the western nations their present mixed identities? This is especially true of the United States, which today can only be described as an enormous palimpsest of different races and cultures sharing a problematic history of conquests, exterminations, and of course major cultural and political achievements."

In words that might provide an epigraph to this series, Italo Calvino once said that a classic is a book that has "never finished what it wants to say". *Orientalism* is such a book.

Three to compare:
Albert Hourani: *A History of the Arab Peoples* (1991)
Ammiel Alcalay: *After Arabs and Jews: Remaking
        Levantine Culture* (1993)
Edward Said: *Out of Place – A Memoir* (1999)

94. THE RIGHT STUFF
BY TOM WOLFE (1979)

Newspapers and magazines often provide an indispensable patronage for writers. *The Right Stuff* is one of several great books in this list that derive from the interaction of high journalism and a higher literary ambition. In 1972, *Rolling Stone* commissioned its star reporter to cover the launch of Nasa's final Apollo moonshot, one of many moments that marked the end of the 60s.

Tom Wolfe responded with what he later described as just "some ordinary curiosity". What was it, he wondered, that would make a man "willing to sit up on top of an enormous Roman candle, such as a Redstone, Atlas, Titan or Saturn rocket, and wait for someone to light the fuse?"

Wolfe decided, he says rather disingenuously, "on the simplest approach possible. I would ask a few astronauts and find out. So I asked a few in December of 1972 when they gathered at Cape Canaveral to watch the last mission to the moon, Apollo 17."

The upshot was a four-part piece entitled "Post-Orbital Remorse", which appeared in *Rolling Stone* during 1973. There was, however, an afterlife to Wolfe's "ordinary curiosity". He had stumbled on a "psycho-logical mystery" – the motivation of the men involved, and his fascina-tion with his own response. "I discovered quickly enough," he wrote later, "that none of them, no matter how talkative otherwise, was about to answer the question, or even linger for more than a few seconds on the subject at the heart of it, which is to say, courage."

And so, with his unfailing instinct for a good story, Wolfe spent the rest of the 70s in "a rich and fabulous terrain that, in a literary sense, had remained as dark as the far side of the moon for more than half a century: military flying and the modern American officer corps". Wolfe's account of "one of the most extraordinary and most secret dramas of the 20th century", became *The Right Stuff*, his best book in any genre.

A classic of reportage, *The Right Stuff* is both a showcase of Wolfe's remarkable gifts, as well as a book of its time. Below the waterline, it was also, as Michael Lewis has identified in a brilliant *Vanity Fair* profile, all about Wolfe. Lewis notes that: "Wolfe took an interest in the moon landing, but less in the mission than in the men. The early astronauts had some traits in common, he noticed. They tended to be born oldest sons, in the mid-1920s, named after their fathers, and raised in small towns, in intact Anglo-Saxon Protestant families. More than half of them had 'Jr' after their names. In other words, they were just like him. What was it about this upbringing, he wondered, that produced these men? It was another way of asking: What strange sociological process explains me?"

And because, in addition to "courage", "test pilots" etc, *The Right Stuff* is all about Wolfe, it exhibits its author's lifelong – and, let's face it, southern – quarrel with the New York literary establishment. The Thomas Wolfe Jr, born in 1931, who had grown up in Richmond, Virginia, during the Second World War, revered those "adventurous young men who sought glory in war" and who had become fighter pilots. As a young reporter in 60s Manhattan, he found himself an outsider. Towards the record of these pilots' self-sacrifice and heroism, "the drama and psychology of flying high-performance aircraft in battle", Wolfe observes, with some dismay, "the literary world remained oblivious".

On my reading, *The Right Stuff* becomes a triple whammy and Wolfe's home run. It's both an exploration of courage and a medita-tion on its author's background, as well as being a coded rebuke to the Manhattan literati who, in their devotion to the values of the *New*

Yorker (Wolfe's *bête noir*) and also *Partisan Review*, perceived military men as "brutes and philistines". Meanwhile, the Vietnam War was in full, horrendous progress and navy pilots were dying. It was this heroism that Wolfe wanted to salute. "*The Right Stuff*," he wrote later, "became the story of why men were willing – willing? – delighted! – to take on such odds in this, an era literary people had long since characterised as the age of the anti-hero."

Wolfe, meanwhile, remained a child of his times. He could never give up his dream of writing A Novel. "It's hard to explain," he writes in *The New Journalism*, "what an American dream the idea of writing a novel was in the 1940s, the 1950s, and right into the early 1960s. The Novel was no mere literary form. It was a psychological phenomenon. It was a cortical fever. It belonged in the glossary... somewhere between Narcissism and Obsessional Neuroses." After *The Right Stuff* made him a heap of money, a fully self-sufficient Tom Wolfe was going to scale the north face of Parnassus if it killed him. And when *Rolling Stone* (which commissioned him as if he were Dickens) came calling again, we got... *The Bonfire of the Vanities*. But that's a whole other story.

Three to compare:
Norman Mailer: *Of a Fire on the Moon* (1970)
Carl Sagan: *Cosmos: A Personal Voyage* (1980)
Tom Wolfe: *The Bonfire of the Vanities* (1987)

95. A Brief History of Time
by Stephen Hawking (1988)

Curiosity is one of the human animal's essential qualities, and two questions – where did we come from, and how did we get here? – continue to express the insatiable curiosity that animates human consciousness. Today, when we consider our place in the universe, the cosmos remains the supreme frontier of mankind's propensity to wonder at its origins.

In October 2017, an event in a remote corner of our universe, another contemporary reminder of this timeless curiosity, hit the international headlines with the dramatic verification of a concept first predicted by Einstein in 1915: gravitational waves.

In the words of the *New York Times,* "a minuscule jiggle, discovered in an exotic physics experiment" saw two teams of American scientists, in collaboration with British and German partners, overcome almost insurmountable odds "to open a vast new window on the cosmos". This, in simple language, was the wider significance of the moment – an astronomical "first" – when the Laser Interferometer Gravitational-Wave Observatory (Ligo) announced that a signal from gravitational waves had been discovered emanating from the collision and merger of two massive black holes (collapsed stars) more than a billion light years away.

The mind-dizzying scale of this data only begins to come into focus when you remember that just one light year is approximately 5.88 trillion miles. Welcome to Stephen Hawking and his universe.

It was, rather less distantly, in 1988 that Hawking confirmed his place as the most brilliant British scientist of his generation with the publication of *A Brief History of Time,* a succinct, entertaining and brilliantly lucid account of our relationship with the universe. In addition to his review of all the great theories of the cosmos, from Galileo and Newton to Einstein, Hawking, who was already renowned for his work on black holes, took the opportunity to explore and publicise some of the most speculative contemporary ideas about space and time. He devoted the final chapters of *A Brief History* to "wormholes", "spiral galaxies" and, perhaps most controversial of all, "superstring theory", in a complex narrative that was also a sketch for Hawking's goal of a "complete, consistent and unified" theory of physics.

It was his ambition, he wrote, to facilitate "the discussion of the question of why it is that we and the universe exist. If we find the answer to that, it would be the ultimate triumph of human reason – for then we would know the mind of God."

What, you might ask, is the use of such hyperbole? What, indeed, is the justification for a highly theoretical department of science, such as astrophysics, that doesn't contribute to the improvement of the physical world (safer aeroplanes; faster cars; better washing machines)? Here we have to acknowledge the immense but intangible cultural significance of scientific inquiry, especially its ability to change mankind's perspective of its place in the universe.

Who knows what the Ligo experiment or *A Brief History* will achieve? If history is any guide, however, the impact on our consciousness is potentially profound. Already, as my *Observer* colleague Robin

McKie recently reported: "It is now clear that astronomers have created a new type of astronomy: gravitational wave observation." The Ligo breakthrough joins an extraordinary tradition of scientific endeavour. As one of the scientists behind Ligo put it, "This confirms the existence of a range of intermediate black holes, about which we had theoretical doubts. Now those have gone. We're already going places."

Over the centuries, Aristotle, Copernicus, Galileo, Newton, Einstein and many others, often at great personal cost, have changed our understanding of the universe. Hawking's own boastful calculations of his book sales suggest that *A Brief History* will have influenced the minds of a generation as few other contemporary titles will have done. Translated into 40 languages, as he writes in the introduction to the latest paperback edition, *A Brief History* has sold "about one copy for every 750 man, woman and child in the world". Not bad for a book that, Hawking freely admits, he never expected "to do anything like as well as it did".

From its opening page, in which he repeats the apocryphal tale of the little old lady who told Bertrand Russell that "the world is really a flat place supported on the back of a giant tortoise", Hawking's intention is to instruct and entertain. He recounts, tongue in cheek, that when Russell is said to have replied, with a smirk, "What is the tortoise standing on?", the old lady answered, "You're very clever, young man, very clever. But it's turtles all the way down." Plainly, Hawking can appreciate the ironies implicit in the speculative side of quantum physics.

Hawking's own life and his heroic struggle with the debilitating effects of motor neurone disease until his death in 2018, became braided into the world's response to *A Brief History* and many of his subsequent speculations, as if his suffering had somehow sharpened his perception of the cosmos and its mysteries. For the media, the oracular nature of his utterances, and the remarkable courage with which he defied all predictions of his mortality, imbued some of his theories with a quasi-mystical status. The most cursory reading of *A Brief History of Time* will remind his readers that there is nothing fuzzy or untested about the intelligence behind this contemporary classic.

Three to compare:
Isaac Newton: *Mathematical Principles of Natural Philosophy* (1687)
Albert Einstein: *"On the Electrodynamics of Moving Bodies"* (1905)
Aristotle: *On the Heavens* (circa 340 BC)

96. DREAMS FROM MY FATHER
BY BARACK OBAMA (1995)

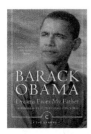

In the run-up to the 2008 US presidential election, that roller coaster primary season in which Hillary Clinton was expected to play a starring, and possibly triumphant, role, I was commissioned by the *Observer* to review the campaign biographies of the principal Democratic and Republican contenders, a slate of candidates that ran the gamut of implausibility from John McCain and Mitt Romney to John Kerry, John Edwards and Joe Biden. Dismal as these politicians appeared to be on the campaign trail, their collected works made an even sorrier catalogue. All the books under review turned out to be either ghosted by party hacks, or "As told to". Every last one of them was a farrago of wonkishness, insincerity, and cliché, polemical half-truths and bits of old stump speeches, mashed-up press releases and policy statements, reheated for popular consumption in some of the dullest American prose imaginable. Was it possible that none of the candidates had even read these books, let alone written them?

There was, however, an exception, a shaft of clarity and brilliance in the prevailing murk. One of the Democratic outsiders, the junior senator from the state of Illinois, a certain Barack Obama, had not only written his own book some years before, he had also executed an affecting personal memoir with grace and style, narrating an enthralling story with honesty, elegance and wit, as well as an instinctive gift for storytelling.

From his opening line, "A few months after my twenty-first birthday, a stranger called to give me the news ...", it was clear that *Dreams from My Father* was something special. It had a voice, and an unmistakable authority. Indeed, at the point at which I picked it up, Obama's memoir had been published for about 12 years, and was belatedly becoming a US bestseller on the rising tide of support for the candidate's winning and optimistic "Yes We Can" campaign.

Back in 2007, among many millions, I had never heard of Barack Obama, though I was vaguely aware that he had made an electrifying speech at the 2004 Democratic party convention. Now, not only did I begin to follow his campaign, I suggested in the *Observer* that a presidential candidate with such literary and rhetorical gifts deserved to be in the White House, and predicted that, against the odds, he might prevail. Anyway, a year later, it had all come to pass. Hillary Clinton (shades of 2016) had been passed over by the voters. "Yes We Can" had become "Yes We Did".

Dreams from My Father is a remarkably candid portrait of a young man facing up to the big questions of identity and belonging. As the son of a black African father from Kenya, and a white American mother from Wichita, Kansas, the young Obama had to make a crucial psychological odyssey, fraught with many conflicting emotions. At first, he traces the movement of his mother's family from Kansas to Hawaii, and thence to Indonesia. One of the many distinctive qualities to the book is Obama's natural and fearless way with dialogue. He animates countless scenes between his young self, his mother and his grandparents with scraps of well-remembered, or possibly well-imagined, conversation that give the narrative a delightful informality.

As the book grows in confidence, young "Barry" finally travels to Kenya to address the painful truth of "the old man", his father's life, and become reconciled to his inheritance as an American of African heritage. Once his parents divorced, he was on his own. "In an improbably short span," he writes, "it seems that my father fell under the same spell as my mother and her parents; and for the first six years of my life, even as that spell was broken and the worlds that they thought they'd left behind reclaimed each of them, I occupied the place where their dreams had been." Here he movingly evokes his "troubled heart – the mixed blood, the divided soul, the ghostly image of the tragic mulatto trapped between two worlds".

It is, he repeats, an attempt at "an honest account of a particular province of my life". As "a boy's search for his father" there is inevitably less of a focus on Obama's mother, Ann Dunham. Her absence is perhaps the most telling feature of Obama's recollections, raising many questions about his relationship to the American component of his identity equation.

Many commentators have rhapsodised over *Dreams from My Father*. Toni Morrison was one of the first to recognise "his ability to reflect on this extraordinary mesh of experiences that he has had, some familiar and some not, and to really meditate on that the way he does, and to set up scenes in narrative structure, dialogue, conversation – all of these things that you don't often see, obviously, in the routine political memoir biography...." She concludes, powerfully: "It's unique. It's his. There are no other ones like that."

More prosaic, according to *Time* magazine, *Dreams from My Father* is "the best-written memoir ever produced by an American politician". In the *New York Times*, Michiko Kakutani described the memoir as "the most evocative, lyrical and candid autobiography written by a future president". At the end of his time in office, it certainly raises many expectations for the retired Barack Obama's presidential autobiography. *The Personal Memoirs of Ulysses S Grant* (No 46) remains a hard act to follow.

Three to compare:
Ulysses S Grant: *The Personal Memoirs* (1885)
Hillary Rodham Clinton: *Living History* (2003)
Barack Obama: *The Audacity of Hope* (2006)

97. Birthday Letters
by Ted Hughes (1998)

Poetry is braided into this series like a golden thread, because in every

generation it is the poets who replenish and tantalise the collective consciousness. As I've written already, this list is a personal inventory of some core texts, the books that I believe shaped our imagination and "made us who we are". *Birthday Letters* fits that template, surviving Ted Hughes as a work of outrageous audacity, astonishing rhetorical and lyrical fervour, mixed with heartbreaking candour. In short, it is a landmark in English poetry.

In any age, the story of Ted (Hughes) and Sylvia (Plath) would be a chapter torn from the playbook of romantic tragedy. Furthermore, in the Anglo-American literary tradition, the marriage of two great contemporary poets from opposite sides of the Atlantic must be a source of endless fascination. At first, the double helix of love and work inspired some remarkable poems, but add the early suicide of one, and the lifelong torment of the other, and you have the makings of a myth. When, in the late summer of 1997, Hughes walked into the offices of his publisher,

Faber & Faber, with the manuscript of 88 poems addressed to his dead wife, he was chiselling the synopsis of a stupendous private drama high into the north face of Parnassus. *Birthday Letters*, the manuscript in question, published in 1998, became the most sensational new collection of poems in living memory.

The collision of art and love, the tectonic plates of any writer's career, creativity mingling with everyday life, must be the San Andreas fault of literature. When the two writers involved happen to be great contemporary poets, artistic equals, the material that explodes from the depths is bound to be incandescent, exhilarating, unearthly and passionate. For Hughes, addressing Plath inevitably had its mythologising dimension. He writes:

> The dreamer in her
> Had fallen in love with me and she did not know it.
> That moment the dreamer in me
> Fell in love with her and I knew it.

A 1998 letter to his friend and fellow poet Seamus Heaney, describes the backstory. From the 1970s, Hughes says that he began to address his "letters to Sylvia", exploring every aspect of their relationship. At first, Hughes reports, he wrote them on the hoof, informally; later, he tried to work at them in a more controlled way but found that he was unable. He went back to spontaneous forays: some of these *Birthday Letters* poems first appeared in his *New Selected Poems* (1995), but in correspondence with friends, he would admit that he found some of the other poems in the series too personal to publish. *Birthday Letters*, written over a period of more than 25 years, was Hughes's own great reckoning – although it would turn out to be incomplete.

When *Birthday Letters* finally appeared, Hughes cast his extraordinary spell, and not for the first time, over an audience which, for two generations, had been brought up on *The Hawk in the Rain, Crow* and *The Rattle Bag*, as well as on the tale of Ted and Sylvia, one of the love stories of the 20th century. The book became an instant bestseller and prizewinner.

There are many ironies in play with *Birthday Letters*. First, there is the unquenchable afterlife of a tragic relationship with which Hughes himself spent half a lifetime grappling. Throughout his career, Hughes was tormented by the vociferous fans of Plath who wanted to hold him to account for Plath's suicide in the winter of 1963, and also for the way in which he administered the posthumous publication of her oeuvre. In death, as in life, Sylvia troubled him still.

Birthday Letters became a painful, at times self-lacerating, tribute to the radioactive power of that legacy, as well as a monument that inexorably reminded readers of Hughes's contemporary status. It was also a career-defining volume. Now, approaching 20 years after his death, Hughes the poet, so often teased and parodied in his lifetime, is emerging as one of the towering literary figures of the past century, to be spoken of in the same breath as *Eliot, Yeats, Auden* and *Larkin*. As the *Observer* put it recently, "he has become the once and future king of the English literary imagination".

Birthday Letters (together with Plath's letters and diaries) describes a now familiar tale. If her beginnings were slow and desk-bound, Plath was soon soaring beyond her lover's reach. But it was a fatal trajectory. Theirs was a tragic match and the relationship turned sour. By 1963 the instability that had dogged Plath's whole life was becoming painfully dominant. The question that feminist critics have endlessly debated is: was she so obsessed with her dead father that her suicide was almost prede-termined, or did Hughes's behaviour, particularly his decision to leave her for another woman after six years of marriage, push her to the edge?

Who will ever know? In Last Letter, a poem with the traumatic line "Your wife is dead", released by the poet's estate after his death, Hughes himself gets sucked into that vortex, declaring that the explanation for suicide is "as unknown as if it never happened". So Plath's tragic death remains a mystery that has already inspired one masterpiece (*The Savage God* by Al Alvarez, the *Observer*'s former poetry editor) and numberless words of exegesis.

Hughes himself went to ground, living in Devon, writing about nature and keeping his counsel. It did not do him much good. "My silence seems to confirm every accusation and fantasy," he once wrote. With Promethean stoicism, he held his ground. "I preferred [silence], on the whole, to allowing myself to be dragged out into the bullring and teased and pricked and goaded into vomiting up every detail of my life with Sylvia."

But he was still wounded. I remember once awkwardly broaching the Sylvia question with him, after several glasses of wine, and being touched and amazed at the flood of loving recollection released by a simple – and tactless – inquiry. He was, in his prime, as compelling a figure as Plath: an unforgettable physical presence with fathomless reserves of feeling and humanity, and a gentle Yorkshire voice that seemed to remake every sentence it uttered.

Birthday Letters was also an attempt by Hughes to nail shut a Pandora's box of prurient, often vicious, speculation. It's easy to forget the vehemence of the opposition. The poet's readings were sometimes interrupted by cries of "murderer"; the American feminist poet Robin Morgan published The Arraignment which began with the lines "I accuse/Ted Hughes..."

Having explored the passage of Plath's short life, Hughes stopped short of revealing the circumstances of the suicide itself, about which there had been endless gossip. He had been wrestling with that lost weekend in the frozen midwinter of 1963, especially the horrifying, almost macabre, detail that Plath had reassuringly burned her suicide note, which had reached Hughes prematurely, in front of him. He distilled the horror of this moment into repeated drafts of Last Letter in a "blue school-style exercise book" that contained versions of several other poems that also appear in *Birthday Letters*. The only person who knew of this poem's existence, because Hughes had given her a typed fair copy of it, was the poet's widow, Carol.

This is where a concluding and redemptive chapter in this story begins. Carol Hughes, with impressive dignity, has chosen never to speak publicly about her husband. For any literary estate, the question of what it is right to publish is always fraught. The second Mrs Hardy burned her husband's correspondence with her predecessor, enraging generations of scholars. Hughes himself had been criticised for his destruction of Plath's last journal. Carol Hughes, however, has always tried to do her best by her husband's work. She had always known about this "last letter", and what it revealed. Biding her time, she chose the right moment to release it, in the pages of the *New Statesman*. On publication, Carol Ann Duffy, the poet laureate, observed that this last poem, the coda to Birthday Letters, is "a bit like looking into the sun as it's dying. It seems to touch a deeper, darker place than any poem he's ever written." Time will tell if Sylvia Plath's spirit has finally been laid to rest. *Birthday Letters* has already become part of the canon.

Three to compare:
Al Alvarez: *The Savage God* (1971)
Sylvia Plath: *Letters Home: Correspondence 1950-1963* (1975)
Janet Malcolm: *The Silent Woman – Sylvia Plath and Ted Hughes* (1993)

98. No Logo
BY NAOMI KLEIN (1999)

Some titles in this list are *"zeitgeist* books", owing much of their

success and influence to the way in which, consciously or otherwise, they channel the mood of the times. *No Logo* is a *zeitgeist* book.

When it was first published in Canada and the USA, just after some well-publicised demonstrations in Seattle against the World Trade Organisation in November 1999 put "anti-globalisation" on the international media agenda, *No Logo* flourished a polemical subtitle ("Taking Aim at the Brand Bullies"), and was hailed as a mix of radical journalism and a call to arms. In hindsight, this response was fuelled in part by a kind of pre-millennial fervour.

To Klein, anti-globalisation was a misnomer. "At the reformist end it was anti-corporate; at the radical end it was anti-capitalist. What made it unique was its insistent internationalism." Meanwhile, *No Logo* became a manifesto for a critique of the way the world worked, embodied in the visionary and articulate figure of Naomi Klein who, in the words of the *Observer*'s review, "positively seethes with intelligent anger".

The secret of Klein's work was the way in which she humanised her argument with fascinating reportage from her quest into Asian sweatshops, and the dark side of western capitalism in Africa. Her voice was insistent but not preachy, her analysis detailed but never obscure. She was hailed by one critic as the "young funky heiress to [Noam] Chomsky". Which, in a sense, she was.

Naomi Klein is the child of militant hippies who moved to Montreal from the US in 1967 as Vietnam War resisters. Her father had grown up in an American communist milieu, loosely connected to Hollywood. Klein's own childhood was partly a protest against her family's radical agenda, especially her mother's feminism.

She has said she spent much of her teenage years in shopping malls, obsessed with designer labels, in a rejection of her parents' values. Klein has also said that it was "oppressive" to have, as a mother, "a very public feminist", and she was slow to embrace the women's movement. But two events, private and public, became the catalyst for her profound change of attitude.

The first occurred when she was 17. Her mother had a stroke, with some serious consequent disability, and Klein took a year off school to help the family care for her. This, she says was the sacrifice that saved her "from being such a brat". Then, while studying at the University of Toronto in 1989, she became understandably traumatised by the slaughter of some female engineering students in a tragedy, (also known as the Montreal Massacre) in which a 25-year-old student ran amok, shouting that he was "fighting feminism". Having denounced the women in his path as "a bunch of feminists," he shot 28, killing 14.

This became Klein's wake-up call as a Generation X intellectual in the making. With the publication of *No Logo*, she was hailed as a freedom fighter for a new and radical post-consumer culture. The great American feminist Gloria Steinem's salute marked the passing of a torch: "Just when you thought multinationals and crazed consumerism were too big to fight, along comes Naomi Klein with facts, spirit, and news of successful fighters already out there."

What singled out *No Logo* was the potency of its reportage. Klein herself observed at the outset that this is "not a book of predictions, but of first-hand observation." As such, it struck a chord with the more socially responsible exponents of popular culture. Radiohead, for example, declared the influence of Klein's work particularly during the making of their fourth and fifth albums, Kid A (2000) and Amnesiac (2001). The band recommended the book to fans on their website and even flirted with calling their Kid A album *No Logo*.

The pop cultural appeal of *No Logo* is not hard to discern. Underlying Klein's observations was the idea that if the world is a global village, then the corporate logo (Nike, Walmart, or Starbucks) constitutes a universal language understood by – though not accessible to – everyone. She analysed the birth of a brand as a corporate means of animating the banal vulgarity of mass marketing. As she followed the progress of the logo, in four sections – "No Space", "No Choice", "No Jobs" and finally "No Logo" – she moved through the negative effects of brand-oriented corporate activity, before developing a central argument about the conflict between corporate dominance and personal identity and the various methods adopted by the individual consumer to fight back.

Ten years after the publication of *No Logo*, but before the emergence of Trump, Klein, looking back, reflected on the lessons of her experience. In part, she seems to recognise that the phenomenon she had identified in 1999 was part of history. "The first time I saw a 'Yes We Can' video … featuring celebrities speaking and singing over a Martin Luther King-esque Obama speech, I thought: finally, a politician with ads as cool as Nike."

Even with her subsequent disillusion – shared by many North American liberals – at Obama's failure to live up to his lofty rhetoric – and the shock of Trump's election, Klein still conceded that the world's love affair with Obama's rebranded America had been timely. "Obama didn't just rebrand America," she writes, in a telling admission, "he resuscitated the neoliberal economic project when it was at death's door. No one but Obama, wrongly perceived as a new FDR, could have pulled it off."

Klein still retains her ambivalence about branding, and its broader social consequences, but she admits that "the global embrace of Obama's brand" continues to demonstrate an extraordinary appetite for progressive change, the kind of social transformation Klein hankers after. At that moment her youthful radicalism seemed essentially intact, albeit with a softening at the edges. "The task ahead," she writes, in language that betrays the influence of the phenomenon she once denounced, "is to build movements that are the real thing." Quoting Studs Terkel, North America's great radical socialist historian, she observes: "Hope has never trickled down. It has always sprung up."

In this new series, we explored the core of the Anglo-American tradition, and discovered fascinating connections between Klein and some of the radical journalists of the past, maverick polemicists such as Daniel Defoe and Tom Paine. *No Logo*, for all its wonky side, is at least partly descended from Paine's *Common Sense*, and Naomi Klein would have plenty to discuss with the author of *A Tour Through the Whole Island of Great Britain*.

Three to compare:
Jeff Ferrell: *Tearing Down the Streets: Adventures in Urban Anarchy* (2001)
William Gibson: *Pattern Recognition* (2003)
Naomi Klein: *This Changes Everything – Capitalism Versus the Climate* (2014)

99. THE YEAR OF MAGICAL THINKING
BY JOAN DIDION (2005)

In December 2003, as an acute, lifelong reporter of her inner states,

Joan Didion was presented with a unique opportunity to examine the experience of bereavement. While love and death are the themes of the great novels, the emotion that links them – grief – is more often the stuff of memoir than fiction. So, you have to be a very special kind of writer to find the detachment to examine a devastating personal loss, especially if you are going to write about it inside out. In *The Year of Magical Thinking* this is precisely what Didion does.

The result is a classic of mourning that's also the apotheosis of baby-boomer reportage, a muted celebration of the enthralling self. "Misery memoirs" are commonplace today – Joyce Carol Oates's *A Widow's Story* (2011) is a typical example – but Didion's contribution to the genre raised it to the status of literature, a point acknowledged by the playwright David Hare, who directed the author's own version in a stage adaptation starring Vanessa Redgrave in 2007.

Cold, clear, precise, and with her emotions mostly held in check through a web of words, Didion narrates a year that began when her husband, the writer John Gregory Dunne, collapsed from a fatal heart attack in the couple's Upper East Side apartment on the evening of 30 December 2003. ("Life changes fast. Life changes in the instant. You sit down to dinner and life as you know it ends.") Surgical in its exquisite precision, and finally serene, Didion's memoir helps to purge her grief and to set her loss in the new context of widowhood.

Interpolated in the agony of this tale is the parallel drama of their daughter Quintana's medical emergency, hospitalised in New York with a case of pneumonia that became septic shock. Indeed, Quintana was still unconscious in the intensive care unit of Beth Israel North hospital when her father died. During 2004, Quintana recovered, then collapsed again with bleeding in her brain. Less than two years later, she died of acute pancreatitis at the age of 39, after a series of traumatic hospitalisations and just before the publication of *The Year of Magical Thinking*, Didion's bestselling book to date. In *Blue Nights*, published six years later, Didion sets out to write Quintana's elegy, but understandably and perhaps inevitably, can scarcely bring herself to face the task.

Taken together, these two books, but especially *Magical Thinking*, consolidate Didion's formidable reputation as one of the US's greatest postwar exponents of first-person reportage. Louis Menand, writing in the *New Yorker*, captures the essence of Didion: "People liked the collection *Slouching Towards Bethlehem* (though it was not, at first, a big seller). People were intrigued by *Play It as It Lays*, Didion's second novel, which came out two years later (though it got some hostile reviews). Mainly, though, everyone was fascinated by the authorial persona, the hypersensitive neurasthenic who drove a Corvette Stingray, the frail gamine with the migraine headaches and the dark glasses and the searchlight mind, the writer who seemed to know in her bones what readers were afraid to face, which is that the centre no longer holds, the falcon cannot hear the falconer, the storyline is broken."

The storyline for *The Year of Magical Thinking* (a title which takes its inspiration from the anthropological use of the term "magical thinking", by which catastrophic events can be averted) is simply the rollercoaster of Didion's grief in the aftermath of Dunne's death. Didion reports several examples of her own "magical thinking", particularly the way in which she cannot give away her husband's shoes, because, she thought, he would need them when he returned.

Slowly, her defences crumble on the page. "I wanted to scream," she writes. "I wanted him back." Then, via her own "apprehension of death" (that offstage nemesis) and her quotidian fears for her own resilience ("I began feeling fragile, unstable … What if I fell?"), she comes face to face with an abyss of grief. It's one of her finest prose passages.

> "Grief turns out to be a place none of us know until we reach it. We anticipate (we know) that someone close to us could die, but we do not look beyond the few days or weeks that immediately follow such an imagined death. We misconstrue the nature of even those few days or weeks. We might expect if the death is sudden to feel shock. We do not expect this shock to be obliterative, dislocating to both body and mind. We might expect that we will be prostrate, inconsolable, crazy with loss. We do not expect to be literally crazy, cool customers who believe their husband is about to return and need his shoes."

The Year of Magical Thinking is an unforgettable *tour de force*. John Gregory Dunne is keenly present on every page, yet absent in character. Didion's version projects honesty yet leaves many areas of legitimate curiosity (how good a marriage? How intimate? How secure?) quite blank and unsatisfied.

In this way, a storyline that begins on the Upper East Side in New York City becomes universal, profound and uplifting, a mirror in which the desolate and the bereaved of all communities can find succour. Finally, Joan Didion has joined that select band of writers, led by CS Lewis, who have transformed grief into literature.

Three to compare:
CS Lewis: *A Grief Observed* (1961)
Joan Didion: *Slouching Towards Bethlehem* (1968)
Joan Didion: *Blue Nights* (2011)

100. THE SIXTH EXTINCTION
BY ELIZABETH KOLBERT (2014)

The human animal knows that it is born to age and die. Together with language, this knowledge is what separates us from all other species. Yet, until the 18th century, not even Aristotle, who speculated about most things, actually considered the possibility of extinction.

This is all the more surprising because "the end of the world" is an archetypal theme with a sonorous label – eschatology – that morphs in popular culture into many doomsday scenarios, from global warming to the third world war. Citizens of the 21st century now face a proliferating menu of possible future dooms.

Elizabeth Kolbert's *The Sixth Extinction: An Unnatural History* is both a highly intelligent expression of this genre and also supremely well executed and entertaining. Her book, which followed her global warming report *Field Notes from a Catastrophe* (2006), is already set to become a contemporary classic.

On the opening page of her investigation into the future of our planet, Kolbert quotes the great biologist EO Wilson: "If there is danger in the human trajectory, it is not so much in the survival of our own species as in the fulfilment of the ultimate irony of organic evolution:

that in the instant of achieving self-understanding through the mind of man, life has doomed its most beautiful creations." This warning note sets the mood for the 13 chapters that follow, an urgent contemporary report on "the sixth extinction".

Kolbert's perspective is both awe-inspiring and fearsome, but utterly engrossing, as you'd expect from a book whose premise is "we're all doomed". During the past half billion years, she tells us, there have been five mass extinctions on Earth, when "the planet has undergone change so wrenching that the diversity of life has plummeted".

The history of these catastrophic events, notes Kolbert, tends to be recaptured just as humanity comes to realise that it is about to cause another one. Sure enough, in our postmillennial century, she finds that scientists around the world are now monitoring the next mass extinction, possibly the biggest devastation since an asteroid wiped out the dinosaurs. With this difference: the impending cataclysm is … us.

In 13 emblematic episodes, exquisitely narrated, Kolbert, a magazine journalist with the *New Yorker*, explores the possibility of our impending doom through the lives of, for instance, the Panamanian golden frog, the Sumatran rhino and the black-faced honeycreeper of Maui, "the most beautiful bird in the world".

Part of Kolbert's concern is to educate the modern reader in the history of mass extinction. While the concept, as she puts it, "may be the first scientific idea that kids have to grapple with", as they play with their toy dinosaurs, Kolbert instructs that, actually, it's a comparatively recent idea that dates to Enlightenment France. Until this moment in the western intellectual tradition, not even Aristotle (in his 10-volume *History of Animals*) had so much as considered the possibility that animals had a past. Later, in Roman times, Pliny's *Natural History* includes descriptions of animals that are real, or fabulous, but none that are extinct. The word "fossil" was used to describe anything dug from the ground, as in "fossil fuel". Even Carl Linnaeus, who pioneered his system of binomial nomenclature in the mid-18th century, catalogued only one kind of animal – those that exist.

It was the discovery of some American mastodon bones in what is now Ohio, during the early 18th century – an unintended consequence of French colonial exploration – that subsequently inspired Georges Cuvier, an anatomist at the National Museum of Natural History in Paris, to ask the essential question: "What was this primitive Earth? … And what revolution was able to wipe it out?"

Revolutionary France celebrated the rights of man. Cuvier was never going to recognise the truth about some later extinctions: that Homo sapiens is the problem, not the solution. Addressing the imminent next catastrophe with a certain grim relish, Kolbert spells out the results of her investigations: "One-third of all reef-building corals, a third of all freshwater molluscs, a third of sharks and rays, a quarter of all mammals, a fifth of all reptiles, and a sixth of all birds are headed towards oblivion," she declares, during the course of her odyssey through our natural world and its human-inspired devastation. Kolbert's indictment of humanity is remorseless, and compelling: "The losses are occurring all over: in the South Pacific, in the North Atlantic, in the Arctic and in the Sahel, in lakes and on islands, on mountaintops and in valleys."

Readers of *The Sixth Extinction* will be unable to evade the conclusion that we do indeed find ourselves on the brink of a great catastrophe, one in which the agent involved is not an inanimate object (such as an asteroid) or a geophysical force (such as the extreme global warming disaster of 250m years ago) but a sentient creature: ourselves. *Homo sapiens* may have enjoyed brilliant success on Earth but we have done so at the expense of virtually every other species. We are, as the *Observer's* Robin McKie has put it, "the neighbours from hell".

The Sixth Extinction ends in a windowless room at the Institute for Conservation Research in California known as the Frozen Zoo, the world's largest collection of species on ice. This, suggests Kolbert, may be the slender thread on which life on Earth will depend in future. Who knows? She underlines her final message with a quotation from the Stanford ecologist Paul R Erhlich: "IN PUSHING OTHER SPECIES TO EXTINCTION, HUMANITY IS BUSY SAWING OFF THE LIMB ON WHICH IT PERCHES."

We have been warned.

Three to compare:
EO Wilson: *On Human Nature* (1978)
Elizabeth Kolbert: *Field Notes from a Catastrophe:*
	A Frontline Report on Climate Change (2006)
Yuval Noah Harari: Sapiens: *A Brief History of Humankind* (2014)

INDEX